Sugar Bowl

The First Fifty Years

Sugar Bowl

The First Fifty Years

by Marty Mulé

Oxmoor House, Inc. BIRMINGHAM

Library of Congress Catalog Number: 83-60428
ISBN: 0-8487-0626-9
Manufactured in the United States of America
First Printing

Sugar Bowl
The First Fifty Years

Editor-in-Chief John Logue
Editor Karen Phillips Irons
Production Manager Jerry Higdon
Design Joyce Kachergis Book Design and Production,
        Bynum, North Carolina
Editorial Assistants Patty E. Howdon, Cecilia Robinson

THE SUGAR BOWL CHARTER MEMBERS

Ralph J. Barry

Herbert A. Benson

J. H. Bodenheimer

M. P. Boebinger, M.D.

George E. Butler

John R. Conniff

Sam Corenswet

Joseph M. Cousins

Joseph B. David

Paul E. DeBlanc

L. diBenedetto

Fred Digby

Joseph Dresner

P. K. Ewing

Richard Fleming

Harry W. Fletcher

A. N. Goldberg

Bernie J. Grenrood

Henry J. Jumonville

Warren V. Miller

A. B. Nicholas

J. M. Niehaus

Herbert Pailet

Irwin F. Poche

T. Semmes Rantlett

F. D. "Hap" Reilly

W. P. Rovira

Frank V. Schaub

George E. Schneider

Leo J. Schoeny, D.D.S.

W. Raleigh Schwarz

W. A. Simpson, Jr.

E. Allan Smuck

Walter L. Snider

Clarence H. Strauss

Albert Wachenheim, Jr.

Douglas S. Watters

P. B. Williamson

Frederick J. Wolfe, D.D.S.

Charles C. Zatarain

Contents

Introduction   3

 1935 Tulane-Temple   12

 1936 TCU-LSU   17

 1937 Santa Clara-LSU   23

 1938 Santa Clara-LSU   27

 1939 TCU-Carnegie Tech   31

 1940 Texas A&M-Tulane   36

 1941 Boston College-Tennessee   41

 1942 Fordham-Missouri   46

 1943 Tennessee-Tulsa   50

 1944 Georgia Tech-Tulsa   54

 1945 Duke-Alabama   58

 1946 Oklahoma A&M-St. Mary's   61

 1947 Georgia-
North Carolina   64

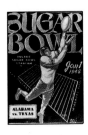 1948 Texas-Alabama   68

 1949 Oklahoma-
North Carolina   72

 1950 Oklahoma-LSU   76

 1951 Kentucky-Oklahoma   80

 1952 Maryland-Tennessee   85

 1953 Georgia Tech-
Mississippi   88

 1954 Georgia Tech-
West Virginia   92

 1955 Navy-Mississippi   95

 1956 Georgia Tech-
Pittsburgh   100

 1957 Baylor-Tennessee   105

 1958 Mississippi-Texas   108

 1959 LSU-Clemson 111

 1966 Missouri-Florida 143

 1960 Mississippi-LSU 116

 1967 Alabama-Nebraska 147

 1961 Mississippi-Rice 120

 1968 LSU-Wyoming 153

 1962 Alabama-Arkansas 124

 1969 Arkansas-Georgia 158

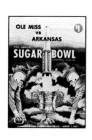 1963 Mississippi-Arkansas 128

 1970 Mississippi-Arkansas 163

 1964 Alabama-Mississippi 132

 1971 Tennessee-Air Force 170

 1965 LSU-Syracuse 137

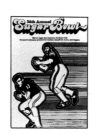 1972 Oklahoma-Auburn 174

1972 Oklahoma-
Penn State   179

1973 Notre Dame-
Alabama   184

1974 Nebraska-Florida   191

1975 Alabama-
Penn State   196

1977 Pittsburgh-Georgia   201

1978 Alabama-Ohio State   208

1979 Alabama-Penn State   215

1980 Alabama-Arkansas   222

1981 Georgia-Notre Dame   230

1982 Pittsburgh-Georgia   237

1983 Penn State-Georgia   244

Acknowledgments

Two major sources—newspaper files and interviews—were used in the preparation of this book. The *Times-Picayune*/the *States-Item* allowed the use of printed and photographic material from the files of New Orleans newspapers, the *Item*, the *Times-Picayune*, the *States*, the *States-Item*, and the *Times-Picayune*/the *States-Item*, without which the book could not have been completed.

The following people were interviewed: Ray Alborn, Ki Aldrich, Ralph "Peppy" Blount, Henry Bodenheimer, Billy Brewer, Frank Broyles, Bear Bryant, Aruns Callery, Dr. Billy Cannon, Fred Cassibry, Clay Cooper, Sam Corenswet, Jr., Denver Crawford, Charles V. Cusimano, Chuck Dicus, Paul Dietzel, Mary Frances Digby, Buddy Diliberto, Glenn Dobbs, Vince Dooley, Phil Dougherty, Charles L. "Pie" Dufour, Rev. Maurice Dullea, S.J., Lloyd Eaton, Dr. Norman C. Francis, Bobby Franklin, Carl Galmon, Joe Gattuso, Jake Gibbs, Harry Gilmer, Hap Glaudi, Bobby Grier, Larry Hickman, Mickey Holmes, Harry Ice, Jill Jackson, Carl James, Darryl Jenkins, Ellis Jones, Charley Justice, Joe Katz, Cliff Kern, John Kimbrough, Armand Kitto, Moon Landrieu, Jim LaRue, Hank Lauricella, Lester Lautenschlaeger, Bobby Layne, Darrell Lewis, Carl Maddox, Archie Manning, Charlie McClendon, Joe McKenney, Felix McKnight, Boyd McWhorter, Abe Mickal, Barney Mintz, Ed Modzelewski, Bill Montgomery, George Morris, G. A. "Goober" Morse, Jerry Nason, Billy Neighbors, Charlie O'Rourke, Tinker Owens, Ara Parseghian, Joe Paterno, Ray Perkins, George Petrovich, Charlie Pevey, Buck Randall, Joe Rault, Stanley Ritinski, Bob Roesler, George Rolfs, Darrell Royal, Fred Russell, Ed Schneider, Ray Scott, Walter Slater, Steve Spurrier, Bob Steuber, Dr. Charles Strange, Billy Sullivan, Walter Tanney, Charlie Thornton, Charley Trippi, Victor Vasicek, Johnny Vaught, Al Wachenheim, Jr., Robin Weber, Joe Wilkins, Barry Wilson, Al Wolff, Walt Yowarsky, and Charles C. Zatarain, Sr.

Also, anecdotal material was obtained from Peter Finney's *The Fighting Tigers*; George Sweeney's *The Green Wave*; Russell Rice's *The Wildcats*; Lou Maysel's *Here Comes The Longhorns*; Robert Rutland's *The Golden Hurricane*; Tom Pagna and Bob Best's *Era of Ara*; and Fred Russell and George Leonard's *Big Bowl Football*.

Sports information directors and their staffs were indispensable in providing leads, information, and photographic material. Many thanks to the SID corps at Air Force, Alabama, Arkansas, Auburn, Baylor, Boston College, Carnegie Tech, Clemson, Duke, Florida, Fordham, Georgia, Georgia Tech, Kentucky, LSU, Maryland, Mississippi, Missouri, Navy, Nebraska, North Carolina, Notre Dame, Ohio State, Oklahoma, Oklahoma State, Penn State, Pittsburgh, Rice, Santa Clara, St. Mary's, Syracuse, Temple, Tennessee, Texas, Texas A&M, Texas Christian, Tulane, Tulsa, West Virginia, and Wyoming.

The Sugar Bowl was often put in perspective by the beat writers who covered the teams after the invitations to New Orleans were extended. The ones not mentioned but whose writings contributed insight to this work were Nat Belloni, Bill Bumgarner, Joe Englert, Tom Gage, John Jones, Bill Keefe, Gil LeBreton, Bob Marshall, Harry Martinez, Larry McMillen, Will Peneguy, Steve Perkins, Bill Rainey, and Jimmy Smith.

Particular thanks goes to Tom Fox for a story he did on Ray Brown. And special appreciation is given George Sweeney for the use of his taped interviews conducted while researching his history of Tulane football. Also, I would like to thank Tom Bloodworth for editing the first drafts into a somewhat cohesive story, and Peter Paul Finney, who opened his arms and heart to this project—and his scrapbook.

MJM

Sugar Bowl

The First Fifty Years

Introduction

"I think . . . the Sugar Bowl . . . I remember best was the first time I sat in the press box high above the west stands and looked across at the double-deck packed with people . . . the Tulane-Texas A&M game . . . January 1, 1940." Fred Digby seemed to hold that moment intact from across 13 years. *"It looked like a beautiful painting hanging from the heavens."* Digby didn't say he painted that picture, that it's his signature on the canvas. The Sugar Bowl couldn't have emerged without the help of others, but it is Digby's masterpiece.

New Orleans, more Mediterranean than American, a blithesome town framed in lacy Old World wrought iron, was and is a city you visit and then go back to for the rest of your life. Its architecture, exotic airs, musical genius, fine restaurants, and mild weather make New Orleans an extremely attractive town.

It was also the birthplace of Paul Morphy, the greatest of the chess masters, and the town where dice, or "craps," was introduced by the Count Bernard Mandeville de Marigny. "Gentleman" Jim Corbett knocked out John L. Sullivan in New Orleans in the first heavyweight championship fought with gloves; Clara Baer of Newcomb College wrote the first set of rules for girls' basketball in 1895; fencing was introduced to America in New Orleans; and baseball's rain check and Ladies' Day were originated by Abner Powell of the New Orleans Pelicans.

At one time, New Orleans was the only city in the country with two racetracks running in opposition for 100 weekdays. A third operated on Sundays. It was the site of the first thoroughbred match race, between Lexington and LeCompte; the legendary Black Gold ran his first and last races at the Fair Grounds and is buried in its infield.

Scads of professional baseball players, golfers, and boxers have emerged from the area; and Tulane and Loyola universities in the 1920s were producing excellent football teams with Louisiana State University's Tigers thriving 80 miles away. Fishing is virtually a year-round activity, and in season there is still abundant hunting. The Louisiana slogan "Sportsman's Paradise" is easily understood. The romance of the city and the Mississippi River, the walkability of the Vieux Carré, and the town's very sporting legacy have made New Orleans an ideal place for a showcase football game.

Fred Digby

The Sugar Bowl has been a goal and a reward for worthy teams, a laurel of champions, for a half-century; it has been a spectacle for fans; it has paid more than $30 million to the universities whose teams have played in the game.

A half-century ago, the world was snarled in economic collapse, the Great Depression. One of every four Americans lost their jobs. What little money there was went for essentials.

New Orleans, not an industrial center, was spared the dramatic shutdowns of other sections of the country. Nevertheless, the crash of 1929 took its toll on life in the city. Banks closed, businesses failed, and people lost their jobs. Yet, Fred Digby's obsession, the Sugar Bowl, was not to flower until the hopeless days of the Depression.

Bowl games were often born, then dead within a few months' time from the turn of the century to the mid-1930s. Many had the appearance of speculative, flimflam adventures. Others were ill-managed projects of well-meaning but incapable civic leaders. The Rose Bowl alone was built on a foundation strong enough to last and to serve as a model for later bowls.

Pasadena's Rose Bowl was an outgrowth of the city's Tournament of Roses. Zoologist Dr. Charles

Frederick Holder conceived the floral parade, persuading members of the Valley Hunt Club that a midwinter caravan of blooming flowers would attract shivering Easterners to Southern California. The first parade was staged in 1890. Twelve years later a college football game was arranged among the blossoms and Michigan defeated host Stanford, 49-0, in the first Rose Bowl. Eight thousand curious persons watched as Stanford literally asked for mercy and Michigan agreed to shorten the game. The lopsided score spoiled the afternoon for almost everyone, and Rose Bowl football lost favor to such holiday diversions as chariot races.

The Tournament of Roses revived its football game in 1916. Its success sparked an alliance between the crusading sports editor Digby and a taciturn New Orleans lawyer named Warren V. Miller. The two of them combined their obsessions to create the Sugar Bowl 18 years later.

Digby, like many youngsters at the turn of the century, was forced to leave school in order to help his family. He worked as a messenger for an insurance company but ran home each evening for a sandwich, then took a streetcar to the Sophie B. Wright night school for needy young men. Of the thousands of students Sophie Wright educated, Digby attained the highest average. He was also an athlete of note, gaining notice as a long-distance trackman in New Orleans' annual Jackson Day runs.

While working as an office boy, Digby began writing sports under the nom de plume "Booster." New Orleans *Item* sports editor H.T. McDaniel paid him by the inch for his copy. Digby joined the *Item* sports staff full time three years later.

Digby was a contradiction. Reserved and quiet, he worked practically every waking hour. Within months he organized the Amateur Baseball Association, a recreational outlet for 1,500 boys. He and Will B. Hamilton, who succeeded McDaniel as sports editor, drew up the 20 boxing regulations that have governed the sport in Louisiana for most of the century. He developed and directed an annual boxing tournament, the winners advancing to national matches in Boston and the Golden Gloves in New York. He proposed the first municipal golf course for New Orleans. He sponsored the *Item's* Junior Tennis Tournament; conducted the Orphans' Football Fund, which allowed underprivileged children tickets and transportation to Tulane University home games; organized the New Orleans Quarterback Club; and staged boxing programs at military camps in New Orleans and Alexandria, Louisiana, during World War I as a member of the War Training Activities Committee.

During a leave from the paper, Digby served as a steward at Sportsman's Park in Chicago, and for a while he managed a stable of prizefighters.

Will Hamilton left the *Item* in 1922 to work for the *Racing Bulletin*. "When he made his decision," recalled Digby's widow, Mary Frances, "Will told

Fred to take a couple of weeks off, not to come around at all. 'And you wait for them to call,' Hamilton ordered. 'You don't call them.' Fred did as he was advised, and the *Item* finally did call and asked him to become the sports editor."

"I worked for Fred 17 years," said Charles L. "Pie" Dufour, "and he was a man of tremendous integrity, a very powerful writer, a reporter who worked like hell. He surrounded himself with people he respected, and people who wouldn't rubber-stamp his ideas. Sometimes I wonder where the Sugar Bowl would be now if everyone around Fred had thought it was such a grand idea in those days."

Warren Miller, five years older than Digby, came from a much more comfortable New Orleans background. He was an exceptional student from grammar school through Louisiana State University, where he studied chemistry, and finished with a law degree.

Miller dreamed as a youngster of becoming a professional baseball pitcher but couldn't last more than three innings. Other than writing an LSU fight song, there was little to indicate he would become one of the most influential persons in Louisiana sports history.

"I roomed with two football captains at LSU," he once laughed about his athletic background. Where Miller did excel was in civil law and as a civic leader. He ran unsuccessfully for mayor of New Orleans on the Republican ticket in 1930.

"I first got interested in the Sugar Bowl idea when Alabama went to the Rose Bowl in 1926," Miller said. "I thought it would be a fine thing for New Orleans to have such a game." Ironically, that same Rose Bowl also planted the seed in Digby's mind for a postseason game in New Orleans.

Tulane ran up a 9-0-1 record in 1925, and Digby felt the school deserved an invitation to the 1926 Pasadena game. He wrote Warren Brown, a friend and the sports editor of a San Francisco paper, asking about the selection process and if an invitation could be presented a Southern team. Brown explained that the Pacific Coast representative, in this case the University of Washington, picked its own opponent.

Digby prevailed upon two friends in Seattle to present Tulane's credentials to the Washington officials. Rose Bowl authorities advised Washington to invite an Eastern team. Princeton got the invitation, but then dazed the sponsors by declining. Washington officials called Digby back asking for assurances that Tulane would accept if invited.

Digby expressed confidence that Tulane would accept. A telegram was dispatched to Tulane President Dr. Albert Dinwiddie which read: "Will you accept a Rose Bowl invitation—if invited?" The answer was *no*. Tulane administrators felt the trip would keep its athletes out of school too long.

Furious and embarrassed, Digby called the unsuspecting Clark Shaughnessy, Tulane's coach, who was

on a trip in Chicago. Shaughnessy, in turn, called the University of Washington and recommended Alabama. The Crimson Tide, on that recommendation, became the first Southern team to participate in the Rose Bowl.

Three hundred and seventy-five dollars had been spent in long-distance telephone calls and telegrams in the aborted campaign. Digby felt he owed an explanation to *Item* publisher James M. Thomson. After a long discussion Thomson approved the charges, then, almost as an afterthought, asked Digby, "Why can't we have a postseason game in New Orleans?"

The torch had been lit.

Thomson's paper was not unique for the time. It was a blend of sectionalism, boosterism, and sensationalism, with murder and the peccadillos of Hollywood and high society dominating its front pages. In many ways the *Item* was the perfect paper for spicy New Orleans; but it also had a flinty, advocate spirit, and to champion such a civic enterprise as a bowl game was within its character.

Digby struggled for more than a year attempting to come up with a format and foundation for the game, though he didn't do it publicly. October 24, 1927, was the first time anything approximating a plan for an intersectional game in New Orleans appeared in the *Item*. Digby wrote that LSU head coach Mike Donahue was attempting to schedule Knute Rockne's Fighting Irish for a 1928 date in New Orleans. "LSU should play one big game in New Orleans every year," said Donahue, "and if we can get the open date, we will arrange the game."

Donahue hit a snag when Notre Dame renewed its contract with Georgia Tech, and after the 1927 season he was no longer the Tiger head coach, falling victim to a 4-4-1 record.

In November of 1928 the subject was broached again, this time by players more than a thousand miles removed from New Orleans. Boston College, en route to a 9-0-0 season, suggested a postseason game with its sister Jesuit institution, Loyola University of the South. Loyola was to host the game, according to the proposal, and Digby used the occasion for his first comprehensive column on a New Orleans bowl game.

"The suggestion from Boston College," he wrote on November 13, 1928, "for a postseason game here with Loyola University in December will get a hearty approval from all football fans. Especially those who have been wondering for years why New Orleans doesn't vie with Los Angeles, Pasadena, and points west for some of the nationwide publicity that such contests secure."

Unfortunately, the suggestion died when it was brought before the authorities at both Boston College and Loyola. "School officials felt it was too long and expensive a trip," explained Joe McKenney, who coached the Eagles in 1928, "and the author-

ities at BC and Loyola didn't feel it was wise to extend the season."

Twelve months afterward, Loyola did extend its season, and in New Orleans. It participated in a postseason game sponsored under the auspices of the Young Men's Business Club and the city's dominant newspaper, the stodgy and haughty *Times-Picayune*.

Loyola of the South and Loyola of Chicago played to a regular season 6-6 tie in what was described by one of the players as a "typhoon" on Armistice Day, 1929. "Players were literally more afraid of drowning than being hurt," Chicago quarterback Corny Collins told Chicago *Tribune* sportswriter Ed Schneider. "The immediate reaction as a man went down was, 'For God's sake, get those people off him before he drowns!' " said Collins.

The Young Men's Business Club, whose initial experience fueled bigger plans, decided to attempt a "real" college match. Loyola of the South and Loyola of Chicago were asked to consider a rematch for the benefit of the Doll & Toy Fund, and both agreed. Tulane Stadium, with a seating capacity in excess of 20,000, would have been the ideal site, but school officials turned down the idea because the game was scheduled for a Sunday. The participating schools then agreed to play at Loyola of New Orleans' home stadium. Despite the game being linked to a rival publication, Digby pushed for its success.

With good weather, the attraction was expected to lure 10,000 fans into Loyola's 15,000-seat stadium. More than 5,000 advance tickets were sold, and prospects of reaching the goal seemed good. But frigid temperatures swept into the South on December 22, the day before the match, and the announced attendance for Loyola of Chicago's 26-6 victory was 6,000. Eight thousand people had seen the same schools play during the regular season, and in equally bad weather.

Most of the principals, considering the circumstances, felt the project was a success. The game—played less than two months after the Wall Street Crash—didn't lose money; it came two days before Christmas; it was played between two teams with less than national mystique; and the weather certainly affected attendance adversely. Clark Shaughnessy, who had left Tulane for Loyola of the South and coached the Wolfpack in the Doll & Toy Fund defeat, agreed. After he became head coach at the University of Chicago, he told Ed Schneider, "That game was really the forerunner of the Sugar Bowl, inasmuch as it opened the eyes of some businessmen in New Orleans to the possibility of a postseason game."

Loyola defeated the University of Detroit 9-6 in the second Doll & Toy Fund game, December 7, 1930, and drew a disappointing 10,000 fans.

Mayor T. Semmes Walmsley earlier in the year sent a delegation headed by Digby to a meeting of

the Southern Conference (the predecessor of the Southeastern Conference). They sought approval of a new concept of Digby's—a week-long carnival of sports climaxed by a football game. It was turned down. "I think the Southern Conference thought this was a fly-by-night deal," said Pie Dufour. "It doesn't reflect on the judgment of those people; they just weren't going to endorse anything until it was established."

Still, the dream of a New Orleans bowl game wouldn't fade. Months after the proposal was rejected, and two weeks after the second Doll & Toy Fund game, Mayor Walmsley opened a Southern Conference convention in New Orleans with the suggestion that an annual postseason football game, along the lines of the Rose Bowl, be held in the South. He said New Orleans stood ready to support such an undertaking.

At the same time, Fred Digby was aboard the Crimson Special with Alabama's Pasadena-bound Tide. He was going to get a look at the granddaddy

of 'em all. The splendor of the Tournament of Roses and its football attraction only made the sports editor more confident that New Orleans could rival it eventually. What he found that California had—and New Orleans lacked—was simply the willingness to do it.

When he returned, Digby found an ally willing to cooperate. The city's Association of Commerce sanctioned the effort to put together a Carnival of Sports and an intersectional football game. Digby called for a week-long calendar that could, hypothetically, include a championship fight, an open golf tournament, midwinter Davis Cup tennis trials, an indoor track and field meet, a special handicap horse race, and the football game.

"What the little city of Pasadena has done with the Tournament of Roses," Digby wrote, "New Orleans can do a hundred times better with a Carnival of Sports."

Weeks, then months, then years went by without any substantive action. It galled the *Item* to realize in the latter part of 1933, two years after the Association of Commerce entered the effort, that Dallas was putting on a postseason game of its own on New Year's Day, the Dixie Classic. Miami had already staged a game in its Festival of Palms attraction and was looking to its second during the holiday season. These were the antecedents of the Cotton and Orange Bowls. Neither had real appeal but were more along the lines of the Doll & Toy Fund enterprises of 1929 and 1930. Centenary and Arkansas competed in Dallas; Duquesne and the University of Miami played in Florida.

The *Item* praised Dallas editorially, and shook an angry finger at New Orleans.

"Dallas and Atlanta," said the *Item*, "usually do the things that New Orleans ought to do, and get the things that New Orleans ought to get, all the way from Federal Reserve banks to 'football classics.' We sweat at Carnival (Mardi Gras) preparations and fuss with each other over local politics while Texans and Georgians go and get what they want, which is very often what we ought to have. The Tulane Athletic Association, not caring for a postseason game itself, has not cared to show the slightest interest and concern in the enterprise as a matter of municipal comity—though its stadium was built by popular subscription in this city."

Digby had information that at least two teams, Pittsburgh and Nebraska, in addition to LSU and Centenary, were interested in playing in New Orleans had the committee acted promptly. And he admonished Tulane for its lack of support. Part of the difficulty in getting Tulane's sanction was the flim-flam image bowls other than the Rose Bowl had at the time. University officials weren't certain the institution should be linked to such an enterprise.

The entire matter seemed to have reached an impossible impasse. There were five noteworthy games on January 1, 1934: the Rose Bowl in Pasadena, the Dixie Classic in Dallas, the Festival of Palms in Miami, the East-West Shrine game in San Francisco, and a charity all-star game in Knoxville, Tennessee. New Orleans had a high school game.

In January, 1934, the sports editors of the *Times-Picayune* and the *States Item*, Bill Keefe and Harry Martinez, with a group of prominent citizens, received the following notice from Joseph M. Cousins, a highly regarded businessman and former president of the New Orleans Athletic Club:

Gentlemen:

Will you please arrange to attend a meeting to be held at my office, 2003 American Bank Building, Monday, January 8, 1934, 12:30 P.M. to discuss plans in connection with the formation of a football league after the regular playing season; also to discuss ways and means of endeavoring to adopt a plan that will mean the staging of a big football game in New Orleans on New Year's Day.

Yours very truly,
J.M. Cousins

Cousins was head of an Association of Commerce group called the Citizens' Committee that had come up with an idea of a semipro football league that would play on Sundays with a championship game on January 1.

At the same time the Co-Operative Club, an organization of executives, had decided to become involved in the formation of a New Year's Day bowl. Both groups, in essence, were anxious to try to get the New Year's Day football concept off the ground. Miller presented his plan to the *Item* asking for the newspaper's approval. *Item* managing editor Clarke Salmon recommended to Miller that the Co-Operative Club unite with Joe Cousins' party.

Fred Digby, of course, was present for the detailing of Miller's plan at the *Item*. Invitations to a meeting with Cousins were sent to Keefe and Martinez because Digby knew full well a venture of this size would need the endorsement of all the papers. Digby was willing to low-key the *Item*'s role for the support—at least for a while.

"We passed a resolution in January of 1934 suggesting a New Year's Day game," said Miller of the circumstances leading up to the official meeting in Cousins' office, "and no sooner had the plan been published than we learned that another group was planning to promote a semipro league and wind up with a big championship game for charity on January 1. We talked it over, and they liked the idea of inviting only college teams, so we decided to get the entire city behind the plan."

Dr. Fred Wolfe, Dr. M.P. Boebinger, Francis "Hap" Reilly, Ralph Barry, and T. Semmes Rantlett joined Cousins, Miller, and Digby in the January 8th conference. They were enthusiastic and confident that business, fraternal, and civic associations would unite behind the undertaking. Others weren't quite as sure. The *Times-Picayune* and *States* sports editors didn't attend and Keefe waited four days before commenting; then he said he doubted the Southeastern Conference would approve the game, pointed out the venture had no guarantees against the weather, and recommended instead a boxing carnival, a rodeo, or an indoor tennis match. Martinez didn't write a word about it, pro or con.

Miller's blueprint was simple. A nonprofit organization would be formed, meaning not a cent would be retained above operating expenses—the associations and businesses involved would volunteer some of their time and labor to the work load of the project; the $30,000 it was estimated necessary to attract top-flight teams would be derived by securing 30 guarantors to pledge $1,000 apiece.

The plan had to be amended because only one of

the organizations, the *Item*, whose backing was pledged by James Thomson, was able to pledge the $1,000. A signing of 300 guarantors at $100 apiece—with assurances of only one thing: their money back or its value in tickets—was agreed to be a more feasible plan.

A coalition of individuals and associations began being molded into one athletic front on February 6, 1934, in a preliminary, organizational meeting. Sixteen organizations committed to the undertaking and selected delegates to work on the project and prepare for the drive for guarantors.

Miller, at the expense of the Co-Operative Club, was in Baton Rouge two days later for a Southeastern Conference meeting. Miller wanted the SEC's sanction for the bowl. Another New Orleans group also attended the league talks, seeking permission to hold a New Year's Day all-star game. Since nothing was known of the second group's existence before the gathering, the SEC must have been somewhat confused. But the conference tabled any decision on the bowl plan because it didn't want to commit itself while the movement was still in the process of mobilization. Miller was encouraged. "They didn't say 'yes,' but they didn't say 'no,'" he reported with a smile.

The *Times-Picayune*'s reportage came across with a slightly different tone, that the proposal by the New Orleans sports *amusement* organization had been voted down.

The Mid-Winter Sports Association was officially chartered at the February 15, 1934, meeting at the New Orleans Athletic Club. Forty members of 23 citywide organizations welded together for the purpose of a December-January sports program. According to the charter drawn by Miller, the Association was stipulated to be a "Voluntary, nonprofit civic organization whose members serve without remuneration; there would be no connection with commercial interest or professional sports; there would be no private profit; and any surplus above the required operating expenses or reserve fund must be devoted to 'charitable, religious, or educational purposes.'"

Miller was unanimously elected president, Joe Cousins vice president, T. Semmes Rantlett secretary, and Harry W. Fletcher treasurer.

Miller hinted broadly that evening that the game would have immediate credibility because he was certain a Southeastern Conference team would be in one corner of the inaugural. He noted that no conference member (meaning the Southern Conference from which the SEC descended in 1933) had ever been refused permission to play in a postseason game. Miller was sure a team invited to New Orleans would not be denied.

"I am sure that if we go back to the Southeastern Conference in November or December with an invitation for one of its teams to play in our game here, that the executive committee will act favorably upon it," Miller said. "We will have no trouble getting a big game for New Orleans every year. What we've got to do is prove to the world that we

An early planning meeting of Sugar Bowl founding members.
Front: Fred Digby, Joseph M. Cousins, Warren V. Miller, Irwin F. Poche, Harry W. Fletcher; Back: Abe N. Goldberg, Dr. Fred J. Wolfe, Albert Wachenheim, Jr., Jacob H. Bodenheimer, Dr. M. P. Boebinger, John Niehaus.

The elegant silver Sugar Bowl trophy.

can put this project over. That job is up to us."

That meant preparing for the hardest part, securing the $30,000 by public subscription. Some still feared it was too steep a task for the times. "We settled that in a hurry," Miller said. "I got Clarence Strauss, who was president of the Co-Operative Club, to try out the plan personally. He went out by himself and got 13 guarantors in 15 visits. We were ready to go ahead then, and soon had guarantees of $32,700."

Miller was next scheduled to attend a convention of Southwest Conference authorities, for there was sentiment the game should be played between the champions of the SEC and the SWC. The visit brought the game's first conference sanction. "We got the approval of the Southwest Conference, providing we had the money in the bank," said Miller. "So we started advertising the game to the world."

Things began falling into place. The Southern Yacht Club agreed to a midwinter regatta, something never attempted in New Orleans previously.

Douglas Watters and Allan Smuck, two tennis enthusiasts among the Mid-Winter Sports Association's members, put together an invitational tournament in conjunction with the football game. It wasn't exactly the carnival Digby dreamed of, but it was a beginning.

Tulane remained standoffish to the idea of its stadium being used. Several donors to the private school were close to the bowl project as well. They privately, but anonymously, allowed Tulane authorities to become aware of their strong interest in the success of the bowl. Tulane acquiesced and allowed rent-free use of its stadium for one day a year by the Mid-Winter Sports Association. The decision was a boon for school and bowl. It would play a role in Tulane being able to continue competing with a major college football program years afterward.

The Sugar Bowl was Digby's suggestion as a name for the game. It was ideal and it was adopted. New Orleans is near the heart of Louisiana's mammoth sugar cane industry, and Tulane Stadium is situated on the site of Etienne de Bore's sugar plantation (which covered the tracts that are now the Tulane and Loyola university campuses and Audubon Park). De Bore's plantation was one of the state's first and de Bore, the first mayor of New Orleans, turned from the cultivation of chicory and indigo to the raising of sugar cane in the 17th century, despite the warnings of others that cane juice would not crystallize. The industry de Bore helped found is alive today; and the area of Louisiana just south and west of New Orleans is known as "America's Sugar Bowl."

An elegant piece of silver became the trophy and personality of the Sugar Bowl, giving the Mid-Winter Sports Association a classical tinge even before consummating its purpose. The sterling silver bowl was handmade in England in 1830 during the reign of King George IV by the silversmiths Rebecca Emes and Edward Barnard. It was probably used as a wine cooler or trophy piece. Samuel Waldhorn, a renowned New Orleans antique dealer, obtained the rare piece on one of his yearly European business trips. The bowl formed part of Waldhorn's celebrated antique silver collection. It was spotted by some Sugar Bowl friends of the Waldhorn family who made a fast-talking appeal to Samuel's civic pride. "I don't know how they did it," said Stephen Moses who now runs the antique concern. "They must have been *very* close friends of my grandfather."

It was decided the striking trophy would be given to the winning football team for a one-year period, then a replica would be donated for permanent possession. Samuel Waldhorn's magnificent generosity gave the Sugar Bowl style from the beginning.

Things were humming until a crisis occurred in October. Paul B. Williamson, whose football ratings service was among the most popular in the country until the wire services began their polls, and Richard Fleming resigned from the Mid-Winter Sports Association, and T. Semmes Rantlett died in the fall of 1934.

A lingering and inaccurate legacy of those formative days is the legend of the "39ers," the 39 men who founded the Sugar Bowl. The loss of three men from the original 40, of course, is 37, though even the listing of the charter members usually totals 39. Two of the three men—and all are mentioned on one list or another—who were unable to continue are added, seemingly to fill the roster.

The combination of circumstances left the Sugar Bowl $5,000 short of $30,000.

"I went out and got Paul E. DeBlanc, new president of the Co-Operative Club, Joseph B. David, and some personal friends to raise the money," Miller said. "In 10 days we collected $5,100 in fresh money and had the $30,000 in the bank when we invited Tulane and Temple for the first game. Ten days later, the guarantors got their money back. Money received from the sale of tickets (was) sufficient to pay the guarantees and expenses of the first game."

With the necessary money in escrow, and Tulane's consent for the rent-free use of its stadium, the Southeastern and Southern Conferences gave the Sugar Bowl their blessings.

Ten years after James Thomson casually asked Fred Digby about the possibility, New Orleans was to host a major postseason football game.

Tulane-Temple

TUESDAY, JANUARY 1, 1935

Cover of inaugural Sugar Bowl program.

Crowds storm ticket counters for 1935 Tulane-Temple inaugural.

"We're only here stooging."

The Mid-Winter Sports Association wanted to annually pair the most evenly matched teams, to create the best game possible. Once the Sugar Bowl realized just how far it could reach for quality teams—despite the new Orange Bowl in 1935 and the well-established Rose Bowl—the somewhat popular sentiment for an annual game between the Southeastern and Southwest Conference champions or a North-South format quickly evaporated. The Sugar Bowl's guarantee of $15,000 to the visiting team was a large sum in the midst of the Depression. The "home" team was assured of $12,500, and $2,500 was alloted for the Association's expenses.

From the start, there were mixed feelings about a conference tie-up, with the SEC being the most logical choice. First, there was the assurance of one corner being filled by a quality team with some familiarity in New Orleans, leaving the Bowl free to concentrate on luring big names from outside the South. On the other hand, if the game was open-ended, it might be possible to pair the most evenly matched teams. This was the route Digby favored and the direction chosen. It was understood, however, that if an area school deserved an invitation, it would be extended.

With the necessary funds deposited in a bank by November 1, the Executive Committee concentrated on the caliber of teams across the country. The Sugar Bowl would not allow the home team a say in selecting its opponent as the Rose Bowl did. After contacting the schools and receiving an agreement, the Sugar Bowl's final decision was expected on Sunday, December 2. But no announcement was made. The Committee went back into session at 5 P.M. the following day at the New Orleans Athletic Club. At 9:30 P.M. the pairing was official: Tulane and Temple.

Although Temple was largely an unknown quantity to New Orleans, it quickly became apparent the Sugar Bowl had done its homework and that gave it credibility. Temple was coached by Glenn "Pop" Warner, already a legendary figure, and the Owls were ranked third nationally in the Williamson Poll. Temple was undefeated, though tied twice, and was considered the "Northern Champion." Its roster included a sophomore fullback, Dave Smuckler, said to be "better than Jim Thorpe" by Warner, who had coached Thorpe at Carlisle Institute. Tulane was the natural attraction for local fans and an obvious choice for the home berth. The Green Wave was 13th-ranked, with a 9-1 record, and could be expected to draw several thousand additional fans from the immediate area. Tulane, in many ways, was a godsend to the first Sugar Bowl. It was the popular choice of the Mid-Winter Sports Association and of Fred Digby.

"All New Orleans is anxiously awaiting word and expecting Tulane to be invited . . . It is inconceivable that Tulane would refuse the invitation since it will offer her an opportunity to provide impetus to an event which the entire city is now supporting with an enthusiasm seldom aroused in an athletic event here," Digby wrote the afternoon of the selections.

Inconceivable or not, Tulane did not want the invitation. School officials did not, players did not. The coaches did. It was later rumored that the Greenies believed they merited Alabama's Rose Bowl berth, or that they wanted a rematch with Colgate, the only team Tulane failed to defeat in 1934. Neither was the case.

Ted Cox's first assistant, Lester Lautenschlaeger, said he was told by Esmond Phelps, president of the Tulane board, to call a team meeting and to "have the team vote down the invitation." Lautenschlaeger would have had no difficulty doing that. His task was to get the team to change its mind on an enterprise the Tulane coaching staff felt could become worthwhile.

Barney Mintz, a junior back on the team, insisted there had been no talk about the Rose Bowl, and it had nothing to do with the Green Wave's reluctance. "In fact," he said, "we were surprised when they called us in the team meeting. The Sugar Bowl naturally didn't mean anything to us then. We didn't know anything about it. They called us in and Lester said, 'Look, we have an opportunity to go to the Sugar Bowl, which is the first time it is being held. We think it would be nice, but we're gonna leave it up to you.' The vote was basically unanimous against it."

The coaches apparently had already signalled the Sugar Bowl the bid would be accepted, because they were aghast. "Well, they were shocked," said Mintz, "because they knew what kind of position they were in. Lester got up again and said, 'Now look, let's think it over, maybe we didn't explain it.' We went through the details, that it was a community undertaking, and that Tulane was in a position . . . and should respond." A suggestion was made by a player that they be given $150 a man for playing and was immediately vetoed.

"We took a vote," Mintz added, "and I would guess the vote was not quite enough for a majority. We got a few more. Then Lester got up again and made a really impassioned plea, that we were going to embarrass the university and such and such, etc., you know, the usual thing. I don't know what the vote was, but it was at least one above a majority. We were gonna go out and play." By then, even Tulane President Dr. Albert Dinwiddie was in favor of it.

There was a chemistry working for the Sugar Bowl now. Certainly Temple, with Warner and Smuckler, aroused the curiosity of a large block of fans. The hometown Greenies, boasting a ballcarrier

the equal of Smuckler, Claude "Little Monk" Simons, accounted for another segment of fans. What will never be known is how many of the half-hearted were prodded into attendance by the *Item's* sports staff.

Pie Dufour recalled with a chuckle, "Scoop Kennedy and I would leave the office at lunchtime and go over to the Maison Blanche ticket office, which was downstairs in the men's clothing department. Scoop and I would go stand in line to make it look longer. Then when we'd get to the window, we'd tell the man, 'We're only here stooging.' After that, we'd leave the line, wait a few minutes, then go back in line again. We did that for a week or 10 days to try to stimulate business, make people think this was the damndest demand they ever saw!"

In two days, the Sugar Bowl sold more than $20,000 worth of advance tickets at $3.50 and $1.50 apiece.

Tulane 20-Temple 14

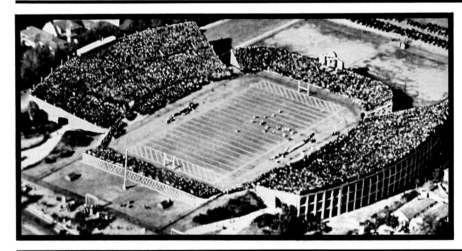

Tulane Stadium on January 1, 1935.

"No one laid a hand on me."

Despite the offensive firepower of both teams, it appeared early on the cool, cloudy afternoon that it would be the pure luck of football that would dictate the outcome. Dave Smuckler was all he was built up to be. Pie Dufour described him as "212 pounds of speed and power who asked nothing more of his own line but that it get out of his way and let him run." That he did, but it was Tulane which allowed him into the end zone.

Toward the end of the first quarter, a period in which the Temple line took command of the game's tempo, Barney Mintz fumbled on the Green Wave 10 and Stan Gurzinski recovered for Temple. Smuckler gained three yards off tackle on first

down. The instant the teams lined up again, the ball was snapped and Smuckler took the handoff. As the Greenies zeroed in, Smuckler rose and zipped a pass to Danny Testa, who had eased just over the goal behind defensive back Monk Simons. Smuckler added the conversion.

Owl quarterback Glenn Frey put Tulane in a deeper hole midway through the second period with an out-of-bounds punt. Stanley Lodrigues then fumbled, and Bill Docherty recovered on the Wave 18. Two consecutive reverses put the ball on the 4. Tulane held twice. Then Smuckler catapulted over center from the 2. Temple led, 14-0.

"In case you hadn't guessed," recalled Assistant

Coach Lester Lautenschlaeger, "we weren't in the best of spirits at the time." But Simons, playing one month after fracturing a shoulder in the act of a game-winning punt return against LSU, proved every bit the match for the heralded Smuckler. Wearing a shoulder pad made partly of rubber to protect the injury, Simons sprinkled the first glitter of Sugar Bowl lore into the classic.

Temple kicked off from within 10 yards of the sideline to keep the return man bottled up on one side. Wave quarterback Johnny McDaniel took the ball at the 10 and ran up a few yards, taking most of the Owl coverage to one side. Then he lateralled to Simons, 5 yards behind at the 15 and running in the opposite direction. A pair of defenders were fooled only for a wink and then rushed over to choke off the ballcarrier from the sideline alley. Unable to shake the pursuing Owls, Simons almost skimmed the sidelines.

Simons vividly recalled a huge cherry-jerseyed figure with outstretched arms that seemed to cover the width of the field and appeared ready to enclose Monk at the 35. "It looked like he had me pinned to the sidelines," Simons said, "and I had just about made up my mind to run over him when Stanley Lodrigues, our substitute fullback, came out of nowhere and wiped him out . . . That was the biggest obstacle in my path . . . the rest of the team set up a wall, and I simply ran down the sideline. No one laid a hand on me."

That block and another by McDaniel made the field appear deserted and by the time he reached the Tulane 40, Simons could have started adding the points. "Johnny and Monk," said Lautenschlaeger, "did a remarkable job of camouflage."

Tulane's Claude 'Monk' Simons, the Sugar Bowl's first hero and, later, its president.

Dick Hardy makes touchdown catch as Wilfred Longsderf dives at his heels.

Tulane starters for the 1935 Sugar Bowl. Linemen, from left, Charles Kyle, Roy Ary, George Tessier, Homer Robinson, Robert Simon, Robert Tessier, and Dick Hardy. Backs, Barney Mintz, Joe Loftin, Claude 'Monk' Simons, and John McDaniel.

It was Simons 11th touchdown of the season and set the tone for the second half, which Tulane stormed.

Bucky Bryan provided the impetus for the tying touchdown with a spectacular 28-yard gain late in the third quarter. Tulane worked itself to a first down on the 4. Bryan dropped back and passed to Dick Hardy, who leaped high between two Owls and came down with the ball in the end zone despite one defender still clinging to his back. Mintz's PAT tied the score.

A second Hardy reception for 12 yards early in the fourth quarter started Tulane moving again. The catch put the Wave at the Owl 48. After Joe Lofton gained 6 yards, Mintz attempted two passes. Horace "Bucco" Mowrey diagnosed the second pass perfectly and stepped squarely between passer and the receiver, Hardy, at precisely the right instant. But the ball brushed his fingertips and bounced up. Hardy rushed over, took the ball on the run, and raced un-

touched the remaining 15 yards as Wilfred Longsderf dove desperately and futilely at his heels. It was the third sensational reception of the day for Hardy. Longsderf kept Temple's hopes alive by blocking Mintz's conversion to keep the score at 20-14.

Simons laughed years later that he could still see Dave Smuckler at the postgame party, wearing a derby and a seersucker suit and smoking a cigar. Members of both squads were given the suits, then a novelty. "It's a helluva thing," Smuckler told Monk, "to come all the way down here and wind up with a pair of pajamas."

Smuckler came down for more than that. The attendance of 22,026 allowed the Mid-Winter Sports Association to present each school with a check for $20,759.20, approximately a fourth again of their guarantee. The quality and derring-do of Temple and Tulane left fans buzzing. The Sugar Bowl was in business.

TCU-LSU

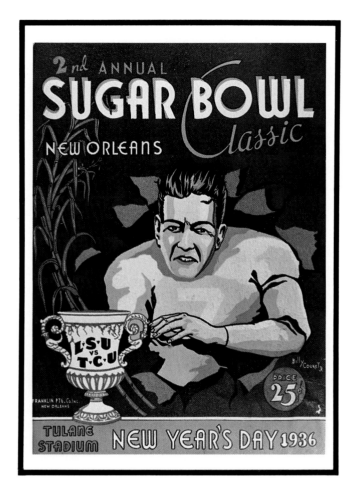

Duck hunting and Slingin' Sammy

Mary Frances Digby remembers her husband coming home the night of January 1, 1935, in a quiet, contemplative mood. "He was very happy," she recalled with a smile. "After a while, he just looked up and said it had been a dream come true."

Almost as soon as the dream of a Sugar Bowl became a reality, it began to build momentum and expand. It was Bill Keefe, noting that general admission tickets weren't put on sale until the day of the game (which put a strain on ticket sellers and forced 2,000 fans away), who called for a 5,000-seat increase of Tulane Stadium. That bit of crusading a couple of days after the Tulane-Temple game must have caused Digby some slight amusement.

Both the *Times-Picayune* and the *States* had given the first Sugar Bowl events as much coverage as the *Item*. The pull of all three influenced the initial wave of popularity that struck as the football game neared.

A February meeting was held to make plans for the following Sugar Bowl. The Sugar Bowl was left with $10,370.61. Half that total was placed in a sinking fund, along with an unsolicited $12,300 already received from eager guarantors for the 1936 game. The other $5,000 was set aside for expenses the Association might need for the coming year.

Also, the Mid-Winter Sports Association became exclusive in 1935. Membership rolls were closed and limited to the original organizers. They had succeeded beyond anyone's belief in less than a year. Four hundred and twenty guarantors put up money for the 1936 game.

Everything the Mid-Winter Sports Association touched at that time was just right. A year after Tulane was the natural selection for the inaugural, LSU emerged as an obvious choice. The Southeastern Conference champions won nine straight after an opening 10-7 loss to Rice and had a flock of exceptional players. They included Abe Mickal, one of the nation's best passers, and Gaynell "Gus" Tinsley, considered the best end in the country. The defensive-minded Tigers had allowed three SEC opponents less than 50 yards from scrimmage.

LSU's probable acceptance was verified belatedly because Athletic Director T.P. Heard returned late from a Tuesday afternoon duck-hunting trip. Heard was asked by a reporter if LSU had a preference of whom it would play. "Our preference is TCU or Nebraska—either would make a great game," said Heard.

Texas Christian was announced as LSU's opponent, and the Sugar Bowl may have backed into its stated goal—the best game possible. TCU was ranked fourth in most polls and had a crowd-pleasing attraction in "Slingin'" Sammy Baugh, whose passing skills had set the Southwest ablaze. The Horned Frogs had finished second to Southern Methodist.

The TCU and SMU match, each team 10-0-0, was the first Southwest football game to be aired on a nationwide radio hookup. Matty Bell's Mustangs had surrendered only three touchdowns and shut out seven opponents. Dutch Meyer's Horned Frogs averaged three touchdowns a game. This game didn't stir just fans; writers from across the country showed up as did three coaches on a busman's holiday—Dana Bible of Nebraska, Lynn "Pappy" Waldorf of Northwestern, and Bernie Bierman of Minnesota. A dramatic 20-14 SMU victory sent the Mustangs to the Rose Bowl, the only Southwest Conference appearance in Pasadena. TCU was more than acceptable to the Sugar Bowl.

More than $40,000 in tickets had been sold before the pairing was announced. Five thousand dollars more came in the day after, and three weeks before the game only a few hundred tickets remained. It was estimated the alphabetical match of LSU-TCU could have drawn 45,000, but the largest crowd to see a sporting event in Louisiana was already assured, despite slightly higher-priced tickets than for the 1935 Sugar Bowl.

The Mid-Winter Sports Association also reached an agreement with the National Broadcasting Company for a coast-to-coast radio hookup. It would immediately precede the Rose Bowl and introduce another estimated 15,000,000 fans to the Sugar Bowl.

Things were going so well it must have been scary at times. The only possible problem could have been the weather. But Warren Miller and Fred Digby ran a check on New Orleans' New Year's Day weather the year before for the Tulane-Temple match. Cloudy and cool had been the average reading for decades, and it hadn't rained on New Year's in 25 years.

Mid-Winter Sports Association Secretary Herbert Benson, left, and President Joseph M. Cousins stand outside the first official Sugar Bowl office at 722 Common in 1936.

TCU 3-LSU 2

"I had a hand in all the scoring."

It poured the last three days of 1935. "There's no doubt but we'll have a slippery field," commented Texas Christian Coach Dutch Meyer as he looked out at the downpour. Meyer noted his team had not played on a wet field in three years, but said, "We'll throw all our power into the game from the start—passing and running. May the best team win." The rain stopped in the early morning hours of New Year's Day but started again shortly before the kickoff, and all hope of the anticipated Baugh-Mickal aerial circus went swirling into the gumbo-like surface of Tulane Stadium.

Considering the conditions, the crowd may have witnessed the finest touchdownless game ever played. The players started with a handicap. Equipment at the time added approximately 15 pounds to an athlete's weight. When the leather helmets, woolen jerseys and awkward padding became soaked, as happened early in this game, the load increased.

Bernie Moore, the LSU coach, seemed determined to show the Horned Frogs some of the balance the Tigers had used in their 9-game victory string. On the first play from scrimmage, at the LSU 23, Abe Mickal daringly threw a strike down the slot to receiver Jeff Barrett. Sammy Baugh was able to recover and knocked the ball down. The second Sugar Bowl quickly settled into a kicking duel of heroic proportions.

George "Junior" Bowman, one of LSU's captains, carried a second quarter punt to the TCU 18 for the first threat of the soggy afternoon. After 168-pound guard Tracy Kellow threw Jess Fatherree for a 7-yard loss, Bill Crass completed a pass to Barrett on the 5 for what appeared to be a certain touchdown.

Baugh, as good a defensive back as he was a passer, shot over from his safety position and wrestled the end down at the two. Crass went over center and was stood up by Darrell Lester after gaining a yard. It seemed to be a costly play. Lester, an excellent lineman, broke a shoulder on the tackle. Jack Tittle, a virtually untested sophomore, went in to hold down the middle. The Tigers took dead aim at the middle of TCU's eight-man line.

'Slingin' Sammy Baugh had a hand in all the scoring in the 1936 Sugar Bowl.

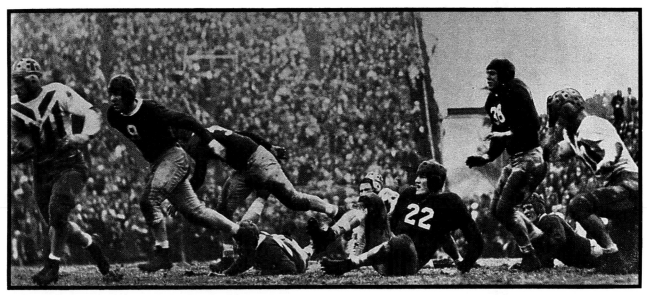

LSU's Rock Reed pulls away from the Horned Frog line.

Six inches separated LSU from six game-winning points.

On second-and-goal from the 1, Crass was smothered almost before he started moving by Tittle and most of the defensive line. A pass went incomplete, pushing the count to fourth-and-goal from the 1. Moore passed up the field goal and sent Crass back into the line, where he was stopped six inches from six points.

The threat did not go unrewarded. Baugh backed up to the end zone on a fake punt. LSU's ends, Barrett and Gus Tinsley, came crashing in and Baugh attempted to get the pass off, but the ball slipped off his fingers and dropped to the swampish end zone turf, an automatic safety.

Will Walls recovered a Crass fumble on the LSU 45 on the Tigers' next possession, and Jimmy Lawrence connected with the same Walls for a 28-yard gain. Three plays lost 4 yards.

"We couldn't get anywhere," said Baugh, "so on fourth down, I called for a field goal. I held the ball, and I believe I was more nervous than Taldon (Manton) was. The kick was from the 26 and, as I recall, it was on the order of a line drive . . . at first I thought it might go wide to the right . . . but it stayed inside the posts."

Manton's field goal put TCU in a 3-2 lead. Pinky Rohm carried for a third consecutive time and was happy when TCU called time, figuring he could catch his breath while the Frogs tried to figure how to stop him.

For the remainder of the half and through the third quarter, the weather and Baugh's sensational punting duel with Mickal and Crass, who alternated kicking duties for LSU, kept both sides at bay.

Micky Mihalic separated Baugh from a Crass punt early in the fourth period and later recovered the fumble on the TCU 32. LSU sloshed its way to the 2—mainly on sweeps by Crass—where Baugh

Sammy Baugh, under pressure from Tiger ends Gus Tinsley (24) and Jeff Barrett, dumps off an incomplete pass in the end zone that accounted for a safety and LSU's points in the 3-2 TCU victory.

The starting LSU line for the 1936 game: from left, John Mihalic, Paul Carroll, Oscar Matlock, Moose Stewart, Wardell Leisk, Eddie Gatto, Gaynell Tinsley.

stopped what appeared to be a sure touchdown by nailing Bowman on an end run. Three plays netted the Tigers a minus 2 yards. "Ernie Seago and I asked to try a field goal," Mickal recalled, "but Coach Moore said he thought we could make it (a touchdown). We didn't."

Baugh, with a sterling defensive (two touchdown-saving tackles and two interceptions) and kicking effort to complement the threat of his offensive skills, pointed to Jack Tittle and little Tracy Kellow for equal praise. Tittle, who had played 39 minutes of flaming football after replacing Lester, was a huge factor in the mild upset. "He came in and did a great job backing the line," Baugh said, "and we sure needed good linebacking. LSU had more good ballcarriers than we'd seen all year."

Slingin' Sammy was the deserved center of attention. In perhaps the finest kicking game ever,

considering the circumstances, he had shaded the LSU tandem with a 47-yard average compared to a 45-yard average. Slight as it was, the difference may have been decisive. Of that remarkable exhibition, Baugh recalled, "Well, I remember doing a little kicking . . . and I guess you can say I had a hand in all the scoring."

Strangely, his biggest thrill was being on the same field with LSU quarterback Ernie Seago. "When I was a kid," Baugh said, "Ernie and I were neighbors. I idolized him, wanted to be just like him. You always enjoy it when you play against someone you've been close to."

Sammy had to be filled in on his enjoyment. He had been dazed by a hard blow in the second quarter and played the rest of the game by instinct. He couldn't remember much of it.

The game knocked out New Orleans, too.

LSU's Pinky Rohm breaks free for a near touchdown against Texas Christian.

Santa Clara-LSU

FRIDAY, JANUARY 1, 1937

"Build big for the future."

Each school collected $30,041, the largest sum either had ever received from a football gate. Texas Christian got something else, too: LSU's top spot in the final Williamson Poll when SMU lost to Stanford, 7-0.

Grantland Rice exclaimed editorially that after two years of existence, "The Sugar Bowl football classic has made the most amazing progress of any sports event developed anywhere in recent years." Rice also noted that the fledgling game needed more room.

It was plain that football interest had exceeded expectations. After the Tulane-Temple game, Bill Keefe saw the need to add 5,000 seats. Fred Digby envisioned a 60,000-seat stadium after LSU-TCU.

Bob Geasey, the Temple sports information director, had returned to New Orleans for the second Sugar Bowl. He told Digby, ". . . Remember, you're not building for next year or the year after, but for 10 and 15 years to come. Build big for the future!"

Digby, characteristically, wasted little time in presenting the case for a larger stadium. Two days after the Texas Christian victory he wrote, "Undoubtedly, the most feasible plan is to enlarge the Tulane Stadium. Its capacity can be boosted to 60,000 before next New Year's Day by making a 'sugar bowl' of the structure."

It was readily apparent a larger football facility was necessary, but that matter would have to wait a little while. The major move made by the Mid-Winter Sports Association after the second Sugar Bowl was to a more centrally located office at 722 Common Street. Also, they hired their first full-time employee.

Edna Engert, a brown-eyed, personable young woman whose interest in athletics was minimal until she met her husband, was hired to run the office. It was a significant decision. Edna would leave a mark on the organization.

For its third game, the Sugar Bowl was initiated into bowl politics. The Cotton Bowl went into operation on January 1, 1937, the first year all of the major bowl games were in business. There were also two lesser bowls and a pro exhibition, but the Sugar, Orange, Cotton, and Rose Bowls were clearly special.

LSU, again the Southeastern Conference champion, ranked No. 1 by Williamson and No. 2 in the first Associated Press poll, was the darling of every post-season game committee. The Mid-Winter Sports Association had several options for the 1937 game. An LSU and third-ranked Pittsburgh game would be in keeping with the North-South formula that some favored. Sixth-ranked Santa Clara, ineligible for the Rose Bowl because it wasn't a Pacific Coast Conference member, was considered the best West Coast

team. This school would broaden the Sugar's horizon. Then there was the possibility of an LSU-Alabama match. Only a tie in the conference had kept the Tide from sharing the title with the Tigers in a year when those teams did not meet. LSU-Alabama would have been attractive but sectional.

LSU was the key and high on the Rose Bowl list. Meanwhile, the Rose Bowl pondered an opponent for the University of Washington. But the Rose Bowl bypassed LSU for Pittsburgh, giving the Sugar Bowl the season's plum in a game with Santa Clara. The *Item* ran a series of nationwide sports editorials ridiculing and laughing at Pasadena. A typical piece was written by John Lardner of the North American Newspaper Alliance, who took some light jabs at the two once-defeated, once-tied schools matched in the Rose Bowl. "For instance," wrote Lardner, "there is the one about the two football teams named Pat and Mike. 'Have you been asked to the Rose Bowl?' says Mike. 'Hell, no,' says Pat. 'I'm undefeated.' "

The Southeastern Conference felt snubbed because two of its teams, LSU and Alabama, were overlooked in California. The SEC hinted that perhaps it and the Sugar Bowl ought to join hands. However, the Sugar Bowl saw the risk of a conference tie-up as the Rose Bowl demonstrated in choosing Washington.

Santa Clara was invited and accepted the Sugar Bowl invitation on December 6; at the time, it was the nation's only undefeated, untied (7-0-0) major college team. Sammy Baugh, the hero of the 1936 Sugar Bowl, tarnished the Broncos' unbeaten aspirations with a 9-0 Texas Christian victory on December 12, showing New Orleans the two-edged sword of bowl politics.

Still, Santa Clara, an old mission school founded in the 1700s, brought some glitter. The Broncos were coached by Buck Shaw, who was renowned for developing outstanding lines and was a tackle under Knute Rockne. The team included an All-American quarterback, Nello Falaschi, and an end, Jim "Mississippi" Smith, who gave Santa Clara a down-home flavor.

Five thousand additional seats had to be installed in Tulane Stadium, which brought the capacity to 41,000. It still wasn't enough.

Possibly the only fans unaware of what was building in New Orleans were Californians. "We were extremely happy when we got the invitation," said Al Wolff, a sophomore tackle for Santa Clara. "We had heard of the Sugar Bowl, but not a great deal. The papers on the West Coast concentrated only on the Rose Bowl. But we felt we were good enough to play in a bowl game, against a really good team."

Santa Clara 21-LSU 14

Cotton Milner is tripped up by the Bronco defense.

"Find a pair that fits and put 'em on."

Incredibly, it rained for the second consecutive year on New Year's Eve and continued until just before the kickoff. LSU, which would suffer the most from the weather because of its passing attack, turned up the wrong card at every occasion.

Nello Falaschi took the opening kickoff on the Santa Clara 17 and returned to the Bronco 41. Pat Coffee, who was LSU's best passer, made the tackle but was jarred on the play. He put in only nine minutes the rest of the game.

On Santa Clara's second possession, on second and 10 from the LSU 44, halfback Don DeRosa, out of the Notre Dame box, ran right, looking for a receiver. Tiger end Bernie Dumas broke through and grabbed the runner. Somehow, DeRosa was able to shed the tackler, and he reversed his field, picked up some blocking, and raced to the LSU 32 before being stopped. It may have been the pivotal play of the game.

Fullback Charles Pavelko gained 3 yards at left tackle before Bill Crass batted down a sure touchdown pass from DeRosa to Mississippi Smith. Falaschi faked a handoff to Pavelko, then dropped back and passed to Manuel Gomez. The halfback took the ball on the dead run at the 5 and strolled over the line.

After forcing LSU to kick away, Bruno Pellegrini booted the ball 51 yards out-of-bounds on the Tiger 1-foot line. Taking no chances, Coach Bernie Moore ordered Crass to kick out. Under pressure, Crass hurried the kick and it was downed on the LSU 28. Three plays lost a yard, but Santa Clara went for it all on fourth down and made good. Pellegrini started right, then stopped and shot a pass down the middle to Santa Clara's Norm Finney, who stealthily got behind the secondary and into the end zone.

Eleven minutes after it began, the outcome of this game seemed as obvious as the mounds of mud on the uniforms. The best gauge of what was happening wasn't just a glance at the scoreboard. One of the country's most efficient offenses was being dismantled. LSU went 25 minutes before gaining a first down. Shaw had trusted center Phil Dougherty to keep LSU off-balance with defensive calls, and the 180-pound junior performed flawlessly.

Gus Tinsley put LSU back in the hunt late in the second quarter when he caught a 10-yard pass from Crass; then, seeing the right side overloaded with defenders, he reversed field, picked up a convoy, and went the distance. The 50-yard play cut the difference to 14-7 at the half.

The agility of both teams was affected by the waterlogged and mud-caked togs. Shaw was determined to give his Broncos their best shot, and during the first half had sent an assistant to talk to coaches from Loyola who were in attendance.

"When we got to the dressing room," recalled tackle Al Wolff, "there were dozens of shoes sent over by Loyola, just scattered around the floor. The coaches said, 'Find a pair that fits and put 'em on.' Then we changed into our practice uniforms for the second half, and we were ready to play again."

At the beginning of the second half, Santa Clara moved in for the kill. Gomez intercepted another Coffee pass and returned it from the LSU 40 to the 15. After the Broncos edged to the 4, Mississippi Smith tried an end run, but a yard from the goal with two defenders ready to scissor him, he threw the ball straight up in the air.

"I just looked up and saw that thing flying out of there," Dougherty remembered with a hearty laugh. Falaschi and DeRosa, several yards to the side of the runner, each went up for it as if going for a rebound, and their combined momentum carried Falaschi, who made the catch, into the end zone. The PAT snap was botched, but Falaschi picked the ball out of the mud and passed to Smith for a successful conversion.

Although LSU was not doing much, the Broncos cracked the door for the Tigers in the fourth quarter. LSU's Bernie Dumas rushed Jules Perrin as he punted from the Santa Clara 12. The kick went straight up and came down on the 18. Guy "Cotton" Milner gained 6 yards; then Crass hit LSU's Rocky Reed on the dead run for the touchdown.

It added some excitement to a finish radio listeners didn't hear. NBC cut to the Rose Bowl with about two minutes to go. "A lot of people in northern California were furious," said Wolff. "My mother said it seemed forever before it was announced that Santa Clara had won."

Santa Clara won in a record-shattering manner. The two teams combined for 10 fumbles, a statistic never achieved in a bowl before.

The media hovered around Falaschi, without whom it was felt the Broncos couldn't have won. Nello said, "I asked them (his teammates) to dedicate the game to Mrs. Shaw (Buck's wife, who was ill and had to remain at the hotel) and to win it for her, and they made good."

"We used five different defenses against the Tigers," explained Shaw in praising Dougherty who called the defensive sets. "We didn't know what to expect, never having scouted them. So we planned to shift around a lot so as to keep them off-balance. Dougherty's job, therefore, was to try to outguess the LSU quarterback. He showed considerable shrewdness in guessing what defense to use. We used two quarterbacks to beat LSU. Falaschi called the offense, Phil Dougherty the defense. Both did a great job. Every boy out there did his best, and some did better than their best."

Buck Shaw, coach of the Santa Clara Broncos.

Santa Clara-LSU

SATURDAY, JANUARY 1, 1938

Youngsters pose for photographer Josef Cermak who wanted to il-
lustrate the happy condition of the sold out LSU-Santa Clara game
in 1938. Models were brothers Bobby, left, and Junior Schmitt.

"Let each play and prosper."

Nearly a quarter of a million fans attended football games on the first day of 1937. The Rose Bowl drew 87,000; the Sugar Bowl 41,000; the East-West Shrine game 40,000; the first Cotton Bowl 17,000; the Orange Bowl 12,000; and the Bacardi Bowl in Havana, Cuba, had an attendance of 6,000.

Thoughts of an SEC-Sugar Bowl tie-up rose again with a degree of sheer nastiness when Alabama's Coach Frank Thomas brought up the issue less than a week after the LSU-Santa Clara game. Thomas predicted the South "will choke the Rose Bowl to death if the (Sugar Bowl) situation is handled properly." "Properly" to Thomas meant a tie-up with the SEC and the Southwest Conference, with an agreement to reject any and all invitations to Pasadena. Thomas pointed out that 7 of the last 10 visiting teams to the Rose Bowl were from the South.

Thomas was irked because Pasadena had passed up his Crimson Tide; the comments were embarrassing to the Mid-Winter Sports Association, which was not anxious to see the demise of the Rose Bowl. Pasadena was respected for the example of what it had built. Pie Dufour wrote plainly and simply, "Let each play and prosper." Then, too, there was the feeling by the Sugar Bowl that a tie-up would not necessarily help in assuring the best game possible each year.

Fred Digby said he felt the Rose Bowl preferred Eastern teams. "The purpose of the Tournament of Roses," he reminded, "is to interest the rich men of the East and induce them to move out of the snow and ice and into the sunshine of southern California. That was the reason Pittsburgh got the bid over LSU and Alabama." Digby added, "But the Sugar Bowlers shouldn't enter into any agreement like the one the Pacific Coast Conference has with the Rose Bowl. The Sugar Bowlers shouldn't let anyone take control of their classic now that they've put it on a firm foundation after three years of toil."

It was plain almost from the opening kickoff of the first game that the Sugar Bowl would eventually need a larger football stadium. Interest in the game was astounding. The fledgling Sugar had to expand its facility (mainly with temporary arrangements) for each of its first three games. The stadium size would affect the growth of the Sugar Bowl.

There was talk early in 1937 of expanding City Park Stadium, which seated 25,000 to 70,000, and of moving the bowl site there. It was also reported that state authorities were negotiating with the Works Progress Administration for money to erect a 100,000-seat stadium near Lake Pontchartrain. The Mid-Winter Sports Association wanted little to do with either project. Proud that what it had accomplished was free of any political entanglements, the Sugar Bowl wanted to keep it that way.

Tulane had tried to obtain WPA funds to make its football facility horseshoe-shaped; efforts failed because of its private status. Sugar Bowl officials, realizing that Tulane was the best site for their attraction, approached university authorities with a deal. Tulane's north end zone wooden seats would be taken out and a steel stand would be erected, pushing the stadium's permanent capacity to 37,000. With the temporary seating, a crowd of several thousand more could be accommodated.

Tulane loved the idea, but there was one slight hitch: The Sugar Bowl didn't have the estimated $180,000 for the project. The Association wanted the university to loan it the money. Tulane administrators were a bit put out by the suggestion. Albert Wachenheim, Jr., a member of the executive board, recalled, "We had to persuade Tulane that it was to their benefit, too."

Tulane was persuaded to loan a total of $164,768.84, and notes would consist of a $20,000 payment for each of the following eight years, plus five percent interest. Tulane would bear the responsibility of stadium upkeep, and the Sugar Bowl would continue its rent-free status.

Southeastern Conference officials, in a March session in Atlanta, listened to a warning by league President R.L. Menuet of Tulane that bowl games were growing to a "most menacing extent." The SEC then went on record as sanctioning only the Sugar Bowl and the Rose Bowl and "no other so-called 'bowl' games." The move, in effect, said SEC members would be granted permission to play in no postseason games other than in New Orleans and Pasadena. As the Orange Bowl screamed 'foul' and 'politics,' the Sugar Bowl membership had to feel pretty smug. But Miami and the other bowls would have the last laugh on this matter.

Alabama and LSU were again the premier SEC football teams. The Crimson Tide was the conference champion; the Tigers were a notch behind with one loss. There was some argument over which was the best team, but the Sugar wanted 'Bama for two reasons: 1) It was the champion. 2) LSU had been in the game two consecutive years. Pittsburgh, which brought snickers when it was picked for the 1937 Rose Bowl, was the hottest prospect in the country.

The Sugar wanted a match between the Tide and the No. 1 Panthers. But the Rose Bowl flexed some muscle in these pairings. California was the Rose Bowl host of 1938 and stated it wanted to play a school with "comparable academic standards."

Alabama and Fordham were apparently each given the impression they were the Pasadena choice, but the Tournament of Roses made no announcement.

Fred Digby believed the Rose Bowl was trying to

embarrass the Sugar Bowl by delaying their own selection and at the same time attempting to keep Alabama and Fordham out of New Orleans. The Sugar Bowl gave those schools 24 hours to make up their minds: Take the Sugar or gamble on the Rose. When time was up, the Sugar extended invitations to LSU and Santa Clara. The Rose had still not made its selection.

Frank Thomas, who 11 months before was talking about the demise of the Rose Bowl, gambled and won. Fordham gambled and stayed at home.

The biggest jolt of December came when Auburn asked for permission to participate in the Orange Bowl. In granting the request, the Southeastern Conference also voted eight to five to rescind the February resolution which looked favorably only on Sugar and Rose Bowl participation.

Digby, whose views certainly reflected that of the Mid-Winter Sports Association membership, was angry. He revealed that a week before, at the suggestion of Alabama and LSU, the Association seriously discussed the advisability of presenting a plan for a definite agreement with the SEC for a tie-up. At the last minute, the Sugar Bowl was asked to hold the plan in abeyance. Obviously, one of the Sugar's guidelines would have been that the SEC would compete only in New Orleans, and the Conference must have known of Auburn's forthcoming request.

Digby wrote that the Sugar Bowl was now free of any obligation—real or imagined—to the Southeastern Conference. It could now look to all corners of the country to fill its berths.

Santa Clara 6-LSU 0

"And that was the way the game was played all day."

Cotton Milner of LSU carries to the Santa Clara 4 on a fake punt.

Santa Clara became the first undefeated, untied team to perform in the Sugar Bowl. Al Wolff, the junior Santa Clara tackle, said, "The year before, we knew we'd have to play over our heads to beat LSU in 1937. But for the 1938 game, we were the better team. Our feeling was LSU would have to play over their heads to stay close to us."

In many ways the rematch seemed a continuation of the 1937 Sugar Bowl. Thirty-nine thousand fans watched in less than ideal weather. It was drizzling for the kickoff, but the field was in excellent shape. As a precautionary measure, it had been covered several days in advance.

After an early punt exchange, Pinky Rohm kicked to the Santa Clara 23 where Orv Hanners bobbled the wet ball, lost it, regained possession, and then lost it again to Barry Booth at the 28. Rohm flicked a pass to wingback Cotton Milner for 11 yards, then cut back off tackle for 13 yards more. Wolff prevented a touchdown by dropping Pinky at the Bronco 4.

"I was able to save that touchdown because I broke one of our fundamental rules," Wolff said. "Something just told me they were going to try something wide, and instead of penetrating, the way we were coached to do, I just ran laterally across the field. As it turned out, I was able to prevent a touchdown."

On three of the five plays, starting with Rohm's jaunt to the 4, Wolff was Santa Clara's sole protector. "I'm convinced," he said, "that series made me an All-American. All those sportswriters remembered it the following year when, in all honesty, I didn't have as good a season."

Both coaches substituted entirely new lineups in the second quarter, and the Tigers began losing ground in the kicking game. LSU was pinned to the 6 and, with the aid of a penalty, the 1. LSU's Young Bussey punted to James Barlow at the LSU 45, and Barlow carried it back 24 yards. Jimmy Cajoleas made the tackle at the Tiger 21. Bruno Pellegrini tried to get off a pass, but LSU's Ken Kavanaugh threw him for a 9-yard loss. Coach Buck Shaw then pulled out a play he had used the year before against LSU.

Barlow, a substitute halfback, took the ball on what appeared to be a developing sweep to his left. As he reached the end position, Barlow wheeled and threw diagonally across the field to quarterback Ray McCarthy. The play covered approximately 50 yards, but the 20 officially credited to Santa Clara gave the Broncos a first-and-goal at the LSU 9. Mississippi Smith gained 5 yards in two plays. Pellegrini took the snap, leaped, and blazed a pass over end Jimmy Coughlan's shoulder in the flat. Coughlan, in almost one motion, made the reception and bounded into the end zone, despite the jolt of being hit by three Tigers. Pellegrini's conversion was wide.

Rohm seemed to have LSU primed by the fourth quarter. He quick-kicked the ball 56 yards, out at the Bronco 9. Jack Roche, on first down, barely averted an LSU safety when Ogden Bauer threw him down inches from the goal. Barlow dropped behind the end zone to get the ball out of the danger zone, and then kicked it 55 yards.

Pinky had LSU right back in position with a return to the 32, where George Locke prevented a possible touchdown. The Bronco defense stiffened again, forcing a punt. But Santa Clara jumped offsides on the kick, giving LSU a first down. Santa Clara again held until fourth down. Rohm went back in kick formation, but as his leg arched he handed the ball to Milner, who raced 21 yards to the 4. In what must have been one of the most frustrating days in LSU annals, the last man, John Schiechi, stopped Milner.

A 6-yard loss and two successive incomplete passes to Milner in the end zone turned the ball over to Santa Clara on its 20.

The teams surged at each other for most of the remainder of the quarter, but with less than three minutes left, Buck Shaw seemed to have matters well in hand. He sent in Charles Pavelko to spell Pellegrini, then he looked up to see Pavelko not only kicking from the Santa Clara 29 but getting off a terrible kick that went out-of-bounds at the Bronco 45. Santa Clara, in essence, had given LSU a free chance at victory.

"I called plays for both the offense and the defense," explained Phil Dougherty. "It was highly unusual for a center. Now, the rules at the time stipulated that no one but the signal caller could speak in the huddle . . . and there was a penalty attached to a violation. Pavelko came in as a quarterback, so I wasn't sure Coach Shaw hadn't sent him in with a play. I looked over to him in the huddle and said low, 'You call the play.' His eyes got as big as half-dollars and he didn't say anything for what seemed like a long time. Finally, he said, 'We'll punt.' I was shocked. He could have called anything, but he called for a punt." As it turned out, it was a 16-yard punt.

Any possible repercussions ended when Hanners intercepted a Bussey pass and returned it to the Bronco 44. Shaw then opened himself up to criticism as his team tried to kill the clock by inching toward midfield. He ordered his troops to go for the yardage on fourth and a long four at the 50. The play fell short.

On the game's final play, Bussey connected with Kavanaugh, who briefly looked as if he were getting away. Bill Gunther brought the big end down at the 23. "We just figured they would go to him," said Wolff. "We were waiting on that play . . . but he still nearly did it. And that was the way the game was played all day."

Indeed it was. LSU out first-downed and outgained the Broncos by wide margins. But in the end, Santa Clara belted the Tigers with a shutout, LSU's first in 50 games. That little stat allowed LSU to become the first school to lose three bowls in successive years.

TCU-Carnegie Tech

MONDAY, JANUARY 2, 1939

End zone view of Tulane Stadium during the 1939 Texas Christian-Carnegie Tech Sugar Bowl.

"I'm gonna play in the Sugar Bowl!"

It didn't take long for the Sugar Bowl to even up with the Southeastern Conference over their snit. Many choice teams were available during the 1938 season, enough for everyone. The University of Tennessee won the SEC championship with a 10-0-0 record and was the favorite to fill the host berth in New Orleans. Possible opponents from the North were Carnegie Tech, Villanova, and Fordham. Texas Christian and Duke (undefeated, untied, and unscored upon) were more than acceptable, but the Mid-Winter Sports Association seemed to be interested in a North-South game.

Pasadena vacillated between Duke and TCU. The Cotton Bowl panted over the possibility of the No. 2 Horned Frogs, with Heisman, Maxwell, and Camp trophies winner Davey O'Brien, the 5-foot-7 glamour player of the year, as quarterback. All-American center Ki Aldrich and All-American tackle I.B. Hale added more tinsel to the TCU trappings. "If the Sugar Bowl can get Carnegie Tech," wrote Flem Hall of the Fort Worth *Star-Telegram*, "the boys might prefer such an opponent to a beaten California or a twice-beaten Southern Cal team."

The conjecture was startling because it precluded an SEC team, which everyone assumed the Sugar preferred. The Rose Bowl was certainly a strong consideration for the TCU staff and squad. The Cotton Bowl wasn't. "The boys and fans would rather go to New Orleans than Dallas," wrote Dick Freeman of the *Houston Chronicle*. "Get TCU in there with Carnegie Tech and the state of Texas will move to New Orleans."

Carnegie Tech's appeal stemmed from its winning the No. 6 ranking and the Lambert Trophy, symbolic of Eastern supremacy.

Tech was playing a midseason game with Notre Dame in South Bend, Indiana. In the fourth quarter of a scoreless game, with the ball placed near the 50, quarterback Ray Carnelly lost track of the downs. He asked referee John Getchell, who said it was third down. Carnelly ran a play that was stopped short of first down yardage. Getchell—realizing then he had made a mistake and that it was a fourth down play that had just been run—turned the ball over to the Irish. Notre Dame was able to use its field position in the fading minutes to push across the game's only points. Acidly, Skibo Coach Bill Kern assessed, "It was the biggest bonehead I ever saw pulled by any official. I don't know if he will quit or not, but I know what I'd do in his place." To Tech's credit, it went on to win its next four games. Carnegie Tech finished 7-1-0 and was acclaimed the best in the East. Notre Dame rose to the No. 1 spot nationally after defeating Carnegie Tech.

After TCU defeated Southern Methodist in its

final game, the Cotton Bowl extended its invitation, though the Frog staff said nothing official.

On November 29 the Sugar announced its pairing, TCU and Carnegie Tech. Duke accepted the Rose Bowl challenge against Southern Cal.

With an excellent Tennessee team expecting bids from the Sugar or the Rose, the SEC appeared shaken by the New Orleans selections. Georgia Tech Coach Bill Alexander told the Associated Press he was "amazed." Joel Hunt, the University of Georgia coach, was quoted by AP to the effect that the selection "might be a little act of independence." Fred Digby wrote piously that the Sugar Bowl felt free to invite anyone, indicating that getting the best game possible was most important to the Mid-Winter Sports Association. He also subtly chided those who snubbed New Orleans the year before.

The match turned into what Grantland Rice called "The Game of the Year." Southern Cal defeated Notre Dame the week following the selections, which lifted TCU to No. 1. Tech retained its No. 6 spot.

New Year's was bringing to New Orleans the nation's No. 1 team (TCU), the nation's No. 1 player (O'Brien), the nation's No. 1 coach (Bill Kern), the nation's No. 2 coach (Dutch Meyer), and the nation's No. 1 official, Johnny Getchell.

That's right. Getchell was one of the officials submitted to be considered by Carnegie Tech. Shortly after the Notre Dame game, Coach Kern sent a telegram to Getchell which read, "Forget it. It's all in the game. Best regards."

Several questions arose about the game. What in the world was a Skibo (a Tech nickname—the other was Tartans)? Would Ki Aldrich be able to play? The anchor of the imposing TCU line had been hospitalized with an ulcer on the cornea of his eye.

The Skibos, a team of 42 engineering students and 1 musician, were named for Andrew Carnegie's manor, Skibo Castle, in Dunfermline, Scotland. Carnegie, it was said, delighted in being referred to as "The Laird of Skibo Castle." Tech students picked up the nickname.

Aldrich had recurring eye problems after being involved in some freshman-sophomore class horseplay his first year at TCU. He led a group of freshmen up a flight of stairs in a night "raid," but a "guard" at the top of the landing turned a fire extinguisher on the invaders. The spray caught Aldrich in the eye. His screams broke up the prank. For some strange reason, Ki yelled for salt water. When some was obtained, he bathed his eye in it and then was brought to the infirmary. It healed slowly, and from time to time eye difficulties would flare up on the youngster. Between the end of the regular season of his senior year and the Sugar Bowl, he again had to be hospitalized.

However, TCU got an emotional lift on the day the team was to leave for New Orleans. Aldrich's injured eye opened, and his vision was restored. Ki jumped into his clothes, ran out, and raced across campus until he spotted Dutch Meyer. "Coach, coach," Ki yelled joyfully, "I can play! I'm gonna play in the Sugar Bowl!"

TCU 15-Carnegie Tech 7

"Coach, we got 'em on the run now!"

Almost everything about the Texas Christian-Carnegie Tech match-up was different from the first four Sugar Bowls. For the first time the SEC wasn't represented; for the first time a Louisiana school wasn't playing; and for a first time the game was not played on New Year's Day, which fell on a Sunday. A crowd of nearly 50,000 was in the stands for the kickoff, anxious to see a team that lived by the pass and another that had completed only 16 passes all season.

The smaller, quicker Tartans opened the game by surprising TCU with four successive power plays that carried to the Horned Frog 45. But, running at left tackle, George Muha fumbled and Allie White recovered for TCU.

Tech's defense against the air-minded Davey O'Brien, who threw for 1,509 yards and 19 touchdowns during the regular season, was based on generating extreme pressure from its ends. Karl Striegel went to work, smothering the diminutive quarterback. O'Brien countered the Carnegie pressure by calling plays that required his ends to come back behind the line or to move into the short flat. Quickly, the Horned Frogs drove to the Skibo 12. Just as the fast noose looked like it was going to drop on Tech as many expected, the Skibos fended off the threat. Earl Clark dropped a pass at the 5 on fourth-and-four to allow Carnegie Tech a deep breath.

Carnelly, who meant as much at quarterback to

George Muha wheels into the Texas Christian line.

Tech as O'Brien did to TCU, was lost before the first quarter ended with a severe ankle injury. Carnegie Tech drove to the Frog 49 early in the second period, though, in a modest march that concerned TCU. The defense called time-out.

"That was the first time," said Ki Aldrich, "that anyone made us do that all season, the first time we had to call time to adjust." The drive extended only 5 yards more.

Jack Odle, with TCU's only punt of the day, slammed Tech against the wall with a 40-yard kick to the 6. When Merlyn Condit kicked back to the Tech 47, the Frogs were poised for a strike. After nudging his unit to the Tech 19, O'Brien unleased a fourth-and-five bullet to Johnny Hall, who was brought down at the 3 by Henry Pyznski. Connie Sparks lost a yard when guard William Rieth penetrated. O'Brien ran a keeper and gained 3 before Sparks again slammed over right guard. It took several minutes to unravel the mass at the goal, but finally the officials signalled a touchdown. Sparks got in by an inch. Unbelievably, O'Brien, who kicked 28 extra points during the regular season, missed the PAT.

Condit dropped into punt formation after Tech gained 4 yards, to its 36, on the ensuing possession Instead of kicking, Condit arched a pass to a streaking Ted Fisher, who made the catch and a 21-yard

gain before Aldrich made the tackle. George Muha picked up 5 yards before Pete Moroz was substituted for Condit at left halfback. Moroz immediately put the ball up and Clark intercepted on the 26, returning it to the 37. TCU was offsides, and the ball was brought back to the 32 where it was third and one yard to go.

TCU took another time-out. There was 1:10 remaining until the half. Muha got nothing at right guard, but the Skibos were in motion and penalized to the 37. Moroz backpedaled almost to midfield, waited for Muha to work past O'Brien, a natural target because of his 5-foot-7 height, and looped a pass. Muha took it at the 1 without breaking stride and went over. Muha's PAT made the score Tech 7, TCU 6, marking the first time the Frogs had been behind all season.

"I yelled, 'Coach, we got 'em on the run now,' " Aldrich remembered exclaiming to Dutch Meyer as the squads broke for the dressing rooms. "Meyer replied, 'Boy, I hope you're right.' We could sense that we had solved their offensive strategy," said Aldrich, "that if they hadn't scored by the half, they weren't going to. They simply were charging high. Once we adjusted, we felt we'd have them."

TCU's first second-half possession started at the 20. In five plays, the Frogs were back in front. An O'Brien to Clark pass pushed the ball to the Skibo

44. Three plays later Davey flung a darter to Durwood Horner, who made a nice grab at the 29 after beating Condit; Horner wheeled and went the distance untouched. O'Brien again missed the PAT, keeping Tech in striking distance.

O'Brien finally got his mates over the hump by whipping the Frogs downfield in the fourth quarter. A drive went from the 50 to the 1, but the Skibos again grittily protected the goal. Meyer finally sent in orders for a field goal attempt, which O'Brien kicked from the 9 to put TCU ahead, 15-7. Considering his PAT attempts, it could be assumed there was some consternation about O'Brien's attempt. Aldrich said no. "The extra points were just one of those things," he said. "Nobody thought Davey couldn't kick the field goal. We had a lot of confidence in Davey. I don't think I even thought he wouldn't make it."

The excitement wasn't over. Muha took the kickoff at the 4, picked up a convoy, and steamed 57 yards before Aldrich caught him from behind, almost certainly preventing a tighter finish. Shortly, O'Brien intercepted a pass at the TCU 21 and ran it back to the Skibo 47. Moments later the game ended with the Frogs on the Carnegie Tech 34.

'L'il Davey,' with a 17-for-28 passing performance for 225 yards, was the afternoon's darling. Tech's George Muha was the leading rusher with 73 yards. But Aldrich, who nearly didn't make the trip, was just as impressive with 19 tackles (13 unassisted) and an interception.

For the second time in four years, Meyers' Horned Frogs left New Orleans as consensus national champions. And, for the first time, a favorite had won the Sugar Bowl.

It didn't come easy. Admitting he was on edge until the game's final stages, a drained Dutch Meyer sighed, "I think I'm going fishing."

Davey O'Brien, 1938's football darling.

O'Brien, a 5-foot-7 passing marvel, unloads against Carnegie Tech.

Texas A&M-Tulane

MONDAY, JANUARY 1, 1940

"Let us strike while the iron is hot."

The original purpose of the Sugar Bowl from the businessmen's standpoint was to fill hotel rooms and restaurants and to stimulate commerce during a traditionally slack period. It was clear after five years that the concept was sound. Texas Christian-Carnegie Tech drew a crowd that spent more money during the four-day period leading up to the game than any group had at any other event or convention in New Orleans for the year, including Mardi Gras.

Mike O'Leary, manager of the St. Charles Hotel, said, "It came in the slump between Christmas and New Year's when every hotel in the country has a slump . . . It was just as though Santa Claus filled our stocking with the biggest crowd we've ever seen." Ray Alciatore, proprietor of the world-famous Antoine's restaurant, said his business had prepared 6,012 orders of Oysters Rockefeller in three days. "That's as many as we serve in an ordinary month," Alciatore exclaimed.

As usual, it was Fred Digby who saw beyond the contentment of the present to a cornucopia of the future. After the game, in a column on the front page of the *Item*, Digby sought to enlarge Tulane Stadium to 60,000. He suggested the issuance of debenture bonds to cover the $200,000 project.

Favorable reaction came from far and near, including an endorsement from former World War I flying ace Colonel Eddie Rickenbacker, then president of Eastern Airlines. Louisiana Governor Richard Leche wrote Digby an eight-page letter and promised that the state would take $5,000 of the issuance. Mike O'Leary spoke for many when he declared, "Let us strike while the iron is hot."

After weeks of studying sketches, the Sugar Bowl membership, with Tulane's approval, decided to build the capacity to 70,000 seats backed by $550,000 in debentures, which were to be paid off at the rate of $25,000 a year.

Each purchaser of a $100 bond would be given the option of buying two choice Sugar Bowl tickets prior to public distribution, and two percent interest would be paid after five years. It doesn't sound like much now, but 40 days after the drive began on March 7, the goal was reached.

The contract was awarded to Doullut & Ewing, Inc., and the firm itself purchased $40,000 in debentures to guard against any contingency that could possibly arise. "We'll have that stadium ready for January 1, 1940," said Jim Ewing to the Sugar Bowl when the company got the contract. "It will be a close fit, but we won't let you down."

The fit was even closer than Ewing thought. Originally, it was thought the enlargement would be of concrete, but the cost would have exceeded the $550,000. So the addition to the bowl and the double-decking of the side stands would be made of steel. The war in Europe threatened to skyrocket expenses in steel, and it became mandatory that the steel needed for the stadium be obtained without delay. This could be done only with a cash outlay above the partial payment already made. It was June when the first piling was driven. Working constantly, except on Saturdays when Tulane played home games, using steel from the Virginia Bridge Company of Birmingham, the contractors Doullut and Ewing met the deadline between the end of Tulane's season and prior to January 1, 1940. Tulane Stadium was now a complete bowl and the largest stadium in the South.

Sugar Bowl President Herbert A. Benson, fourth from left in straw hat, and Joseph M. Cousins, next to Benson, attend the driving of the first piling for the 1939 expansion of Tulane Stadium.

The only problem with expanding a stadium is the filling of it after it is completed. In 1940, the Sugar Bowl was lucky. A three-way tie between Tennessee (undefeated, untied, and unscored upon), Georgia Tech, and Tulane put the Sugar Bowl in fine position.

Texas A&M, the Southwest Conference's second consecutive national champion, was the prime choice for the visitor's berth. Heavyweight competition from the Cotton Bowl was a hurdle which stood in the way of the immediate signing of the Aggies after the regular season.

A&M Coach Homer Norton had an invitation to New Orleans tucked in his pocket right after his final regular season game. Dallas businessmen had put together a package of $170,000, to be split by both teams, as an inducement to A&M for a game with second-ranked Tennessee.

A&M's acceptance was contingent upon Tennessee's appearance. The Volunteers had the inside track on the Rose Bowl but did not want to say anything formally until their last game with Auburn a week later. So Norton let his players vote, and they chose New Orleans. On December 5 it was announced that A&M would meet fifth-ranked Tulane in the Sugar Bowl. It was the first Sugar Bowl pairing of two undefeated teams. Tennessee spent its holidays in Pasadena.

Getting Texas A&M, as it turned out, was easier than getting Tulane. Just as in 1935, the Greenies were hesitant about playing what amounted to one more home game. Halfback Fred Cassibry told New Orleans *States* sportswriter George Sweeney years after, "(Coach) Red (Dawson) worked us to death during the season. He was a hard taskmaster, but a fair one. He was the type of guy who felt you were at Tulane on scholarship, so you should play your best at all times or he would take that scholarship away. And that meant 100 percent at practice. Some guys just didn't feel like going through three more weeks of practice.

"We wanted some assurance that if we played, we would get something out of it ($150 a man was what the team wanted, Cassibry said later). No one could give us an answer, so we sent word that we didn't want to play in the game. Dr. (Rufus) Harris (Tulane's president) and the coaching staff said that we would always regret it if we turned the invitation down. They would have been right."

The Sugar Bowl was billed as a David (Tulane) and Goliath (A&M) match. Although Tulane was a bigger team physically, the Wave had 6 tackles ranging from 215 to 240 pounds and standing between 6-foot-3 and 6-foot-5. What brought on the David and Goliath comparison were the measurements of the featured runners—Tulane's 160-pound scatback Bobby Kellogg and A&M's 210-pound fullback John Kimbrough, who had played 60 minutes in every Texas A&M game.

Coin toss before the 1940 Texas A&M-Tulane classic.

Texas A&M 14-Tulane 13

A&M's 'Jarrin' Jawn' Kimbrough jars Tulane with a touchdown run.

"Anyone who tackles Kimbrough doesn't feel like talking."

A record southern crowd of 73,000 poured into the gates while Red Barber prepared for his broadcast on the NBC Blue network. The expanded stadium wasn't big enough to match the enthusiasm for Texas A&M-Tulane. Even Arch Underwood, a director of the Cotton Bowl, was in attendance.

This, of course, was the scene that stayed with Fred Digby the rest of his life: fans flooding into a huge Sugar Bowl stadium to see the cream of college football. "Other than having my baby," said Edna Engert, "sitting in that packed stadium, listening to all of those people cheering, was the biggest thrill of my life."

As skywriting planes, hired by Louisiana politicians, wrote messages of the on-going gubernatorial campaign against the clear blue heavens, A&M sent an early warning to Tulane: The Aggies meant business. A&M rode a fiery passing attack by quarterback Walemon Price to camp on the Green Wave 10 with a first down. In three plays, two raw power plays by "Jarrin' Jawn" Kimbrough, the Aggies were

a foot away from the goal, setting a classic strength-against-strength situation. Kimbrough hit the center of the line, the teeth of the Wave defense. He was hurled back with no gain, and the ball went over to Tulane.

When Stan Nyhan tried to kick out, he kicked against a stiff wind and the ball bounced out-of-bounds on the Greenie 32. Price went right back to the air, tossing an 8-yard completion to Herb Smith, a diminutive 153-pound end. Kimbrough came busting out of the Tulane line at tackle to the 16. On a no-gain end around, Tulane center Pete Mandich drove Derace Moser out-of-bounds, finally bringing the ballcarrier down with a fierce tackle. Referee Ted Arnold measured off 15 yards for unnecessary roughness. Kimbrough hurdled the Greenie line, his heaving shoulders landing three feet beyond the goal. Seven and a half minutes after the kickoff, Texas A&M led, 7-0.

Bobby Kellogg made Tulane hearts thump harder in the third quarter. Moser quick-kicked from the

Tulane's Bobby 'Jitterbug' Kellogg returns a third quarter punt to put Green Wave back in the hunt with Texas A&M.

Tulane takes the lead against Texas A&M on Monette Butler's 1-yard run.

The decisive play: Herb Smith, the smallest man on the field, blocks Jimmy Thibault's PAT.

Aggie 33. Kellogg retreated to handle the flat-arced kick. It bounced high at the 24 while the Aggies bore down on Bobby. He took the ball, sidestepped the first tackler, then took off for the west sidelines. "I came up the middle," Kellogg said, "then cut for the sidelines . . . I went right past the Tulane bench. A block by Buddy Banker sprung me loose, and another by Al Bodney cleared the last man in my road . . . I had missed some practice because of injuries and when I reached the end zone I was a pretty sick boy." It was the longest Sugar Bowl run since Monk Simons' kickoff return in 1935. Jimmy Thibaut tied the game with his placement.

Tulane went into a near-blood frenzy when Moser fumbled and Mandich recovered on the A&M 39 as the third period ended. With Fred Cassibry and Monette Butler knifing through the suddenly shaken Aggies, Tulane pressed to the 1. Butler scored, and the Green Wave seemed totally in command. Little Herbie Smith, the smallest man on the field, popped through and blocked Thibaut's PAT. At that point, the miss didn't look important.

Starting from its 31, A&M came back. Price flipped a 9-yard pass to Smith, then a 10-yarder to end James Sterling. Kimbrough, taking a pass directly from center, barreled off tackle with Greenies bouncing off at all angles and plowed to the Tulane 27. Then he went wide to the 24. A&M's double-wing offense had shifted to high gear.

Smith then latched onto a pass at the 15 and lateralled to the streaking Kimbrough. "Jarrin' Jawn" ran straight into the cluster of Greenies and either left them sprawling or carried them with him into the end zone. Price's PAT put A&M back in front, 14-13.

Texas A&M completed an undefeated national championship season by the thin margin of one extra point and one blocked extra point. Wave Coach Red Dawson was convinced the Aggies benefitted from some crucial noncalls, including one on Kimbrough's winning touchdown run.

"They used the same pass play several times during the game," Dawson stewed. "The ends came across the line and blocked the middle linebacker out of the play. The rule states there can be no blocking downfield before the pass is thrown."

Dawson's last look at Kimbrough was something to remember. The Aggie fullback finished with 159 yards on 25 carries, a 6.9 average.

Kimbrough told Kellogg after the game, "You're the cleanest little tackler I ever saw." Kellogg didn't reply. He later said he couldn't say anything because "anyone who tackles Kimbrough doesn't feel like talking for 5 or 10 minutes."

Boston College-Tennessee

WEDNESDAY, JANUARY 1, 1941

Coach Frank Leahy, standing third from right, and Sugar Bowl Vice-President Joseph B. David, standing far right, introduce Boston College players to Santa Claus.

Boston College's Fred Naumetz, left, and Henry Woronicz serve part of the feast at Sugar Bowl party after the 1941 game.

"That's the way things were then."

In October of 1940 Fred Digby covered a University of Tennessee football game. Immediately after filing his story, he sent a telegram to the Sugar Bowl urging consideration of the Vols. He informed the Mid-Winter Sports Association that no one on its schedule was capable of defeating Major Bob Neyland's squad.

Then, as the year before, there were many good football teams from which the bowls could choose: Boston College, Texas A&M, Nebraska, Mississippi State, or Fordham. All were outstanding.

Tennessee was the key. The Cotton Bowl again considered a Texas A&M-Volunteer match, while in Pasadena there was strong sentiment to invite Tennessee back a second consecutive year. Neyland's

team again finished undefeated and untied Southeastern Conference champions. Only a loss to Southern California in the 1940 Rose Bowl spotted Tennessee's record over the course of 35 games.

The Tournament of Roses requested that Neyland hold off making a decision until it could decide. The coach saw no reason why he should gamble and take a chance of being shut out. On the evening of November 30, it was announced that Tennessee would play Boston College in the Sugar Bowl.

Boston College, under a 32-year-old firebrand coach, Frank Leahy, had run roughshod over the East and wiped out a 24-game Georgetown winning streak to wind up with a 10-0-0 record, identical to

Tennessee's. An early-season 27-7 victory over Tulane in New Orleans first alerted Sugar Bowlers to Boston College's potential. Neyland was famous for putting his faith in a strong kicking game and defense, but the Vols' offense was extremely potent, having scored 319 points in 1940. Only one team in the country scored more. That was Boston College with 320. Two weeks after the announcement, the Sugar Bowl was declared a complete sellout. Despite the statistics and close rankings, Tennessee opened a touchdown favorite and stayed there.

New Orleans, for the third consecutive year, had come up with the best game possible. The Vols and Boston College were ranked fourth and fifth in the final Associated Press poll. But Minnesota and Michigan were first and third, and their conference, the Big Ten, did not allow bowl participation. Stanford, committed to the Rose Bowl, was second.

Billy Sullivan, then the Boston College publicist, remembers John Drummey, an athletic department treasurer, making the trip. Drummey was not a football fan, as Leahy found out in Bay St. Louis, Mississippi, where Boston College set up its pregame camp at St. Stanislaus High School. Drummey pulled up in the middle of an unusually tough scrimmage while the intense Leahy bombasted the players. Drummey left his car, cheerfully walked to Leahy and said, "Don't worry about it, coach. It doesn't make any difference. I have the biggest check we've ever received for a football game."

Leahy turned a cold glare on the accountant and softly said, "John, it's just too bad you don't realize that this may be the greatest mismatch in history. This (Tennessee) is one of the greatest teams in history, the undefeated heavyweight champion. And all you're worried about is a check."

One observer at St. Stanislaus was Louis Montgomery, who knew full well what it would take to beat Tennessee: the best from every man on the Eagle roster. Montgomery's name was on the roster, but he would not be in uniform. He was a reserve running back, and he was black. In the South of the early 1940s, there was never any thought that Montgomery would suit up with his teammates.

"It's embarrassing to talk about it now," said the Rev. Maurice Dullea, S.J., then the faculty-moderator at Boston College. "But the (Sugar Bowl) committee made it quite clear that a Negro would not be allowed to play. It was kind of touchy . . . But that's the way things were then . . . One of our graduate managers was afraid someone would shoot at Louis

from the stands if we even let him on the sidelines with us. . . . Certain things didn't go with certain people in certain parts of the country. It was simply reality. Even the United States Army was segregated."

Jerry Nason, who covered the Eagles for the *Boston Globe*, said, "I'm almost ashamed to say it, and I was a guy who didn't mind stirring things up over an injustice, but it was just taken for granted when a team went South to play. I think the attitude was, 'We're gonna play in the South. They are our hosts, and we are their guests. We will play by their rules.'"

Montgomery was at least able to see his teammates in the Sugar Bowl. A black family in Bay St. Louis, people with ties to Boston College, wired Father Dullea offering a place to stay for the running back. When the Eagles played in the Cotton Bowl the year before, Montgomery wasn't able to make the trip. For the Sugar Bowl he was given a job spotting for reporters in the press box. Nason and some of Montgomery's teammates were able to see him display his athletic talents in a black All-Star game played on the Xavier University campus.

Neyland seemed skittish about his opponent, even holding secret practices. His armada of football talent didn't appear as impressed. Bob Suffridge was considered the premier guard in the country, and he overshadowed Ed Molinski only slightly. Bobby Foxx was the backfield scourge of the SEC. These were the sort of specimens that have come to be associated with the image of great football.

George Kerr, a brilliant Greek and Latin student studying for the priesthood, was a standout in the Boston College line. Charlie O'Rourke, weighing about 147 pounds by the time of the Sugar Bowl game, was the Eagles' offensive trigger. End Gene Goodreault made most All-America teams, but even here the gladiator image didn't fit; he had been struck with a form of paralysis as a child. Several relapses nearly killed him. He had heart problems by the age of 11.

Goodreault overcame it all to become an All-American. However, a knee injury threatened to, but did not, keep him out of the Sugar Bowl.

This was not the look of a team to be sent against Neyland's three-deep legions. "We'll be satisfied with anything better than a tie," said Suffridge, who won the Knute Rockne Memorial Trophy as the outstanding lineman of the year, "but I believe we'll win by at least a touchdown."

Boston College 19-Tennessee 13

James Coleman (31 in light jersey) of Tennessee is covered on all sides by Boston College's Charlie O'Rourke (13), Henry Toczylowski (22), Joseph Zabilski (44), Mike Holovak (12), and Chet Gladchuck (45).

"But the play O'Rourke scored on was a Tennessee play."

Frank Leahy, as well as Bob Neyland, became somewhat surreptitious as the Sugar Bowl drew near. "Two days prior to the game," said Leahy, "we had a live scrimmage, mainly to give our first team a last . . . look at Tennessee's single-wing offense. Our team succeeded in stopping everything except one of General Neyland's bread-and-butter plays . . . it was a fake pass run inside the end. During our final scrimmage it averaged seven yards per try against our first line. It was used approximately seven or eight times. We became impressed to the point where we decided after prac-

tice to incorporate the maneuver into our repertoire of plays."

On New Year's Eve, Leahy had the Eagle first stringers work on what they called "shift right, Tennessee special." Wearing sneakers and sweat clothes, they ran through it at the Bay St. Louis High School gym. The doors were locked; in fact, the session was so secret that Boston College's trainer didn't know about it.

The Tennessee special was quickly forgotten early the next afternoon as Boston College found itself in a hole shortly after the kickoff. Charlie O'Rourke

Tennessee's Bob Suffridge, the premier guard in pre-World War II football.

General Bob Neyland brought two undefeated, untied football teams to the Sugar Bowl and lost both times.

grabbed Bobby Foxx's first punt, attempted to run, was smacked, and fumbled. Center Norbert Ackerman recovered for the Vols on the Boston College 27. Van Thompson crashed the Eagle line for 11 yards, but four downs later Tennessee gave the ball up at the Boston College 15. O'Rourke punted back out-of-bounds at the Vol 46. A pass from Thompson to end Ed Cifers was allowed when O'Rourke, beginning to sprout goat horns, interfered on the Eagle 32. Thompson, five plays later, wading in behind superlative blocking by Marshall Shires and Bob Suffridge, scored. Foxx kicked the PAT. The score was 7-0 at intermission, but at that point there was no question which was the better team.

Very early in the third quarter something took place that was downright rare in southern football: Tennessee had a kick blocked. End Henry Woronicz rushed in as Foxx attempted to punt from the Tennessee 19. The ball bounced off Woronicz's chest and Joe Zabilski recovered. Mickey Connolly, in for O'Rourke, pulled Boston College even with a 12-yard sprint.

Center-linebacker Ray Graves, later the head coach and athletic director at the University of Florida, said, "We felt we had 'em beat at halftime. We were ahead 7-0 and pretty much in control. I

can still see the guy coming in from the left side. They blocked Bobby Foxx's kick, got the ball, and went in to make it 7-7. After that they were a different ball club, and we were sort of in a trance."

If Tennessee was in a trance, it didn't immediately show. Chester Gladchuk shanked the kickoff out-of-bounds at the Vol 45, and Neyland's team flowed downfield. Connolly allowed Tennessee to get to the three by interfering with Ed Cifers on a pass from the 14. Fred Newman scored in two downs. On the conversion Newman took a bad pass from center, tried to run with the ball, but failed to get across.

Boston College took its turn at the tennislike form the game had taken. Connolly skirted right end for a 9-yard gain after Donald Currivan returned the kickoff to the 31. The Eagles picked up an additional 15 yards on Connolly's sweep when Tennessee was penalized because substitute Don Edmiston talked to a teammate before the play was run. Then Connolly connected with Fred Naulmetz down the middle for 20 yards at the Vol 22.

The Eagles were at the 10 in two plays; after a 6-yard pass completion, Mike Holovak carried to the 1, then scored the tying touchdown. Tennessee jumped offsides when the teams lined up for Francis

Charlie O'Rourke eludes Ed Cifers (47), left, and starts Boston College's game-winning run on a play right out of the Tennessee playbook. Right, the scoreboard tells the numbing story.

Maznicki's PAT, placing the ball at the 1. Holovak tried to hit the line for the conversion but missed.

There were six minutes left when Boston College took over at its 20 with O'Rourke back at the controls. After gaining exactly 10 yards in three downs, O'Rourke threw two incomplete passes. He then connected with Ed Zabiliski for 20 yards. A second pass from O'Rourke to Zabiliski worked for 19 yards. When O'Rourke threw his third consecutive pass to Maznicki for 7 yards, the Vols called time out and changed their defense to send three men deep. For Boston College, it was time for the Tennessee special.

O'Rourke faded, raising his skinny arm as if to throw. Instead he cut sharply between Tennessee's tackle and end. Like a shadow he glided through a maze of flailing Volunteers 24 yards and into the end zone. There were two minutes remaining.

"I had a clear shot at him and missed," said Ray Graves. "He kept going parallel to the line of scrimmage, but coming back toward the sidelines. I had another shot at him—and missed. When he got to the sidelines, he turned downfield and scored just inside the boundary line. It really killed the general. We not only had a punt blocked, but the play O'Rourke scored on was a Tennessee play . . ."

Boston College missed on the extra point, but the game ended soon after with O'Rourke making an interception. The loss secured a strange Tennessee football fact. In three years the Vols had outscored its regular season opposition 807 to 42. And following those three seasons, bowl opponents had defeated Tennessee twice, outscoring the Vols 33-30.

The victory made a national name of Frank Leahy and within a month his alma mater, Notre Dame, sought out the coaching wunderkind to lead the Fighting Irish. The Sugar Bowl was the fuse to a spectacular career.

"Can you imagine," drawled Graves a quarter century later, "I missed O'Rourke twice and Frank Leahy has never thanked me for helping him get to South Bend."

O'Rourke found a spot in Edna Engert's heart as much for his actions after the game as during. "A friend brought him over to my house the night of the game," said Edna. "You know how he celebrated? With a glass of milk."

A standout in Boston College's team photo of the 1941 Sugar Bowl champions is the face of the figure standing second from the right in the second row. Just as proud as the others is Louis Montgomery.

Fordham-Missouri

THURSDAY, JANUARY 1, 1942

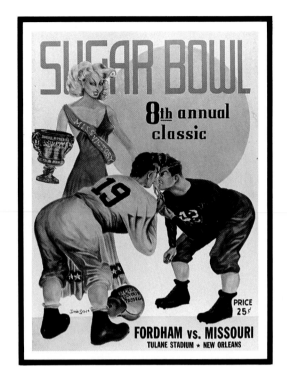

"Japs call home 2 attachés."

Picking the 1941 bowl teams was more of a guessing game than in the preceding few years. Mississippi State and Alabama were the logical SEC candidates; Texas A&M and Texas were the best bets from the Southwest Conference. A late-season loss to Vanderbilt eliminated Alabama. Mississippi State, the conference champion, had a game left with San Francisco after the pairings were to be announced. The Sugar Bowl was afraid to take a chance on the Bulldogs. Neither SEC team finished in the Associated Press Top 10. A similar situation occurred in the Southwest Conference. When the Longhorns upset the Aggies, the Sugar Bowl became interested, but was nervous about inviting Texas due to a late game.

Late Saturday, November 30, the Associated Press ran a story indicating that sixth-ranked Fordham would play in the Rose Bowl opposite Oregon State. But later the Sugar Bowl announced the Fordham Rams would play seventh-ranked Missouri. For the first time, New Orleans had a game without an SEC or SWC team. Public reaction was unfavorable at first, but on New Year's Day the Sugar Bowl was the only game with two Top 10 teams.

The champion of the Third Army and the Pensacola (Florida) Fliers, champions of the Eighth Naval District, were scheduled to meet in Tulane Stadium on January 3, 1942, in a service championship game approved by the War and Navy departments. The day after the announcement was made, however, the front page headline crowning the ominous global news read: "Japs Call Home 2 Attachés From U.S." Less than 24 hours later, the Japanese Empire attacked United States Navy and Army installations at Pearl Harbor. There would be no service championship game in 1942.

The war brought an immediate change in the suddenly inconsequential world of college football. Because California was believed to be a danger zone, the military demanded that the Rose Bowl and the East-West Shrine game be relocated. The Tournament of Roses shifted its game to Durham, North Carolina, home of Duke University. The Shrine game was also relocated to New Orleans. Tulane Stadium would be the site of the January 3 East-West Shrine game.

Some foresaw an offensive circus in the 1942 Sugar Bowl. Fordham, a 6-to-5 favorite, had a rock-like defense and a swirling passing game. Ram statistics were high, and they had a knack for the big play. The Tigers, with a strong split-T offense and a dynamic backfield, were the nation's best ground-gaining team, averaging 307.7 yards per game. The Tiger's coach Don Faurot said an opening loss to Ohio State led to revamping the offense. "The Ohio State game sold me on the split T," he said. "We ran 30 single-wing plays and averaged 1.8 yards per try. We ran 10 split-T plays and averaged 10 yards per carry."

Ram Coach Jim Crowley planned to counteract the split T with a Rockne defense, the Box and Seven, a seven-man line. This would allow the Ram ends and linebackers to "wait" for a play to unfold while the guards and tackles rushed. "If the seven and box made coaches stop using the T formation a dozen years ago," Crowley assessed, "it should do it again."

Fordham 2-Missouri 0

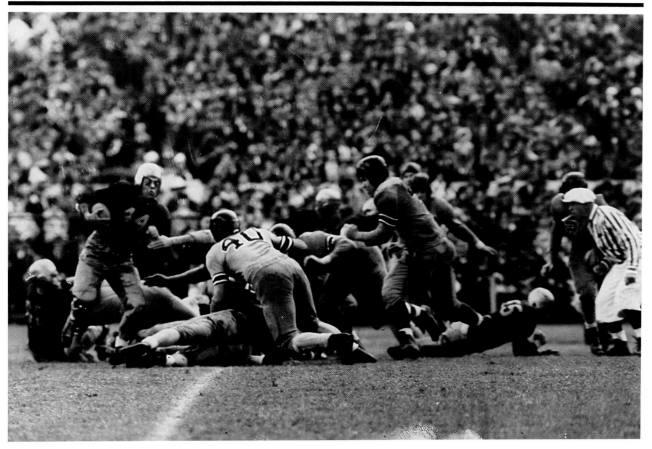

Waterlogged James Blumenstock (44) has precious little room to run against Missouri.

"Coach, two's enough. Don't pour it on."

It rained New Year's Eve, and just before the kickoff, it began to drizzle; clouds darkened the field. Missouri wasn't too concerned about the rain because the Tigers had won several games on wet fields during the season. "We were good mudders," said Harry Ice, a 157-pound quarterback. He had touchdown runs of 90, 76, 57, 21, and 16 yards during the season, and still finished second on his team to Maurice "Red" Wade, who averaged 6.6 yards a carry. The rain would later cripple the Fordham air game, however.

Tackle Alex Santilli was a big problem for Missouri, stopping the Tiger runners on their first possession. Ice got off a 59-yard punt that went out-of-bounds at the Ram 42. A driving rain swept Tulane Stadium as Fordham took over. Jimmy Blumenstock punted into the end zone after the Rams moved to midfield. By this time, Ice explained, "It was raining so hard, you couldn't see the ball until it was coming down and right on you."

Wade, on the first Missouri play from its 20, mishandled the ball, fumbled, and recovered for an 11-yard loss. Bob Steuber gained a yard, and Coach Don Faurot hustled in a substitute punter, Don Greenwood. Ice, the regular kicker, said the substitution was "just strategy."

On a low snap, Santilli flashed through and the ball hit him in the chest and bounced crazily back toward the end line. End Stanley Ritinski heard the "whomp" of leather against Santilli's soggy jersey and "just reacted to the situation."

Ritinski chased and finally corralled the ball by diving on it in the end zone and sliding off the field. Subsequent photographs showed that Ritinski had control of the ball before he went out, but the referee ruled otherwise and credited Fordham with a safety. Coach Jim Crowley said a player on the sidelines turned to him and cracked, "Coach, two's enough. Don't pour it on."

The two points meant different things to the players. Ice said it didn't mean a thing to him at the time. "No bother," Ice recalled. "We had been outplaying them, and had every reason to expect that to continue." Steuber had the same reaction. Ritinski said he was "just so thrilled to get anything

James Landing (88) of Fordham hightails it across the soaked Tulane turf.

on the board . . . we felt we had enough defense to hold them." James Lansing, the opposite Fordham end, concurred.

Missouri showed its vaunted ground game the next time it got the ball. Ice took a lateral and instantly seemed clear. "I made a crucial mistake," Ice explained. "I cut toward the sideline instead of the middle of the field." That decision allowed Joe Sabasteanski to barely catch Harry's arm from behind 34 yards upstream at the Fordham 47 just when it looked like he was open.

"When Harry went down," laughed Steuber, "I swear he looked like a powerboat sliding across that field."

Desperate, the Tigers decided to gamble at midfield in the opening moments of the fourth quarter. On a fourth-and-two situation, Missouri attempted to pick up a first down with a line play that failed. Fordham kept the Tigers bottled for the next two possessions. When Missouri got the ball on its 34 with five minutes remaining, the Tigers junked the split T and went to the single wing. Then they rattled off three first downs in succession, the last an 18-yard run by Ice that put the ball at the Ram 23.

Steuber attempted a reverse, but Santilli threw the runner for a 5-yard loss—a crucial play. As Missouri fans roared, Ice was held to no gain around right end. Jimmy Hearn knocked down another pass.

The field goal unit readied for its chance to pull a victory out of the quagmire. Ice knelt to hold for Steuber at the 35. The ball was snapped, Steuber got his foot into it, and the ball sailed straight toward the goal. Steuber and Ice began jumping up and down, hugging each other.

But the ball seemed to die, dipping just under the crossbar, and the referee signalled it was no good. Then the Tigers began to wonder about the 5-yard loss Santilli had inflicted a minute earlier.

Ice steadfastly maintained the field goal was good. Steuber said, "It looked good, but, heck, the official had the best look at it and he said no, and that's the way it was."

Fordham, the passing team, had won a Sugar Bowl without completing a single pass. It was the weather that got most of the press, however. United Press reporter Henry McLenmore wrote, "At the end of the game, the field was ready for stocking with trout and bream, and tarpon were reported to be leaping in the end zone." Another writer quipped, "Last time I looked up I saw a Fordham player penalized for doing an Australian Crawl."

"The way was paved."

Dallas was about to change the look of New Year's football—it had always urged a tie-up with the SWC. The Cotton Bowl had lost two stellar Southwest Conference teams, Texas Christian and Texas A&M, to the Sugar for the 1939 and 1940 bowl games. The Cotton Bowl got the SWC champion Aggies in the 1942 game only because the Rose and Sugar didn't extend invitations. Both Texas A&M and Texas were worthy bowl teams for the 1942 games, but A&M's 1941 loss to the Longhorns and a later Texas game made the Sugar Bowl back off.

Until then there was some division among the Southwest Conference officials about whether a tie-up was in the league's best interests. Two of the staunchest opponents had been Coach Dana Bible of Texas and Coach Homer Norton of Texas A&M. However, when those coaches and their schools felt snubbed by the other bowls, they began to listen more attentively to the Cotton Bowl offer.

Fred Digby assessed, "When the Rose Bowlers passed up the Aggies and Longhorns, the Dallas scribes took it as an insult to Southwest Conference football and blasted the Pasadena promoters. That done, they turned their guns on the Sugar Bowl and fired away. Thus the way was paved for a change in attitude by Texas A&M and Texas and the tie-up that is ahead."

So, the Cotton Bowl became the holiday nesting spot of the Southwest Conference champion. It has been a wonderful merger and in many ways the best of the bowl tie-ups.

Tennessee-Tulsa

FRIDAY, JANUARY 1, 1943

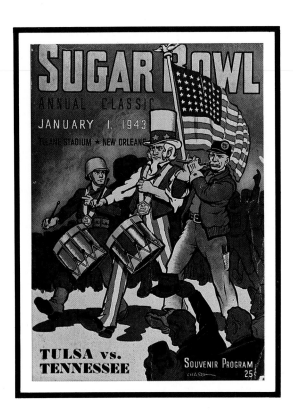

"Lock the door and stack the furniture."

Obviously, the war put a crimp in the sports scene; the quality of competition fell. But the luck of the Sugar Bowl continued. Before the final big week of the 1942 regular season, the Mid-Winter Sports Association was angling for Boston College and either Georgia Tech or Georgia, the best two teams in the Southeastern Conference.

Pasadena flexed its considerable muscle and stepped in with an agreement to take the winner of the Tech-Bulldog fight, snatching a plum right out of the hands of the Sugar. New Orleans then quickly glanced to the Midwest where Henry Frnka's Tulsa Hurricane was blowing over everything in its path. Fourth-ranked Tulsa, the only undefeated team eligible for a bowl and averaging an incredible 42 points a game, would have made an ideal opponent for No. 1-ranked Boston College. Tulsa was invited, and accepted.

Eerie things were taking place at Chestnut Hill, Massachusetts. The program cover of the November 28, 1942, Boston College-Holy Cross game showed a photograph of the schools' captains shaking hands. The Holy Cross captain wore No. 55, the Boston College captain wore No. 12. On that day twenty-six-point underdog Holy Cross drummed the Eagles 55-12. Until Northwestern, a 32-point underdog, defeated Minnesota 31-21 in 1982, this was college football's biggest reversal of form. Boston College instantaneously lost its glitter and national championship aspirations.

The Sugar Bowl appeared to be wiggling on a hook, especially after Boston columnist Bill Cunningham indicated that Boston College might have made an agreement with New Orleans before the game. "So far as I'm concerned," Cunningham said, "the Sugar Bowl is stuck with Boston College. Apparently they can't get out of it, even with that awful drubbing this afternoon."

Cunningham was as close as a reporter could be to the Boston College athletic situation, so his words were taken as an imprimatur. But he was wrong. Seventh-ranked Tennessee received and accepted the Sugar Bowl invitation. It may have been the best thing that ever happened to the Boston College athletic family.

A party celebrating its victory and the Sugar Bowl invitation had been scheduled to follow the Holy Cross game. The crushed Eagles, without victory and without a Sugar Bowl bid, cancelled the affair. That night the Coconut Grove, site of the called-off celebration, burned down and over 500 people were killed.

Tulsa, the Missouri Valley champion, didn't appear to need anything extra in its high-velocity offense, featuring a do-it-all tailback named Glenn Dobbs. The Hurricane had 2,339 yards passing that season, 4,261 yards in total offense, and ranked eighth nationally on defense, surrendering an average of 148.7 yards.

The Hurricane did pick up a lot of what normally would have been neutral fan support in New Orleans. Bill Cunningham, apparently irritated that Boston College had not gotten the Sugar Bowl invitation, wrote that one of the participants was a "fine semi-pro club, peopled with several gents whose eligibility wouldn't pass muster in some of the politer circles." The howl that arose in Oklahoma caused Cunningham to back up and say he was actually speaking of Tennessee, though he seemed to be simply covering his tracks. Tulsa received a great deal of sympathy nationwide for being in the line of fire through no fault of its own. New Orleans went out of its way to show hospitality to the Hurricane.

The game itself had a slightly odd look. Coach John Barnhill had taken over the Volunteer reins for General Bob Neyland. Frnka had been a longtime assistant at Vanderbilt and had crossed swords with Tennessee for years. "I used to scout them so often I sometimes stood up when their band played their alma mater," he laughed.

Tennessee, in the Neyland tradition, emphasized its kicking game and defense. The Vols had a fine running attack and were deep in reserves, accounting for their pick as a three-point favorite. Tulsa, however, was not deep and wasn't a consistent ground threat. "We were a bunch of greyhounds with a lot of heart," said Dobbs. Some felt Tulsa was a little more than that. One sportswriter led off a story with, "Lock the door and stack the furniture because Glenn Dobbs & Co., otherwise known as the University of Tulsa football team, are in town." Not only was Tulsa exciting, but it had a coach who didn't overlook anything. Frnka brought 300 gallons of drinking water from Oklahoma with the team. "We aren't taking chances," he explained.

Tennessee 14-Tulsa 7

"I swear, that ball went straight up in the air about 70 yards."

A crowd of 68,361, which didn't quite fill Tulane Stadium, marked the first Sugar Bowl that wasn't played before capacity or above capacity seating. One of the missing seats belonged to Warren Miller, who had to be content with listening to Harry Wismer's broadcast after he broke an ankle.

The early play was strictly a groping for position and a soaring punting duel between Bobby Cifers and Glenn Dobbs. Cifers kicked a ball out-of-bounds at the Tulsa 14 after the second Tennessee possession. Dobbs, who led the nation in punting, jolted the Vols with a quick-kick that zoomed over Cifers' head and came to rest 76 yards away from the line of scrimmage at the Vol 9.

Startled, Tennessee called time-out and then kicked right back. Cifers got off a 51-yard punt to the Tulsa 40. Dobbs, with excellent field position, was ready for business.

Dobbs uncranked the Hurricane offense with consecutive pass completions of 5, 6, 13, 5, and 21 yards. End Saxton Judd nearly scored with the last pass, but stumbled, allowing three of the Volunteer secondary to catch up and pull him down at the 10. Left end Johnny Green caught Dobbs' next attempt and went down to the 2, where the quarter ended.

The Volunteer defensive backs started moving with Dobbs as he took the snap and began moving toward the right end. But he pulled up and flicked a

Vols look for a crack in the Tulsa forward wall.

pass to Cal Purdin for the touchdown. Clyde Le-Force kicked the PAT that put Tulsa ahead, 7-0. The passing drive was a seven-for-seven display by Dobbs. He had also completed his last attempt before the drive started and would complete his next attempt, giving him nine consecutive completions.

Walter Slater, the Vols' single-wing signal caller, began probing the noticeably tiring Tulsa line. Slater broke through left tackle and gained 16 yards. A 17-yard pass put the ball at the 14 and, after Jim Gaffney made a catch, Bill Gold slashed into the end zone from the 3. Charlie Mitchell's conversion was wide, leaving Tulsa in front, 7-6. The half ended with the Hurricane one point up.

"We were darned glad to be where we were," said Dobbs. "Tennessee had shut down our running game completely, and all the moves Coach Frnka made weren't working. All season long he would come up with something new for our opponents, but they weren't working this time. And we were pretty tired, but he didn't tell us anything at the half."

"What we did," explained Tennessee tackle Denver Crawford, "was drop the ends off and rushed

with four men. Tulsa's running game wasn't tremendous, and we concentrated on stopping Dobbs' passing."

A mild Tennessee threat opened the third quarter, and Slater eventually dumped a punt out at the 10. Two Tulsa plays lost 3 yards. Dobbs then prepared to punt from his end zone. The center was low. Denver Crawford roared in, threw blocking back N.A. Keithley aside, and felt the sting of the ball on his chest.

"I swear," said Crawford, "that ball went straight up in the air about 70 yards. I thought I was gonna be a star and get my first touchdown. I ended up standing on the end zone line waiting for that thing to come down. When it did, I tried to jerk it in bounds, but I just couldn't fool that official."

"Why Keithley, the lightest back we had, was back there blocking, I don't know," mused Dobbs of the safety that put the Volunteers in the lead.

Dick Jordan intercepted Dobbs on the 24 and returned it 11 yards. In three plays Clyde Fuson carried it over from the 1. Mitchell again missed the conversion, leaving the score 14-7.

Slater later fumbled after a 15-yard gain, and

Tulsa gained possession on the Hurricane 42. Keithley, in for Dobbs, ignited a gallant late attempt to salvage a tie. LeForce lost 3 yards, and Tulsa was penalized 5 more before Keithley completed an 18-yard pass to Judd. Johnny Green made a sensational catch at the Tennessee 29 before Keithley, hemmed in by storming defenders, got off a pass to Judd that netted 16 yards.

Jim Powell cut in front of Keithley's next pass, intended for Judd, at the 5, intercepted and returned it to the 13. One play later the game ended.

Frnka's offensive plans might have had better success on another day. The Hurricane finished with a minus 139 yards rushing. "Tennessee has won a lot of games playing defense," said Walter Slater. "This was one."

Coach John Barnhill felt he had discovered the key during pregame practices in which he stressed the kicking game. "We knew," he said, "that if we didn't run those kicks back each time for about 15 yards, Tulsa would be camping on our 5-yard line all afternoon."

Tennessee averaged 17.5 yards per punt return against Tulsa, as the Volunteers became the first Southeastern Conference team to win in the Sugar Bowl since Tulane in the inaugural game.

Georgia Tech-Tulsa

SATURDAY, JANUARY 1, 1944

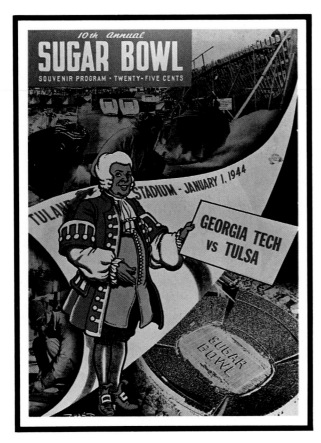

Eddie Prokop, Joseph B. David, and C.I. Pontius, president of Tulsa University, at 1944 Sugar Bowl party at the St. Charles Hotel.

"Rejected, Deferred, Unbeaten."

There was wide speculation during the week following Tulsa-Tennessee that the Sugar Bowl might be scrapped until the end of the War. Fred Digby doubted anything that severe would be done. "They'll do whatever Uncle Sam thinks best," he wrote. "Two years ago the Sugar Bowlers announced their policy would be to carry on unless the government thought it best to call a halt. To date, the government has not asked anything except that ticket sales be confined to the New Orleans area. This was done, and to the letter."

When the Association met that January, there was no official mention of temporarily suspending the Sugar Bowl other than to refute the idea had substance. President Joseph B. David said, "We held our regular monthly board meeting tonight, and no discussion of the matter was had."

Selecting bowl teams was a chore in the 1943 football season. The best teams were those whose

schools were involved in military training, such as the Navy V-12 program, and those on military bases whose participants were still amateurs. Washington and Southern California, both members of the Pacific Coast Conference, were announced early as the Rose Bowl combatants. The reason for the choices was the travel that would be involved for an Eastern or Southern team.

Iowa Preflight and Southwestern Louisiana Institute, a strong team with a military program, appeared the favorites for one berth in the Sugar Bowl. Georgia Tech, a Navy training school, was the Southeastern Conference champion. It was the choice for the other spot, though badly beaten by No. 1-ranked Notre Dame. Iowa Preflight was eliminated because the Navy had a 48-hour limit on furloughs. The Mid-Winter Sports Association disclosed its pick in late November. Georgia Tech—with the most defeats, three, of any team that had ever competed in the Sugar Bowl—was pitted against the undefeated, once-tied Tulsa.

Receiving and accepting the invitation was a historic occasion for Georgia Tech. It completed Coach Bill Alexander's circuit through the four major bowls. He had taken Tech to the Rose Bowl (1929), the Orange Bowl (1940), the Cotton Bowl (1943), and now the Sugar. Tech became the first school to complete the cycle.

This would not be the same Tulsa team that competed in New Orleans in 1943, although its roster did carry a couple of familiar names. Maurice "Red" Wade, who had played with Missouri against Fordham in the 1942 Sugar Bowl, was now with Coach Henry Frnka's Hurricane. Ed Shedlosky, who had played with Fordham in 1942, had also transferred to Tulsa. Only six members were back from the previous Tulsa squad, and 24 of the 40 team members for 1943 were classified 4-F by the draft or had medical discharges. Nine others were 18 years old and expecting draft notices, or under draft age.

Guard Ellis Jones was missing an arm. Another player had one lung. A third had one kidney. Coach Henry Frnka had one athlete who had a large area of scarred tissue, and another who had to play in a special shoe because of a severed Achilles tendon. Red Wade, who suffered an attack of osteomyelitis when he was 13, had back and ankle problems.

This team surprised everyone, including Frnka. *Time* magazine ran a story on the Hurricane headlined "Rejected, Deferred, Unbeaten." Embarrassed about 'Frnka's 4-Fs', Washington authorities asked for a quiet review of draft physicals.

Georgia Tech 20-Tulsa 18

"Give me that ball!"

In practically every close football game, one play can be the turning point. It came early in the 1944 Sugar Bowl.

Following the opening kickoff, Clyde LeForce took Tulsa from its 14 to the Georgia Tech 15. The Golden Tornado had the Hurricane stopped, but on the fourth down, with Tulsa lined up for a field goal, LeForce faked the kick. He flicked a screen pass to halfback Ed Shedlosky who scored. LeForce missed the extra point, the only mistake the Hurricane made in the early going.

On Tech's first series, halfback Eddie Prokop, blocking for Frank Broyles, was rushed by the one-armed guard Ellis Jones. On the collision, Prokop took an accidental crack in the face. "We didn't have big face guards then," recalled Broyles, who played fullback and halfback for Tech. "I looked at Eddie, with his bloodied mouth already beginning to swell, and it was plain he was as angry as anybody had ever seen him. 'Give me that ball,' he told us. That may have been the biggest play of the game."

If it was, it would take a while to manifest itself. Prokop began punching out yards at every point of the defense, but the Engineers couldn't sustain anything.

Near the end of the opening period, Tech gave up the ball at the Tulsa 24. Beginning the second quarter, Jimmy Ford, in for LeForce, faked a pass and found a hole at right tackle. He fired for the sidelines and went 76 yards with the Tech defense in faint pursuit. It was the longest run from scrimmage in the 10 Sugar Bowl games, and staked Tulsa to a 12-0 lead as LeForce missed his second extra point. Prokop, Broyles, Ed Scharfschwerdt, and Malcolm Logan returned the fire, going 73 yards in 12 precision plays. Broyles carried from the 1 to chalk up Georgia Tech's first touchdown. Prokop converted.

Ford made his presence felt again when, shortly after the Tech touchdown, he launched a 68-yard punt that flew over Broyles and went out at the Engineer 6. Broyles tried to kick it back out of the danger zone, but the weak snap grazed the leg of a blocking back and the ball came to rest at the 1 where Tulsa end Barney White recovered. A delay penalty put the Hurricane back on the 6, but LeForce made it academic by slicing off tackle and scoring on the first down.

"I thought Barney White recovered for a touchdown," explained a sheepish Henry Frnka later. "It looked to me as if one official raised his arms. I sent LeForce in to try the extra point, and I was as much surprised as anyone to see us draw a five-yard penalty for excessive time. Of course, LeForce scored from the 6, but if Tech held us it would have made us look awful dumb. It was no time to substitute, I'll admit."

When it was time to do what he was originally sent in for, LeForce missed his third PAT. The half-time score stood: Tulsa 18, Georgia Tech 7.

Prokop pushed Tech back in the contest shortly after the second half began when he arched a pass just over the straining fingers of Camp Wilson to Phil Tinsley, who made the grab, whirled at the 30, found himself alone, and ran 46 yards for a touchdown. It was a pivotal play because Wilson came so close to intercepting with a chance to put the Sugar Bowl in the cooler with a good return.

"Wilson cried after the game over his failure to intercept," said Frnka. "We have a signal on intercepted passes for the men to form in front of the man intercepting. Wilson actually gave the signal, so sure was he that he had the ball. He must've jumped too soon and missed it coming down. He probably missed it by inches. That's how close it was. We all thought he had the ball."

Depth, the dimension that played such a crucial role in Tulsa's 1943 defeat, began to have an effect. "We began having some injuries," said Jones, "and we weren't real deep to begin with. Georgia Tech was gaining momentum, you could feel it, but we kind of felt we could hold them off."

Prokop's team started running Tulsa ragged with laterals and scrambles. Prokop moved the ball inside the 50. He lateralled to Logan, who hit left end and, as he was about to go down, lateralled to Scharfschwerdt who carried to the 29. At the four after four plays, Scharfschwerdt went over and Prokop kicked the extra point to make the margin 20-18 for Georgia Tech.

Ellis Jones was sobbing on a bench in the Tulsa locker room when Notre Dame coach Frank Leahy walked in and shouted "Buck up, boy. You played well enough to win, but didn't. You gave it a good shot, that's all that counts. These things happen in life." Jones said, "I never forgot that."

Prokop set Sugar Bowl records for number of carries (43), yards gained rushing (199), and total yards (256). Georgia Tech's 373 rushing yards, 456 total yards, and 25 first downs were also records. Ford's 76-yard run from scrimmage, Tulsa's 3 touchdowns in a half, the 38 combined points, and 135 plays by both teams were all Sugar Bowl records.

Georgia Tech's Frank Broyles breaks free against Tulsa.

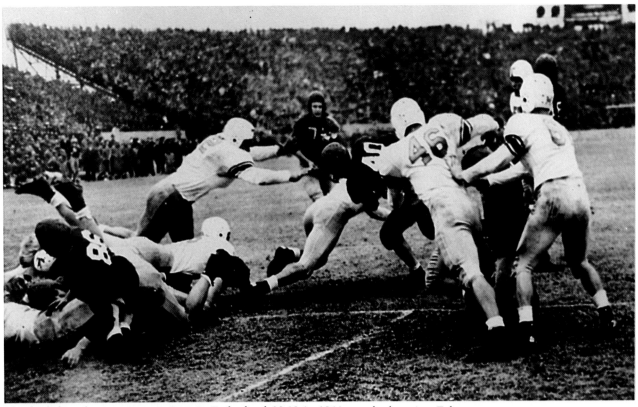

Ed Scharfschwerdt scores to put Georgia Tech ahead 20-18 in 1944 comeback against Tulsa.

Broyles about to be roughed getting a punt off against Tulsa.

Duke-Alabama

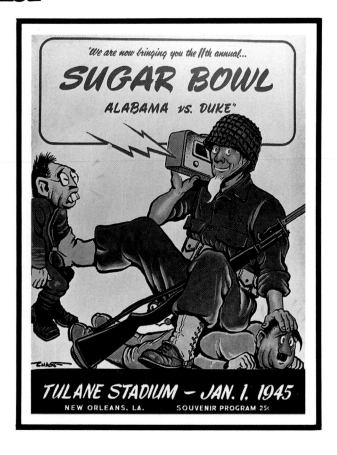

"They're too young to know any different."

The 1945 Sugar Bowl was an almost complete reversal of form from the previous 10 pairings. This one, at first glance, looked to be a pumpkin; but at the stroke of midnight, it was transformed into the princess.

Again, the war made for odd pairings, but Georgia Tech again had a representative team in the South, one in which the Mid-Winter Sports Association was definitely interested. The Orange Bowl made a bold bid and invited the Engineers to Miami for a rematch of the 1944 Sugar Bowl with Tulsa. Tech still had two games to play, including one with Notre Dame.

Tennessee was on its way to an 8-0-1 season but quickly committed to the Rose Bowl, the big winner in the holiday sweepstakes with the only two ranked teams (7th-ranked Southern Cal and the 12th-ranked Volunteers). The Sugar Bowl was sent scrambling. Alabama, an SEC also-ran with one loss and two ties, was eventually selected. Coach Frank Thomas was surprised when the invitation arrived. The Southern Conference champion Duke, beaten four times, would be the opponent. Duke was also a Navy training team.

Alabama, a civilian school that didn't even field a team the year before and started the 1944 season with only one backfield regular as old as 18, came under some pressure not to accept because it didn't appear to be an equitable match. Thomas resisted initially but finally accepted.

Thomas, the second coach in two years to complete the major bowl circuit in New Orleans, knew full well what he was getting into. Asked how his team felt, Thomas replied, "They're too young to know any different than they're going to win. I'm not going to tell them any different."

For the first time since Pearl Harbor the Sugar Bowl would be an absolute sellout of 73,000. It may not have been a stellar attraction compared to the other bowls, but a lot of fans wanted to see Alabama-Duke.

Other than the buoyant atmosphere prevalent toward the end of a war, it is hard to see how Alabama-Duke would create much excitement. Purely and simply, it appeared to be a case of men against boys, as the Blue Devils' two-touchdown pick reflected. Alabama's line had only one man who weighted as much as 200 pounds—center Vaughn

Mancha. Eighteen-year-old Harry Gilmer guided the Crimson Tide offense. In contrast, the older, heavier Duke trainees looked to 23-year-old Tom Davis for leadership. Davis was a Marine lieutenant who had been discharged in September and had returned to school.

Coach Eddie Cameron, who had taken over at Duke while Wallace Wade, also a former Alabama coach, was in the service, realized he could be stepping into a trap. Coach Cameron said the odds were "silly" and read a letter to his team from Colonel Wade, a field artillery officer in France, who wrote that he would be listening and was "setting up a special cheering section over here to help the boys along." In reference to two previous Duke bowl losses, Wade added, "Tell the boys they've got to win this one. We don't want to be three-time losers at anything—especially football."

Thomas, on the other hand would have made the odds higher. The Alabama coach, speaking to the New Orleans Quarterback Club, couldn't contain a gush of praise for his team. Chairman Lester Lautenschlaeger reminded Thomas that it was a bit out of his character to do that before a big game. "I believe in giving the kids the credit they deserve," Thomas reflected. "The boys are young, and are just about the hustlingest team I've had. I wouldn't say it is the greatest team I've coached, but they have more enthusiasm and love to play."

When asked for a prediction, Thomas thought for a few seconds, then answered, "Duke 21, Alabama 6." Lautenschlaeger said, "I understand you told somebody before it would be 21-0." "I did," Thomas admitted with a smile, "but I've become enthused myself since coming to the Quarterback Club and now I think we'll score!"

Duke 29-Alabama 26

"You can plainly see him beat the ground."

As the chilly, golden afternoon began to fade, Grantland Rice searched for the precise words to describe what he had just witnessed. He settled on a simple and succinct lead: "The Sugar Bowl classic of 1945 must go down in the book as one of the great thrillers of all time."

At the same time in the Duke locker room, Blue Devil captain Gordon Carver was sighing, "I sure was glad to hear that final whistle." In a game filled with memories of men being in the right place at the right time, Carver had been the most conspicuous.

Immediately after the kickoff, George Clark lit a fuse to a game that would go off like a Roman candle. He broke off a 52-yard run from the Duke 33 to the Alabama 15 where he was knocked out-of-bounds by Lowell Tew. Three plays later, Clark faked a pass, then knifed through the Crimson Tide for 13 yards and the first touchdown of the day.

Soon after the kickoff, freshman Harry Gilmer punted to Tom Davis at the Blue Devil 27. Davis carried to the 34, but Clark fumbled on the next play. Ralph Jones recovered for Alabama on the Duke 36. Norwood Hodges gained 17 and then 9 yards more in two plays to plant the brazen young Tide at the 9. Gilmer was held to 3 yards on two carries. Then he reared up and passed to Hal Self, who was stopped by Davis a foot from the goal. Hodges took it in from there, but Hugh Morrow missed the conversion.

It didn't matter. Later in the first quarter, after a Carver punt to the Tide 32, Gilmer took off on a 25-yard gallop over right tackle. The drive reached the Duke 24 before Davis dropped Tew for a 3-yard loss. Gilmer, back to pass, was shot down by Fred Hardison 14 yards behind the line of scrimmage, bringing on a third and 27 from the 41. Gilmer was chased back again, but during the chase he spotted Jones open downfield. He leaped high, arched his body, and flung the ball to the end, who made the catch and was bumped out-of-bounds by Carver at the 1.

"He wasn't supposed to throw to me . . . just picked me out," marveled Jones afterward. Hodges scored on the next play. Paul Stephanz blocked Morrow's kick; but the first period wasn't over yet, and three touchdowns were already on the board. Things were just heating up.

Tew and Hodges did most of the damage as another Alabama threat began to boil in the second quarter. The pair chewed up yardage, moving from the Alabama 21 to the 49. Gilmer, again being rushed by the tormented Blue Devils, jumped up on the dead run and duplicated his bull's-eye to Jones. Clark tackled the end at the 10. Hodges slipped and lost 6 yards after Gilmer gained 3. Alabama went into a spread formation and Gilmer threw over the middle to Jones who then stepped into the end zone from the 2. This time Gilmer kicked the PAT, making the score 19-7, Alabama, and putting the crowd —not to mention Tide coach Frank Thomas—in a frenzy.

Harry Gilmer of Alabama tests war-hardened Duke.

Smarting, the Blue Devils struck right back. Starting from its 37, Duke began cutting up the Tide defense (as it was expected to do before). Duke picked up 5, 13, 0, 2, and 15 yards in succession. Cliff Lewis picked up a wall of blockers as he swung out and raced 26 yards to the Tide 1. Davis scored, but Harold Raether failed to convert. The half ended with the Crimson Tide in front, 19-13.

Tom Davis put on an extraordinary display early in the third period when Duke gained possession on its 36. Davis carried 10 consecutive times and scored from the 1. When Raether kicked the PAT, Duke was in the lead, 20-19.

Duke was given a chance to win by recovering a fumble at the Tide 33. The Blue Devils got down to the 12, but Alabama continued playing tough. Lewis, on the first play of the fourth quarter, threw a fourth-down pass to Carver in the end zone, but it was ruled the catch was out-of-bounds and the Tide took over.

Nothing came of the possession. But after a punt was returned to the Tide 44 and an ensuing Duke first down, Morrow eased in front of a Lewis pass, picked up some interference, and galloped 75 yards for a 26-20 Alabama lead.

The Duke power was asserted again. The Devils drove inside the Alabama 1 where Davis, instead of running a slant, tried to hurl himself across and missed. Alabama took over two feet from its goal, then was penalized even further back for an excessive time-out. Frank Thomas was mulling over a suggestion by one of his players.

Thomas would take an intentional safety and have Gilmer kick out from the 20. Harry took the first-down snap and went to one knee in the end zone, giving Duke two points. Alabama now led only 26-22. The strategy fell short when Clark took John Wade's darter kick on the Duke 46 and slammed upfield to the Alabama 39. On the play Duke coach Eddie Cameron felt was decisive, second-string half-back Jim LaRue raced wide around left end on a reverse, bounced off a pair of Alabamians, and carried two with him until he finally went down at the 20.

"The play was run precisely as called and diagrammed," LaRue recalled. Clark, on a spectacular burst, went off tackle and covered the remaining distance to put Duke in front 29-26 with only seconds to play.

Gilmer moved from the Alabama 23 to the 43 and, with time for one last play, heaved a shot to Jones at the Duke 30. Jones pivoted and had a clearing for an instant. He only had to beat Duke safety Carver and 'Bama was home. Carver managed to grab and hold on to the receiver's woolen stocking and finally bring him down on the 24 as the gun went off.

Gilmer, who was eight-of-eight passing for 142 yards, said, "The sad thing is that I had another receiver further downfield, Jack McConville. I got off a weak pass to Jones, but McConville recognized instantly what to do and turned to block the only defensive back that had a chance of getting Ralph. But when he turned he slipped. On the film you can plainly see him beat the ground."

Oklahoma A&M-
St. Mary's

THURSDAY, JANUARY 1, 1946

We're off—for the 12th annual
SUGAR BOWL

January 1, 1946
TULANE STADIUM
New Orleans, La.
SOUVENIR PROGRAM 25¢

THE WAR YEARS

ST. MARY'S vs. OKLAHOMA A. & M.

"I'll be right here for it, too."

A letter from Wallace Wade to Fred Digby after Duke-Alabama cut short the tale of his Sugar Bowl listening post while in the war. Wade wrote he was involved in military operations on January 1, 1945.

Undefeated Alabama was the southern choice of all the major bowls. Little St. Mary's was embarrassing the Goliaths of California. Army was the best team in the country, and there was talk of the Cadets breaking their bowl ban for a holiday in Pasadena or New Orleans.

Army favored a Rose Bowl invitation but was reluctant to decide before the Navy game. The Sugar Bowl pressured Pasadena to extend an early bid. The Sugar Bowl told Alabama to make up its mind or forget a New Orleans trip. Pasadena, with no answer from Army in the offing, was afraid of coming up empty with both the Cadets and the Tide.

Frank Leahy told Fred Digby, ". . . I have no interest in St. Mary's, nor is Jim Phelan more than an acquaintance; but if the Sugar Bowlers invite the Gaels for their game, I am sure they'll give the fans a show such as they've never seen. I'll be right here for it, too." St. Mary's and Oklahoma A&M were extended Sugar Bowl invitations the following day.

Both accepted. The undefeated Aggies, Missouri Valley Conference champions, were the nation's best ground offensive team, averaging 287.7 yards a game. St. Mary's, a tiny (enrollment under 300) Christian Brothers school in northern California, ran a sleight-of-hand offense and averaged 170 yards passing. A&M's Bob Fenimore, in the era of Glenn Davis and Doc Blanchard, was the nation's leading rusher (1,641 yards), followed by none other than Hawaiian Hurricane Herman Wedemeyer (1,428 yards) of St. Mary's. Both were first team All-Americans. Oklahoma A&M finished fifth and St. Mary's seventh in the final Associated Press poll, giving New Orleans the only major bowl match-up of the Top 10 teams.

Ticket demand was incredible. Seventy-five thousand fans, the highest Sugar Bowl attendance in its 12 games, were cramped into Tulane stadium. The governor of Oklahoma strolled into Sugar Bowl headquarters a couple of days before the game, spotted President Sam Corenswet and other bowl committeemen, walked over, and said, "Gentlemen, I'm a man of few words. I want tickets." Corenswet replied, "We're men of few words, too, governor. We haven't got any."

Oklahoma A&M 33-
St. Mary's 13

Bob Fenimore turns upfield as St. Mary's defender dives at his heels.

"Too much power—too much speed."

"I remember we went onto the field in just T-shirts and pants with no pads," Herman Wedemeyer recalled years later. "Bob Fenimore and the big Oklahoma A&M team was already out there. The entire stadium was full. How many were there, 72,000? Well, they all laughed at us. We looked like midgets on the field. No wonder people laughed. But that sort of set the stage for what was to come later."

Oklahoma A&M was a team that started seven war veterans, including fullback Jim Reynolds who flew 52 missions over Germany, and tackle Bert Cole who had been shot down over Yugoslavia and spent months among the Chetniks while making his way back to Allied lines. In contrast, St. Mary's was a lot like Alabama in 1945 with seven 17-year-old starters on a team and an average age of 18 and a half years. Also, A&M, the heaviest team to play in the first 12 Sugar Bowls at a 203-pound average, was man-for-man 15 pounds larger than the Sugar Bowl's youngest-ever team. And St. Mary's was bitten severely by the flu bug four days before.

However, the Gaels fired the opening salvo. Very early in the game, Fenimore punted to Wedemeyer—the 21-year-old Honolulu native. He scampered 10 yards along the sidelines and then lateralled to the trailing Wes Busch. Busch was instantly clear and apparently heading for a touchdown before slipping untouched on the A&M 46. Spike Cordeiro swung wide to the left on the next play, then flipped to Wedemeyer who faded back and waited for Dennis O'Connor to work his way behind Fenimore. O'Connor took the ball at the 10 and scored.

After being penalized for being offsides on a successful onsides kick, the Gaels kicked to Jim Parmer who returned to the 36. The methodical Aggies answered the St. Mary's touchdown in five plays. Fenimore passed to Cecil Haskins at the Gael 45, then flashed around end to the 30. He ran for another yard; then he passed to Haskins to the 1. The receiver fell in with Wedemeyer and Cordeiro hanging on.

Fenimore set things in motion for more points by returning a second quarter punt 15 yards to the St. Mary 30. Also capable of razzle-dazzle, Oklahoma A&M picked up 11 yards on two Parmer carries. Then Parmer, Nate Wilson, and Fenimore each handled the ball on a one-play series of laterals that Fenimore delivered to the 1. Cutting off right tackle, Fenimore scored.

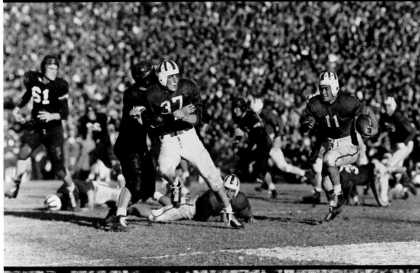

Herman Wedemeyer (11) carries for 'Galloping Gaels' against war-toughened Oklahoma A&M.

Wedemeyer accounts for two touchdowns but they aren't enough.

Not to be outdone, Wedemeyer returned the kickoff to the Gael 34 and then passed to O'Connor at the Aggie 44. He wheeled around right end, cut back to the middle of the field, and pounded out 24 yards before latersalling to guard Carl DeSalvo. The lineman picked up a horde of blockers to escort him the remaining 20 yards. The weary Wedemeyer missed the extra point, leaving St. Mary's behind 14-13. Oklahoma A&M drove to the 9, but that was all the scoring in the first 30 minutes.

"The half ended with us trailing, 14-13," Wedemeyer remembered. "The feeling of the entire stadium had changed. Now, they all seemed to be rooting for St. Mary's."

In the second half, the Gaels drove to the Aggie 27, but Fenimore intercepted a pass at his 20 and returned it 7 yards. Fenimore got off a 60-yard punt that sailed over Cordeiro's head to the 10. Spike returned it to the 22, but St. Mary's was guilty of clipping and was penalized to the 7.

When the Gaels kicked, Fenimore took in the ball at midfield and weaved his way to the 7. Wedemeyer, the last man between runner and goal, brought him down. For three downs the St. Mary's defense staved off the touchdown. On fourth down

from a half-yard out, Fenimore slammed in. Don Schultz blocked the PAT, and St. Mary's remained within waving distance, 20-13.

A&M, at last showing superiority over the tiring Gaels, was handed its next opportunity on a freak fourth-quarter play. Wedemeyer slipped while attempting to punt from his 39 and missed the ball completely. Neill Armstrong recovered on the 35. Seven plays later Jim Reynolds went over the goal from the 1.

The Sugar Bowl, heard for the first time over the American Broadcasting Company, was a settled matter. A&M got another touchdown as the horn sounded. The Aggies drove to the 9, but a penalty and a sack placed them back at the 20 in the waning seconds. Reynolds went for more points and threw deep. St. Mary's Paul Crowe batted the ball into the air, seemingly breaking up the game's last play. Alert Aggie reserve back Joe Thomas grabbed the tumbling ball and crossed the goal, making the final score 33-13.

Coach Jim Phelan, after locking the press out of the dressing room for 30 minutes, explained, "Too much power—too much speed. And, above all, too much Fenimore."

Georgia-North Carolina

WEDNESDAY, JANUARY 1, 1947

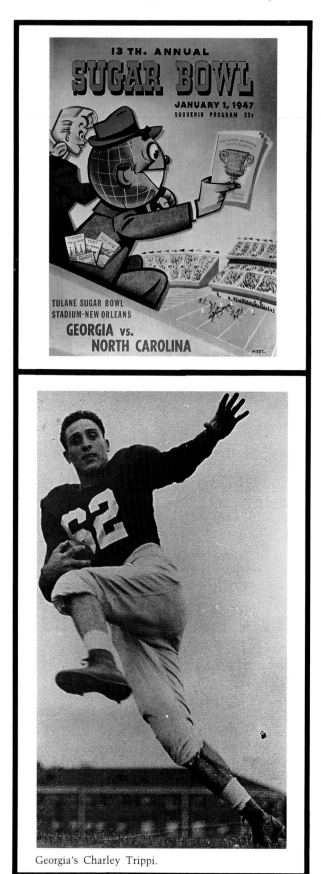

Georgia's Charley Trippi.

"It would have been interesting."

Notre Dame and Army, two traditional giants with bowl bans, were No. 1 and 2 respectively in 1946. Despite the postseason taboo by both schools, there was some hope the administrations might not be as adamant as before. The Western Conference (the Big Nine), long opposed to bowl games, agreed to a five-year contract with the Pacific Coast Intercollegiate Conference, permitting one of its schools to participate annually in the Rose Bowl.

There was some sentiment in New Orleans for Army. It was rumored that Army wanted to select its opponent. The Cadets were eyeing Rice, but the Sugar Bowl wanted unbeaten, untied Georgia—the SEC co-champion and No. 3-ranked team. When Sugar Bowl representatives attended the Bulldogs' last game with Georgia Tech, fans unfurled banners which read "Beat Army." Whether it was the selection issue or not, Army turned down all bowl invitations, and so did Notre Dame, which did not have the change of heart its Midwestern brothers did.

Actually, Army, Notre Dame, and Georgia all had claims to national championships. Bulldog Coach Wally Butts wanted Associated Press poll notice to go with his Williamson System No. 1 tag. Army was ranked first by the Helms Athletic Foundation and the Football Thesaurus. Notre Dame was champion in the eyes of AP, the Dunkel System, and the Litkenhous System.

"I was prejudiced," Butts admitted, "but I thought we had the No. 1 team in the nation. Georgia and UCLA were the only teams with perfect records, for Notre Dame and Army had played their famous tie. It would have been interesting to see (Charley) Trippi competing against Doc Blanchard and Glenn Davis of Army. But neither Coach Red Blaik of Army or Coach Frank Leahy of Notre Dame was interested in playing that Georgia team."

Georgia's firepower was fantastic for the postwar years. Only one team (Alabama) held the Bulldogs under four touchdowns during its 10-game schedule. The Georgia T formation pulverized its opposition with a 37.2 point-per-game average.

Two of the nation's best backs, Charley Trippi and John Rauch, drove the Bulldog offense. Trippi had a 6.4-yard-per-carry average with 1,366 total yards. Rauch was the country's top-ranked passer, and five Bulldogs were ranked among the top receivers. Defensively, Trippi and Rauch were tied with five players nationally with five interceptions apiece.

Seventh-ranked North Carolina, with legend-in-the-making Charley "Choo-Choo" Justice who had gained 1,213 total yards, was paired with Georgia. It was the Tar Heels' first bowl trip and, despite being Southern Conference champions, 14 points separated the teams in the odds. It was plain most felt Carolina would need luck to stay close to Georgia.

Tar Heel Coach Carl Snaveley gives instructions to 'Choo-Choo' Justice.

Georgia 20- North Carolina 10

Charley 'Choo-Choo' Justice (22) follows his blocks against Georgia.

"Congratulating you! Ain't that rich."

What Harry Wismer told his listening audience on New Year's Day, 1947, what 73,000 witnessed, and what the sportswriters conveyed was extraordinary.

Carolina played superbly. The teams sparred for better than a quarter before Georgia moved to the Tar Heel 32. Charley Trippi called a screen; Bob Mitten laid back and kept John Rauch, the intended receiver, in the corner of his eye. As Trippi's pass was released, the tackle flew in front of Rauch, caught the ball at the 30, and set sail for the Georgia goal.

Mitten was caught from behind at the Bulldog 25, though the 'Heels were quickly inside the 5. Justice faked as if he were hightailin' it for the end, but Walt Pupa cut in the end zone as the Carolina line leveled everything in his path. Bobby Cox's conversion put North Carolina on top, 7-0. The Tar Heels continued the battle until the half, holding the Bulldogs at bay.

Coach Wally Butts was infuriated by his team's performance. "Why, in the dressing room between halves," Butts said, "I told them I found it hard to believe I was seeing what I was seeing. I said, 'Here you boys are getting smacked around and you act like it's all right because those North Carolina boys are patting you on the back, kidding you, and congratulating you after knocking the heck out of you. Congratulating you! Ain't that rich! Those boys are not as gentle and kind as they are trying to make you believe. Junk that congratulation business until after the game. Go on like this and they're going to beat us to a frazzle.' "

Trippi recalled, "We hadn't played against a single wing team all year, and we had a hard time adjusting. We made changes in our line spacing. That got us untracked."

North Carolina drove to the Georgia 34 to start the third period. Pupa threw a 15-yard pass to Cox, but the play was nullified. Carolina was in motion and Georgia was offsides, so the third down was replayed. Another pass to reserve back Jim Camp was called. Georgia's end Joe Tereshinski picked the pass off at the 25. Camp recovered enough to turn and tackle Tereshinski as soon as he caught the ball. As he was going down, Tereshinski pitched the ball forward to Dick McPhee.

The ball should have been dead at that point, and the field judge Gabe Hill appeared ready to mark the spot. Center Dan Stiegam realized he had not heard a whistle and chased the fullback down at the UNC 14.

Charley Justice remembers arguing so long and loud with Hill that he was threatened with expulsion from the game. The end result of the missed call was a 4-yard touchdown run by Rauch. George Jernigan's extra point tied it 7-7.

Enraged, the UNC offense tore off four successive first downs and moved to the Bulldog 7. Tackle Jack Bush ended the touchdown threat by sacking Pupa for a 3-yard loss on third down. With the ball directly in front of the goalposts, Cox dropped back to the 17 and kicked a field goal to nudge the Tar Heels ahead.

Georgia immediately retaliated. Dan Edwards returned the kickoff from his 20 to the 31. Two running plays netted 2 yards, so Trippi took a handoff, pulled up to throw to Edwards, and found him covered. The scrambling Trippi at last was able to get the pass off. Edwards caught the pass at the 50 and outmaneuvered the frantically clutching hands of Justice before zigzagging to the goal line. Jernigan's PAT was blocked, but the 67-yard Sugar Bowl record scoring pass put Georgia in the lead for good.

Georgia gained a cushion in the fourth period by driving 80 yards. Rauch picked up his second TD of the afternoon on a quick opener from the 13. North Carolina had a chance to close the gap. Another official's call proved disastrous.

Justice gathered in the kickoff on the 7 and very nearly broke it, clearing the wave of Bulldogs thundering on him. Then he picked his way to the Georgia 44 before the last man, Trippi, prevented a touchdown. Two quick passes netted 26 yards. Then Justice went to Ken Powell in the end zone. Powell made the reception in front of defensive back Charlie "Rabbit" Smith, who came up to prevent the completion. With Smith hanging on, Powell turned and fell face forward.

Powell was unconscious, apparently the result of a hit by Smith. Head linesman George Gardner threw his flag. Interference was called on Powell, who was being helped from the field. Gardner ruled Powell had instigated the contact before making the catch. The ruling put a practical end to a 20-10 Georgia victory.

Fred Digby refused to let it go at that. He quizzed Smith, who answered, "I would rather not discuss it." Gardner said to Digby, "The minute I saw the play was to be a pass, I went downfield to cover. On a pass the ball is a free ball, and every player has a right to try for it. Interference can be by the offensive or defensive player. The North Carolina boy struck the Georgia boy as they went into the air. I called interference immediately and returned to my position."

"With what hand did Powell strike Smith?" Digby asked. Gardner said, "I refuse to answer that question." "What happened to Powell? How was he injured on the play?" pressed Digby. "I don't know. I made my decision and left. I never stay around after a ruling to argue with the players," Gardner replied.

The films later showed Gardner's call incorrect and also that Hill had missed a call on the lateral.

It was a disappointing afternoon in some ways. The game had little of the anticipated Justice-Trippi juice. Camp was the leading rusher with 68 yards. Trippi had 54 and Justice a meager 37. Trippi and Rauch played 60 minutes, the last to play the distance in the Sugar Bowl.

It was also the last Sugar Bowl Fred Digby would cover, and the last Warren Miller would see.

North Carolina Coach Carl Snaveley and halfback Charley Justice, and Georgia halfback Charley Trippi and Bulldog Coach Wally Butts before 1947 Sugar Bowl.

Texas-Alabama

THURSDAY, JANUARY 1, 1948

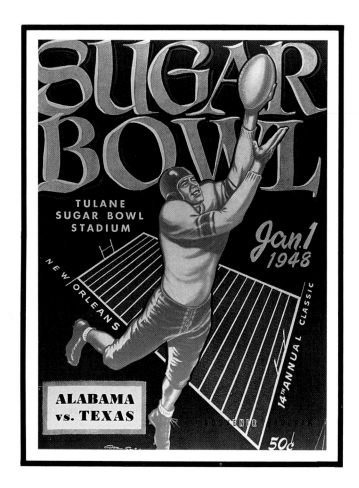

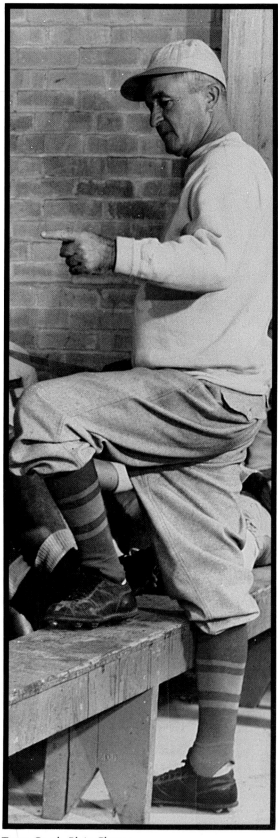

Texas Coach Blair Cherry.

"He later realized it was the right decision, and he was happy."

It was evident for some time that Tulane Stadium still wasn't adequate for the Sugar Bowl demand. In early 1947, Mid-Winter Sports Association President Sam Corenswet appointed a committee to look into the feasibility of further expansion. Committee Chairman Joseph David presented a plan to extend and double-deck the north end zone stands, which would add 12,241 seats and make Tulane a complete bowl.

The expansion committee was the last Sugar Bowl project for Warren Miller. He suffered a heart attack late on the night of June 21, 1947. The first president of the Sugar Bowl died at 4:30 A.M. the next morning at Touro Infirmary. He was 59.

Herbert J. Schwartz, president of Maison Blanche Co., a New Orleans department store, and Roy Bartlett proposed a memorial to Miller. Schwartz offered to underwrite a substantial sum toward a memorial. It was decided the Most Valuable Player trophy for the Sugar Bowl's outstanding player each year would be named in Miller's honor.

As one pioneer passed from the scene, another was wrestling with his future. The year before, the Sugar Bowl membership asked Fred Digby to become the general manager. The responsibilities had simply become too large for these businessmen to run on a part-time basis.

Digby had been with the *Item* 35 years. Journalism was his vocation and avocation. The Sugar Bowl, at the same time, meant more to him than just some venture; and after he took this position, it became the apex of Digby's fruitful career.

"Leaving the paper was the hardest thing he ever had to do," said Mary Frances Digby. "Finally, I said, 'You'll still be with the same type of people you've always been with, coaches, athletes, etc. I really don't think you'll feel too bad leaving it.' He said maybe I was right. At the time we had two boys in college, and the money sounded good."

Hap Glaudi succeeded Digby as *Item* sports editor. "He later realized it was the right decision, and he was happy," said Mrs. Digby.

Alabama had a $50,000 guarantee from the new Dixie Bowl in Birmingham, Alabama. Alabama's team preferred to play in New Orleans. After the victory over LSU which secured the Sugar's invitation, the Dixie Bowl offered Coach Frank Thomas a check of $60,000 for the Tide. Thomas went along with his players' wishes.

The Crimson Tide's opponent turned out to be Texas. Texas and Alabama, ranked fifth and sixth nationally, was not a bad attraction. But neither was a champion; it was the first time since 1938 that New Orleans didn't have one. Still, a game between Harry Gilmer, eight-for-eight passing in the 1945 Sugar Bowl, and Longhorn Bobby Layne, 11 of 12 in the '46 Cotton Bowl, promised to be a torrid duel, perfectly suited for a new medium—television.

It was at this Sugar Bowl that America's first woman sportscaster was assigned. Celebrity reporter Jill Jackson did the halftime color. But there was one problem: Women were not allowed in the Tulane press box, and Jackson could not get to the telecasting booth without walking through the press box.

Jackson wrote in 1978, "A meeting was held. It was decreed that Miss Jill Jackson could walk through the press box if she went through before any male member of the press had arrived. Then she must wait until after the game was over, and the press box was cleared of its male content."

Texas 27-Alabama 7

Bobby Layne executes the Texas offense to a T.

"It was the softest landing I had all day."

The Gilmer-Layne aerial display didn't materialize because Harry Gilmer misfired, although he did complete his first two passes. After four years and two Sugar Bowls, Gilmer was 10-for-10. That was also virtually the end of Alabama's offense. Texas' wasn't much better, but the combination of an alert defense and the swashbuckling Layne served the Crimson Tide its worse defeat in 10 bowl appearances.

Nine minutes and forty seconds after the opening kickoff, Texas scored. Layne drove the 'Horns 85 yards, including a 44-yard pass to Billy Pyle. The touchdown came on a 4-yard pass to Ralph "Peppy" Blount, who was a 21-year-old war veteran and Texas legislator.

"Don't get the idea this was a picnic, despite the score," Blount said. "I made one catch and was knocked out-of-bounds into a pile of photographers on the sidelines. It was the softest landing I had all day."

The Longhorns quickly came back for more points as Layne hit Blount for a first down at the Alabama 27. Alabama's Ray Richeson, who played a superb

game in defeat, prevented any damage by recovering a fumble at the 39. Gilmer returned a punt by Norman "Monk" Mosley to the Texas 41. Finally, Alabama drove to the 8, and Gilmer threw to end Ed White. Jim Canady nearly intercepted the ball as it crossed the goal line, but White wrestled it away for the TD. Texas threatened one last time before the half, driving to the Tide 12 before losing possession on downs.

Texas pushed to the 'Bama 27, but again could get no points. Alabama couldn't do anything either. And when Mosley punted this time, George Petrovich broke through to block it. He and his roommate, Victor Vasicek, beat a herd of other Longhorns to the ball in the end zone.

Layne missed two field goals, one at the end of the third period and one at the start of the fourth. Alabama saved another TD from inside its 1. Several series later, Lewis Holder anticipated a Gilmer pass from behind the end zone, intercepted at the 20, and returned it for a touchdown. On the next possession, Gilmer, attempting to pass from his 20, was thrown for a 10-yard loss and fumbled. Holder

Texas quarterback Bobby Layne
was recipient of first
Miller Memorial Trophy as
the Sugar Bowl's MVP.

recovered at the 5. Layne scored the game's last points on a dive.

"Thing about it was Bobby hit about everything he put up," said Gilmer, who ended a sterling college career with his worst statistical performance, 3 completions in 11 attempts and 5 yards rushing. Layne was 10 of 24 for 183 yards. The Texas quarterback was the first recipient of the Warren V. Miller Memorial Trophy.

"That was the first year they gave out the MVP award," said Blount, "and I seem to recall walking into Pat O'Brien's (a French Quarter night spot) and seeing ol' Bobby drinking Hurricanes out of that trophy." "I don't remember that," said Layne, "but I guess it's possible."

That game and Tulane Stadium became sort of enshrined in Blount's memory. Nearly 30 years after the 1948 Sugar Bowl, Blount was in New Orleans while his wife was being treated at a local hospital. One afternoon Blount took his son for tennis on the Tulane campus. The sight of the magnificent, abandoned stadium hovering over the school grounds intrigued Blount. "Finally," he said, "I said to the boy, 'C'mon, let's go over and see the Sugar Bowl.' "

Father and son walked into the decaying stadium, glanced around at the rusting interior, and walked to the sidelines. As they approached the end zone, Peppy stopped, pointed to a spot, and said, "Stephen, right here in 1948 your 'ole daddy caught a touchdown pass that helped beat the University of Alabama in the Sugar Bowl."

Lost in the glow of his faraway heroics for a moment, Peppy looked a while longer at the field, then down at his boy. "Dad," the lad said, "can I have a hamburger? I sure am hungry."

Jill Jackson found there was something sacred in the press box after all. It was the passageway to the little room she was allowed to visit after every last man had filed the last word of every story. "Needless to say," she explained, "after several hours in that booth, on a cold, cold day, I was a stretcher case when I finally made it to the *other side of the press box*. I almost died. It wasn't long after that I relinquished my role as America's only female sports commentator. It has been much easier that way."

Oklahoma-
North Carolina

SATURDAY, JANUARY 1, 1949

Myrle Greathouse, Oklahoma linebacker, starting back with his 69-yard interception of Charley Justice's pass in 1949 game.

"But I'm of the opinion."

Dallas apparently was slightly embarrassed. Southwest Conference runner-up Texas pulled down a check from the Sugar Bowl more than $20,000 larger than champion Southern Methodist from the Cotton Bowl game. And SMU had to share its Cotton Bowl receipts with the SWC to help maintain the office of the executive secretary. Texas, because it played in an "outside" bowl, was under no such obligation. What eventually evolved as a result of that situation was the sharing of all SWC bowl revenues with all conference members.

The Sugar Bowl had created an associate membership in 1946 to fill its ranks as death began taking a toll on the original founders. Associate membership, limited to sons, relatives, or sponsorship of extremely close friends, called for two years of service on committee assignments. The first group of associates were given full membership in 1948. Joseph B. David, Jr., Moreau Jumonville, and C. Norman Schwartz constituted the first incoming group. Claude Simons, Jr., (hero of the first Sugar Bowl),

Dr. Fred Wolfe, Jr., and Robert Gunsaulus made up the second.

It was tough to select opponents for the 15th Sugar Bowl, the first in the 82,000-seat stadium. Tulane put the squeeze on by unleashing one of its finest teams.

Georgia, Tulane, and Ole Miss were the best of the SEC in 1948; but of these teams, only the Bulldogs were listed in the national Top 10. The Bulldogs were ranked eighth in the nation. The Sugar Bowl wanted a pairing of third-ranked North Carolina and fifth-ranked Oklahoma, led by 33-year-old whiz-kid Coach Bud Wilkinson. Days before the bowl process began to fall into place, Hap Glaudi wrote, ". . . I'm presently of the opinion that for the Sugar there can be no finer selection than North Carolina and Oklahoma."

This game then would feature Charley "Choo-Choo" Justice in a return appearance, and an Oklahoma team so deep its lines alternated every six minutes for a crowd of 85,000.

Oklahoma 14- North Carolina 6

"I'm not allowed to drive to the entrance."

The outcome of the North Carolina-Oklahoma game may have been determined three days before when Charley Justice came down with a virus. For that entire period, a small pregame steak was all he could eat.

North Carolina started like the slight favorite it was. Justice had the Tar Heels moving full throttle at the start, shoving the vaunted Oklahoma line back from the UNC 36 to the Sooner 14 in seven plays. Justice took the pass from center in the Tar Heel single-wing formation, started to roll out, stumbled, and tried to force a pass in the flat anyway. "I made the mistake of throwing off-balance," Justice moaned. "He was in the right place at the right time."

Oklahoma's Myrle Greathouse intercepted on the 17 and brought the crowd to its feet as he picked up three blockers. Dan Stiegman, who chased down Dick McPhee in a similar situation in 1947, slowed

down the interference. While the Sooners tried to take Stiegman out of the play, Greathouse delayed for an instant and Eddie Knox tackled the runner from behind.

The 69-yard run placed the ball at the UNC 14, and quarterback Jack Mitchell carried four successive times to the 3. After making up a 5-yard penalty, Mitchell scored from inside the 1. Les Ming added the conversion.

UNC bounced back when Joe Romano recovered Lindell Pearson's fumble on the Oklahoma 30. Hosea Rodgers completed a 15-yard pass to Bob Kennedy. Then the 'Heels pulled off a spectacular double reverse on which Kennedy, who had taken the ball from Rodgers (who had taken the ball from Justice), carried to the 3. Rodgers scored in two plays from the two. Bobby Cox missed the PAT.

Justice had his teammates on the brink of the lead late in the second period by spearheading a 79-

yard march. UNC looked stalled near midfield, but Buddy Burris was charged with running into the punter, Justice. Charley then gained more on an end sweep. As Justice was about to be tackled, he lateralled to Chan Highsmith, who carried 8 yards more to the 16.

Oklahoma Coach Bud Wilkinson felt that containing All-America end Art Weimer could unlock a victory. He put halfback Darrell Royal to the task. "I went whatever side of the field he did," said Royal, "but, heck, I was 5-foot-11, maybe 160 pounds. He was 6-3 or 6-4 and about 215. Any jump ball was to his advantage. What I had to have was a good pass rush and a dropped pass or two." Cox caught a second-down pass from Justice to the 8. Royal's worst fears were almost realized on the following play. Weimer broke loose in the end zone, and Justice threw just high enough to prevent any chance of interception. Weimer leaped, got his hands on the ball, but dropped it. Justice failed to pick up the two yards for the first on a fourth-down run, and the ball went over to the Sooners just before the half.

Greathouse, who was playing Justice defensively one-on-one, seemed to have an easier time in the second half. "North Carolina never used it as an excuse," said Royal, "but I always felt Charley Justice's strength diminished as the game went along, that his health had a lot to do with it."

Oklahoma took over after a Justice punt on its 47. The ground-oriented Sooners took the Tar Heels and stadium by surprise when Royal unleashed a long pass to end Frankie Anderson. North Carolina's Dick Bunting momentarily had control of the ball, but deflected it into Anderson's hands at the 10. "It was underthrown, like most of my passes," said Royal. "I was not playing quarterback, I was a halfback. But Coach Wilkinson would put me there on that play. I'd move from halfback to under center, and we'd fake a fullback counter and throw a deep pass. That was the only play I'd be under center,

and I just didn't know if we could get away with it as late as a bowl game."

Lindell Pearson sped through a huge opening in the UNC line at the 8. Ming's PAT pushed the scoreboard numbers to 14-6, and then the Sooners concentrated on ball control and defense.

It wasn't a spectacular game, but after Royal planted a kiss on Wilkinson's cheek in the locker room, the young coach mused, "You know, maybe defense isn't a glamorous way to win a Sugar Bowl game. But it will win football games and that's what we were down here for, wasn't it?"

Justice, fighting back tears in the North Carolina locker room, felt he was the biggest factor in Oklahoma's win. "I threw that one away," he said, lip quivering. "I gave them that first touchdown with that bad pass. They've got a great ball club. I lost it —you can say that." One newspaperman, Earl Ruby of the Louisville *Courier-Journal*, did. His lead read, " 'Choo-Choo' Charley Justice's passes won the Sugar Bowl football game, but not for North Carolina." Wilkinson saw it differently. "It took 11 workhorses who played football every second of the game to derail Justice and his teammates," assessed Wilkinson.

The deepest cut for North Carolina was yet to come. The Sooners, flushed with victory, showered and dressed quickly, and boarded their buses to return to their hotel. The Tar Heels took their time, letting the sting of the upset fade. But when the team left the dressing room, the parking area was deserted. The buses assigned to Carolina's team took Oklahoma's cheering contingent by mistake. After a futile search, Coach Carl Snavely and some team members waved down a passing truck. The team stood in the open back end and the driver brought them within the vicinity of the hotel. "Ya'll have to get off a couple of blocks from the hotel," the driver said. "I'm not allowed to drive to the entrance." As dark began to envelop New Orleans, the downtrodden Tar Heels slipped unnoticed into a side entrance of the hotel.

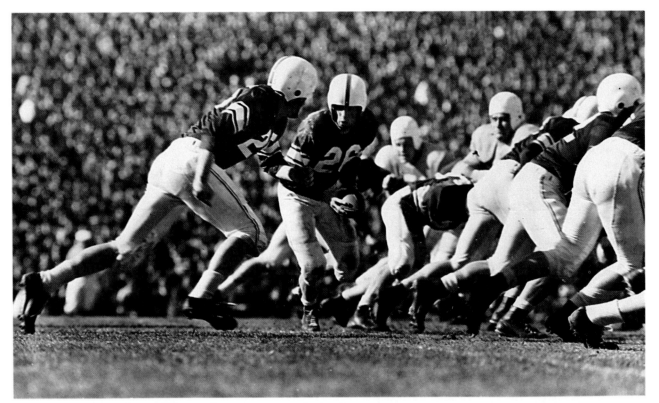

Jack Mitchell hands off as Oklahoma chips away at North Carolina.

Mitchell scores first Sooner touchdown in a 14-6 victory over North Carolina.

Oklahoma-LSU

MONDAY, JANUARY 2, 1950

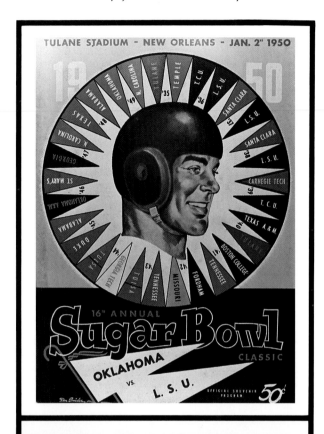

Leon Heath, center, receives the Miller Memorial Trophy from chairman of the Mid-Winter Sports Association's Executive Committee Herbert A. Benson, left, and Sugar Bowl President Frank V. Schaub.

"We just don't know very much about them."

In 1949, the Sugar Bowl became the first bowl to work under new National Collegiate Athletic Association (NCAA) guidelines which included: 1) Two representatives from NCAA member schools must be on any noncollegiate or nonconference committee sponsoring a postseason football game. 2) NCAA members cannot take part in more than one such game in the same academic year, or in any game which lacks NCAA approval or doesn't abide by NCAA rules. 3) Competing schools shall agree on officials. 4) The competing schools shall get not less than a third of the seats in the stadium. Each shall get at least one-sixth of them. 5) The competing schools shall get at least 80 percent of the gross receipts. The sponsoring group shall get no more than 20 percent of the gross. 6) The postseason game must be certified by the NCAA's Extra Events Committee.

The 1950 Sugar Bowl pairing took an ironic twist. Second-ranked Oklahoma, which hadn't lost in 20 games, accepted a second consecutive bid. Filling the other spot was more complicated. Louisiana State University was the nation's most-publicized underdog. After losing two early games, the Tigers finished 8-2 and defeated three (Rice, North Carolina, and Tulane) conference champions. The two losses were to Kentucky and Georgia, giving the Tigers a .667 winning percentage in its six SEC games. The SEC rule stipulated a conference school had to win at least 75 percent of its league games to be eligible for bowl competition.

T.P. "Red" Heard, the Tiger athletic director, anticipated victory, and began phoning around the SEC the day before the Tulane game. By 5 P.M. Saturday, LSU had beaten the Greenies and the rule had been thrown out. Digby informed newsmen, "LSU will play Oklahoma."

Gaynell "Gus" Tinsley, the Tiger coach, was the first former Sugar Bowl player to return as a head coach. Tinsley got as much from a team's ability with his 1949 Tigers as any coach ever did. Although ranked ninth nationally (the highest of any SEC team), LSU did not have anyone on the first team all-conference selection. Oklahoma was the country's best rushing team (averaging 320.3 yards a game) and the nation's best defensive team against the rush, giving up an average of 55.6 yards. Tinsley knew he was in trouble. "We just don't know very much about them. We can't find out much either," the coach moaned two weeks before the Sugar Bowl.

There were others who were curious about the Sooners. A resident glanced out a window toward the Biloxi, Mississippi, High School Stadium where Oklahoma was practicing, and noticed someone hiding on a platform in the rear of the residence at 753 Lee Street. Oklahoma officials shortly received a call with the suggestion that someone hide in the yard of the informer and observe the house that adjoined the stadium.

The next day, a policeman and John "Baby Grand" Scafide, a letterman on Tulane's 1932 Rose Bowl team, closed in on the spy, hidden behind a rigged blanket and ringed with scratch pads and a pair of binoculars. Bill Dennis, a free-lance Biloxi photographer shooting for the *Times-Picayune*, got a picture as the three flushed out the suspect.

Harry Wismer, left, talks over spy incident before 1950 game with LSU Coach Gaynell Tinsley.

Wismer and Bud Wilkinson discuss Sugar Bowl for national audience.

Although his identity wasn't then known, the man photographed was Walter "Piggy" Barnes, a former LSU linesman playing with the Philadelphia Eagles. There was also another person involved, Gustave Adolthus "Goober" Morse, a fan closely associated with the LSU athletic department and who had served in the Navy during World War II with Sooner Coach Bud Wilkinson. Barnes got out of the policeman's clutches and joined Morse on the garage roof where he defied the growing police contingent to come and get him. The police, uncertain as to whether the pair was really guilty of anything or who they were, hesitated. Eventually, Barnes and Morse, buoyed by the uncertainty, climbed down, walked through the police, got into their car, and took off for New Orleans.

"God, they got fighting mad," recalled Morse. "That story just grew and grew all the time we drove to New Orleans until it was front page. Man, we didn't stop until we reached the Roosevelt Hotel. We called Pappy (Art) Lewis (an assistant at Mississippi State about to be named head coach at West Virginia) and asked what he thought we ought to do. 'Well,' he said, 'Your name is M-o-r-s-e, and yours is B-a-r-n-e-s . . . tell 'em to make damn sure they don't leave the 'r' out in the spelling.' He was a big help."

Morse insists even now that he and Barnes were scouting prospects for "Greasy" Neale, the coach of the Eagles. "LSU didn't have a thing to do with it," said Morse. "We just thought it would be a good idea to look 'em over. We could've gone in the main gate, maybe. We didn't exactly scout like we were supposed to. Normally you walk in through the gate and watch 'em work out. So, we didn't do it that way." It's not a defense most lawyers would be eager to use.

"The coaches were furious," said Sooner quarterback Darrell Royal, "really angry. That gave us additional impetus." Wilkinson was angrily shaking his head, saying, "I can't believe LSU would do such a thing. I just can't believe they'd do us this way." At a meeting in New Orleans, Wilkinson refused at first to shake Tinsley's hand. LSU officials argued before Barnes' and Morse's identities were known that it could have been done by Oklahoma to fire up a complacent team.

Morse chuckled, "Later on, the Atlanta Touchdown Club gave Coach Wilkinson the Walter Barnes-Goober Morse Award, which was a pair of binoculars. Every time I see Coach Wilkinson, we laugh about it now." But Bud Wilkinson wasn't laughing January 2, 1950.

Oklahoma 35-LSU 0

"I just kept waiting for the bear to jump on him."

An unintimidated LSU bounced onto the field looking for a fourth conquest of a conference champion. For 15 minutes the Tiger line actually outperformed Bud Wilkinson's alternating fronts. Quarterback Charlie Pevey had the Tigers moving, slowly and cautiously but effectively, to the Oklahoma 19, then the 35. Eight-point favorite Oklahoma was not impressed.

Quarterback Darrell Royal had to change the Sooner offense somewhat in order to get in gear. "Our drop back passes were completely useless because they knew exactly what was coming. The passes I did complete were a new set of plays that we didn't practice."

Nine plays into the second quarter, Royal went to his alternate plan, lateralling to halfback Lindell Pearson who threw to a wide-open Bobby Goad 40 yards downfield on the 8. LSU held the Sooners on fourth down inside the 1 on a fine goal line stand.

Buddy Jones returned Kenny Konz's punt to the Tiger 37, however, and Oklahoma was in business again. After two line plays, Pearson passed 27 yards down the slot to George Thomas for the touchdown. The passing loosened the LSU defense, which had been primarily concerned with the Sooner runners.

Mel Lyle fumbled Ken Tipps' low kickoff, and Delton Marcum recovered on the LSU 38. Thomas bolted to the 21, then dropped a pass in the end zone with no defender in sight. Pearson barreled to the 8, where Thomas fumbled. Royal recovered on the 6. Thomas scored in two plays from the 5.

The score remained 14-0 until the half. Konz gave LSU an opportunity to get back in it with a third-quarter punt that came to rest on the Oklahoma 14. Fullback Leon Heath then wheeled out of the Sooner split-T and blazed 86 yards, the longest scoring run of all the previous Sugar Bowls. Armand Kitto, a 157-pound LSU end, said, ". . . They say on a long run like that, a bear will jump on the runner's back. Well, I just kept waiting for the bear to jump on him, and instead, he jumped on me . . ."

Lyle fumbled on the LSU 14 on the Tigers' first play of the fourth period. Royal, in short order, dove in from the 5 for Oklahoma's fourth TD of the day. LSU went to a desperate air game; Carroll Griffith hit Warren Virgets with two successive completions, but Bert Clark intercepted the next attempt and ran it back to the Tiger 29. Heath, after a loss of 5 yards, cracked straight through right tackle and sped 34 yards for Oklahoma's final touchdown.

In the first 15 games the Sugar Bowl had a remarkable matchmaking record with an average of seven points separating the teams. The 1950 game remains the worst scoring differential in Sugar Bowl history. The headline in the *Dallas News* of January 3 read, "Oklahoma Overpowers Minor League LSU Team," ignoring the fact that LSU had beaten both Rice and North Carolina, the Cotton Bowl participants.

Wilkinson graciously understated the SEC's eighth loss in 12 Sugar Bowls when he said, "If we played LSU a dozen times we'd never play that well against them again, or score that many points. They're too good a team."

This was probably why the Sooner coach didn't take out his regulars until approximately three minutes remained in the game, and the score stood at its final 35-0.

Sooner fullback Leon Heath rambles 34 yards for Oklahoma's final touchdown against LSU.

Kentucky-Oklahoma

MONDAY, JANUARY 1, 1951

"I still wanted them."

While the conquering Sooners enjoyed a holiday in Cuba after the dismantling of LSU, a question arose concerning LSU's propriety in the Sugar Bowl—but not over the spy incident. The school's Board of Supervisors had approved $250 to each player as an expense allotment, "subject to all rules and regulations of the Southeastern Conference." "That may be questioned," said NCAA President Karl E. Leib at the governing body's annual convention in Chicago, "but only to standardize procedure. We certainly wouldn't quarrel about making up money the boys lost by leaving their jobs to play in the Sugar Bowl and to take care of valid expenses."

Innocent and aboveboard though it was, this sort of action couldn't help but be noticed by critics of bowls (there were 12 games on January 2, 1950) who felt college games were becoming too commercialized. Precisely because of such money-making ventures as bowls, the NCAA at a later meeting in Dallas adopted a recommendation from the previous year. A bylaw was enacted requiring sponsors to give not less than 75 percent of the gross, including such ancillary revenue producers as broadcast, concession, and movie money, to its participating teams. The Sugar Bowl had tried to pay the 80 percent suggested in 1949, but was still paying off the bonds issued for the expansions of Tulane Stadium. The NCAA ruled that bowls with a bond issue before August of 1949 were permitted 20 percent payment toward that debt.

The Southeastern Conference produced two superb teams for the 1950 season—Kentucky, in the fifth year of Coach Paul "Bear" Bryant's five-year plan, and Tennessee. Bryant had already secured the Wildcats' first, and to date only, SEC championship when the Vols and Kentucky played late in the season. An early-season loss to Mississippi State was the only blot on Tennessee's record, and Coach Bob Neyland accepted a Cotton Bowl invitation before the Kentucky game.

Charles C. Zatarain was president of the Sugar Bowl and went to Knoxville to view the second-ranked Wildcats play Tennessee in eight-degree weather with four inches of snow. "It was so bad," said Zatarain, "that at the half I could see the special train just getting fans in. They marched downhill like a troop. It was a miserable day. I went to

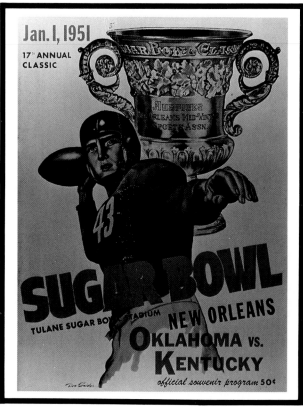

Knoxville for the purpose of inviting Kentucky, but they lost."

It was a day of reckoning for Bryant, who had held the other bowls off in hope of spending New Year's in New Orleans. "I didn't know where we stood," Bryant said, his hopes of a national championship and undefeated season buried under Knoxville's snowdrifts and his personal jinx against Neyland intact. Bryant was never able to beat the General. "The Orange and Cotton had filled, and I couldn't blame the Sugar Bowl folks if they didn't want us after Tennessee whipped us," said Bear.

Bryant and Zatarain wound up in a hotel room with Kentucky Athletic Director Bernie Shively and Southeastern Conference Commissioner Bernie Moore. "We had a line open to the Sugar Bowl office," recalled Zatarain. "I told them Kentucky was a great team, and that as far as my vote was concerned I still wanted them. The committee talked it over, then came back to tell me to ask Bryant if he'd play if he got an invite. Bear reached out, took the phone, and said, 'If you invite me, I'll beat Oklahoma!'"

"If I had gotten shut out of a major bowl after I

Coach Paul 'Bear' Bryant sends Kentucky end Charlie McClendon in against Bud Wilkinson's national champion Sooners.

had passed up several invitations, I would have had a tough time getting back into Lexington," growled Bryant.

The prediction about beating Oklahoma was premature. The Sooners, ranked No. 1 nationally, hadn't been invited yet. It was felt that Coach Bud Wilkinson didn't want to participate in a bowl that year, that he would rather his team retire undefeated after the regular season. His team voted to play in New Orleans a third consecutive year, however, and Wilkinson accepted the invitation. Kentucky dropped to seventh after the Tennessee defeat,

but one statistic provides an insight on just how good these teams were: Kentucky and Oklahoma finished their regular season schedules tied for second nationally in fumbles lost with 27. Despite that horrifying stat, there was one loss between them.

Bryant, aware of his promise and the opportunity to atone for the galling Tennessee defeat, tinkered a bit with his defense. Before the game Bryant cleared the locker room of his underclassmen. He turned, stared, then commanded the seniors in his grumpy, resonant voice, "I want you to give it your absolute all. Play 'til you drop on the field!"

Kentucky 13-Oklahoma 7

Leon Heath (40) pounds the Kentucky line. Heath gained 120 yards, but Bear Bryant keeps his word as his Wildcats stun Oklahoma, 13-7.

"They weren't strong enough to move us out of there."

To offset Oklahoma's flashlike split-T offense, Kentucky Coach Paul Bryant used a multi-defense which often ballooned to a nine-man line. Four Kentucky tackles were usually on the line of scrimmage, including 6-foot-2, 208-pound Walt Yowarsky, who had played one game of defense in his life. He went head-to-head with Oklahoma's highly touted Jim Weatherall, and Yowarsky had a specific task: Shut down the wide option, constantly harass quarterback Claude Arnold, and upset the Sooner offensive precision. No one had done anything approaching that sort of controlled mayhem against a Bud Wilkinson team in a long time. Oklahoma had won 31 consecutive games.

"Coach Bryant wanted his biggest kids on defense to shoot gaps in the Oklahoma offense," remem-

bered Yowarsky, who played end in the defensive scheme. "That's why, I suppose, I was moved to defense. I think the feeling was that Oklahoma could probably move some on us until they got near the goal, but that they weren't strong enough to move us out of there."

Bryant, who was ever-mindful of Oklahoma's devastating speed, decided to use an unprotected punter and a line that did little blocking on punts, believing it was less a gamble than allowing Billy Vessels an opportunity to start flying.

Kentucky received the opening kickoff, couldn't move, and punted to the Sooner 25. Bob Gain cracked Arnold behind the line of scrimmage on the first Oklahoma play, causing a fumble that Yowarsky recovered at the Sooner 22.

Babe Parilli (10) gets a pass away as Oklahoma's Frankie Anderson (82) and Fred Smith (67) rush the Kentucky quarterback.

Parilli of Kentucky sets sail for Oklahoma goal.

Quarterback Babe Parilli dropped back on first down, faked a handoff, faked a jump pass, then threw into the end zone for Wilbur Jamerson, who made a sensational catch in outmuscling Tommy Gray for possession. Gain kicked the extra point with the game barely three minutes old.

"Early in the game," Bryant related in his biography, "Charlie McClendon came off the field with the side of his face torn off. When I turned to call the trainer and looked around, he was already going back on the field with the defense. His tackling caused three fumbles that day." McClendon said, "They put cotton on the thing, then froze it. I remember asking the Lord, to please 'not let that thing fall down in my eye.'"

Leon Heath fumbled a pitchout from Arnold following the penalty and Doug Mosely recovered on the Oklahoma 16. Parilli went for the jugular and passed to Ben Zaranka who was wide open in the end zone. Zaranka missed a chance to end matters early by dropping an easy catch. "I had nightmares, just dreaming about doing what happened in front of all those folks in New Orleans," Zaranka said later. "A child could have caught that ball." The Sooners held without giving up a yard.

Heath, the Sugar's MVP the year before, broke off

a 30-yarder to the Kentucky 31 in the second period, but the threat ended when Yowarsky threw Arnold for a 12-yard loss. Parilli worked the Wildcat offense from its 19 to the Oklahoma 48, then heaved a shot to a streaking Al Bruno. Bruno made an over-the-shoulder reception at the 15, then dragged Jack Lockett several yards before going down inside the 1. Jamerson dove over on the next play for the second Wildcat touchdown. Gain missed the conversion.

Kentucky continued to exert pressure as the half neared. Fucci punted inside the Oklahoma 1. Oklahoma gained 5 yards; then Dick Heatley went into the end zone to kick on fourth down. He got a high pass; when Heatley recovered, a Wildcat was closing on him. On the play of the day, he managed to evade the defender, run 10 yards toward the sideline, and kick on the dead run.

Kentucky went into the dressing room behind in the stats. Although Parilli was seven of nine for 98 yards, Kentucky led, 13-0. Bryant decided to close up his offense and leave the game to his defense to win or lose.

Arnold moved his unit to midfield on Oklahoma's first second-half possession. There the 'Cats braced, but a 15-yard roughing penalty kept the Sooners alive. Oklahoma got to the 4 with a first-and-goal to go. Bryant's defense faced its trial by fire.

Heath got 2 yards, and Vessels was held for no gain. Vessels then went wide and Yowarsky fired through and threw the runner for a monumental 5-yard loss. "I just knifed through," said Yowarsky. "I don't remember exactly what happened, but I do remember feeling this was a fairly large play." A pass just beyond Frankie Anderson's reach finished the series. Kentucky's defense, featuring a line of four tackles and three ends, had held.

Gain missed an 18-yard field goal that could have sealed the victory, and Vessels started the Oklahoma machine up with runs of 20 and 14 yards. On fourth-and-one, Heath inched in for the necessary distance at the 33. The drive reached the 17 where Vessels started wide, drew up, and passed to Merrill Green for a touchdown. With six minutes left, Oklahoma was suddenly in position to win.

Kentucky couldn't move after the kickoff and Fucci punted. Lockett attempted to field the ball on the bounce but lost control and fumbled. Yowarsky recovered on the Oklahoma 32. Taking as much time as possible and three delay penalties, Kentucky

nudged to the 15 before losing the ball on downs. Dick Martin intercepted a last gasp Oklahoma pass at midfield with three seconds left.

Just as Bryant had blueprinted, Oklahoma had won almost every statistical comparison but fell short on the scoreboard. Two Kentucky stats may have been the difference. Bryant's unprotected punter strategy allowed Oklahoma less than a half-yard average on returns; and when Kentucky needed to control the ball, it did. In the 7:04 remaining after Oklahoma's touchdown, only 13 plays were run.

It was Kentucky's finest football moment. Bryant, who always felt a bit strangled by the basketball glitter in Lexington, held the game ball close in the locker room. A reporter asked what he planned to do with it. "Son," Bryant replied in a low voice, "I'm gonna take this here football, get the score put on it in great big numbers and I'm gonna bring it into that new (basketball) coliseum that they've just finished at Kentucky. I'm gonna go right up to where they put all those shiny basketball trophies, you know those shiny round things. Then I'm gonna take this ball and put it right where everybody can see it."

Harry Wismer and Kentucky Coach Paul 'Bear' Bryant read telegrams from well-wishers.

Maryland-Tennessee

TUESDAY, JANUARY 1, 1952

"Coach said to vote again."

What the Sugar Bowl had come to mean was put in eloquent perspective with the 1951 Sugar Bowl. After the game, Babe Parilli gave his Sugar Bowl watch to his father. "It was Dad's greatest treasure," said Parilli. "He wore it every day." When Babe's father died at 82, his son fulfilled a final request. "He was buried with the Purple Heart he won in the war and with his Sugar Bowl watch."

Fans, players, and coaches loved the bowls. The major bowls certainly were a symbol of achievement. However, some influential critics did not love the bowls. They thought the bowls fostered crass commercialism and a win-at-all-costs attitude. These critics sought their abolishment and maintained that collegiate sports belonged strictly on campus.

Ironically, in late 1951 it was the Sugar Bowl that gave the critics ammunition and provided the major bowls' defense.

At a September meeting of the presidents of the Southern Conference, the administrators voted to direct their representatives at a scheduled December meeting to vote against allowing any conference school to play in a bowl game that year.

The Southern Conference vote colored the entire bowl scene. Maryland, under Coach Jim Tatum, was clearly one of the premier teams of 1951 and high on all bowl lists. Tatum wanted his third-ranked Terrapins to play on New Year's Day. He told Sugar Bowl President Charles Zatarain he would resign if permission wasn't granted, and he wanted to play the No. 1-ranked Tennessee Volunteers.

Washington, D.C., newspapers predicted Maryland was going to the Cotton Bowl, but in mid-November—with several games remaining—Maryland and Tennessee contracted to play in New Orleans. The early signing seemed to point to increasing competition between the Sugar, Orange, and Cotton Bowls, although the Cotton Bowl vigorously insisted it would not have taken the Terps until Southern Conference permission had been obtained. Maryland had not taken a telephone poll of its sister schools.

Maryland's defense rested on the fact that any action at the December meeting under the conference constitution would not be binding until September, 1953. The Southern Conference bylaws required, however, that the "consent of the conference" be obtained before any member agrees to play in a

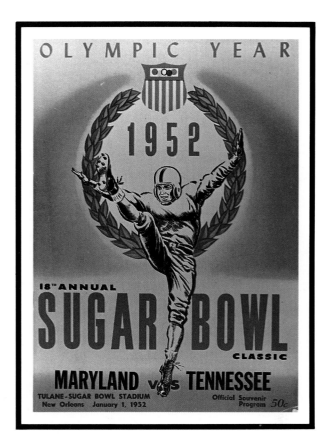

postseason game. Another bylaw read that all new rules adopted by the conference "shall go into effect the 1st of September, following the annual meeting, or on such a date as the conference may direct." Southern Conference presidents, it seemed plain, intended the bowl ban to go into effect before January 1, 1952.

Clemson, which had accepted a Gator Bowl bid, and Maryland were placed on a year's probation by the conference. Neither could participate in a football game with another Southern Conference school in the 1952 season. The Sugar Bowl felt this was a family fracas, and it wasn't the concern of the Mid-Winter Sports Association. Of course, if the Sugar or any of the other bowls hadn't extended early invitations, the difficulty would never have arisen.

Aside from its Southeastern Conference and national championships, General Bob Neyland's Tennessee Vols had an additional New Orleans lure.

Tennessee's All-American tailback Hank Lauricella had prepped in New Orleans and been overlooked by local colleges. Unbeaten and untied Maryland had a unique brother combination, fullback Ed Modzelewski, who personally had outgained Maryland's regular season opponents (834 yards to 680 yards on a 7.8 average), and Dick Modzelewski, a tackle.

A crowd of several thousand spent the eve of the Terrapin-Vol announcement standing in an icy wind waiting to get tickets. The match, as Zatarain had said, was the one everybody wanted. Not until it was over did anyone realize Tatum had convinced his team to take a shot at the No. 1 team—over a stack of cowboy hats.

Although the Cotton Bowl said it wouldn't invite Maryland until the Southern Conference granted permission, it apparently did. An anonymous Terp confided to Hap Glaudi, "We came damn close to not playing in the Sugar Bowl. We had invitations from the Cotton and Sugar Bowls because Dave Cianelli, the Maryland co-captain, asked us to vote where we wanted to go. We had been talking about it among ourselves and decided we would like to go to the Cotton Bowl. We knew fellows who played in the Cotton Bowl came home wearing those big cowboy hats and boots. We weren't worried about the team we would play." So they voted for the Cotton Bowl, and Dave went to tell the coach the vote.

Dave returned and told them Coach Tatum said

to vote again. If they voted for the Sugar Bowl, the coach said he would buy them all the cowboy hats they wanted. They knew the coach really wanted to play Tennessee, so they voted this time for the Sugar Bowl.

The dispute over the value of bowl games had silenced many university employees, including coaches, not wishing to publicly argue with the academicians. The silence generated a sentiment that perhaps the critics were right, that bowls helped foster a win-at-all-costs attitude and contributed to moving college football from a campus activity to a big business. Timed to coincide with a special NCAA meeting, and virtually the only voice heard in defense of the four major bowls, the Mid-Winter Sports Association issued a statement with a list of 15 contributions the New Year's Day games had made to college football. It ended by saying, "We would cease our program at once if we thought we were doing anything harmful to collegiate sports."

No one seriously doubted the integrity of the major bowl sponsors. The Sugar, like the three other major bowls, had always conducted its activities on the highest collegiate plane. When the NCAA tentatively set up a code of conduct for postseason football, the Sugar Bowl immediately and voluntarily adopted it. The 1950 and 1951 games were conducted under that code.

Maryland 28-Tennessee 13

"Lord, what a day that was."

"The closer it gets, the scareder I get," quipped Jim Tatum, who had studied at the knee of General Bob Neyland and fully appreciated the capability of Tennessee's single wing offense and fundamentally sound defense.

The Maryland defense was changed to a four- and five-man line with three linebackers up front in order to cut off Hank Lauricella's wide runs and place additional pressure on the passer. It also upset Tennessee's blocking scheme. "Coach told us over and over again that Tennessee's offense was on the ground," said Terp center Bob Ward. "He told us the Tennessee team had been overpowering teams all season long—four yards, three, five, and four again. So we dug in and did our best to stop the running."

Ed Modzelewski, called "Mighty Mo" to distinguish him from his brother Dick "Little Mo," said the Maryland offense was pared to a fairly simple operation. "Our plays were designed to gain three or four yards at a time," he said. Tatum targeted Tennessee All-American guard Ted Daffer as the point of attack. "We decided to slant our offense at Daffer," said Tatum. "He's built pretty much like Bobby (Ward, who would play on Daffer), about 190 pounds and extremely fast for a lineman. But a study of game pictures showed Daffer couldn't handle plays run straight at him. He could make tackles all over the field but when a play was run straight at him, he couldn't handle it."

Neyland's 6-2-2-1 defense was rigged to stop the option and wide plays, and was tailor-made for

Tatum. "When I saw how they had their defense set, and knew what a great line-buster we had in Mighty Mo," said quarterback Jack Scarbath, "I would have been crazy to call for anything but Mo through guard."

It was a Terrapin day from the start. Mighty Mo cracked the line midway through the opening quarter at the Vol 41, broke into the secondary, was hit, and fumbled at the 29. Teammate Lou Weidensaul recovered on the 25. Scarbath connected on two passes, one just over the fingertips of two defenders to Ed Fullerton to the 12. Modzelewski gained 7 yards with a flock of Vols hanging on, and Fullerton carried on three consecutive plays to score on fourth down from the 2. Don Decker converted, and that was the last time the game was close.

Lauricella gathered in the following kickoff 2 yards deep in the end zone and raced out. At the 13 he was sandwiched, the ball popped loose, and Ed Kensler claimed it for Maryland. After seesawing for a couple of downs, Fullerton took a handoff and tossed a halfback pass to Bob Shemonski over the goal. Maryland, a 7-point underdog to the national champions, was an astonishing two touchdowns ahead with the second quarter barely under way.

Things were to get worse for the Vols. Neyland refused to change the defense the Terps were dissolving. Fullerton recovered another fumble near midfield, and Scarbath eventually scored on a quarterback sneak from the 1.

Hal Payne finally got Tennessee moving in the latter stages of the second period and put the Vols on the scoreboard with a 4-yard pass to Bert Rechichar. Rechichar then missed the PAT.

Maryland spent most of the third quarter trying to make up ground lost by repeated penalties, but Fullerton still managed to post points by intercepting a Lauricella pass and returning it 46 yards for the Terrapins' fourth touchdown.

"Lord, what a day that was," moaned Lauricella, who finished his collegiate career in his hometown with his poorest day as a Tennessee Vol. He had 1 yard rushing, fumbled the kickoff that led to Maryland's second touchdown, and threw three interceptions in five attempts.

For a second consecutive year, a national champion left its bones on the Sugar Bowl field. Ed Modzelewski had personally outgained Tennessee, 153 yards to 81, and Maryland overcame an incredible 120 yards in penalties. General Neyland wouldn't even meet with the press; he simply sent out a release praising Maryland. Tatum was bubbling. Perhaps remembering the cowboy hats, he told his players to take their headgear, have all team members sign them, and keep them as a gift from him.

"Coach called that one for us," laughed Dick Modzelewski. "He told us the story about the man who asked him if he was the toughest guy in town, and he said, 'No, but I'm the guy who beat the toughest guy in town.'"

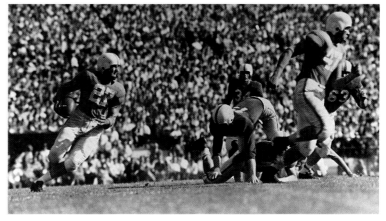

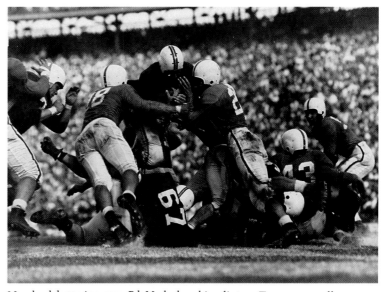

Hank Lauricella (27) searches for running room against giant-killing Maryland.

Maryland battering ram Ed Modzelewski splinters Tennessee wall.

Tennessee's Hank Lauricella, a hometown boy who didn't make good in the 1952 Sugar Bowl.

Georgia Tech-Mississippi

THURSDAY, JANUARY 1, 1953

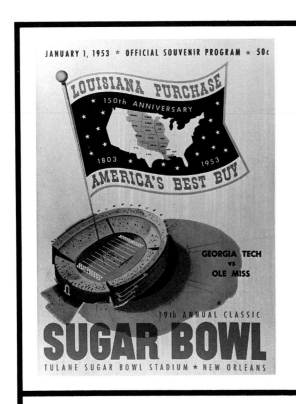

Georgia Tech Coach Bobby Dodd checks in hotel with assistant Ray Graves.

"That made us nationwide."

While the recommendations of the 10 university presidents on the American Council of Education committee were being studied, the NCAA ordered member institutions not to make bowl commitments beyond January 2, 1953. The Southern Conference made its antibowl position official, and punished Maryland and Clemson for their appearances by barring them from participating in Southern Conference regular season games for a year. The Big Seven Conference took an antibowl posture, apparently putting Oklahoma out of the holiday picture. One of the maddest bowl scrambles of all time was the result.

Most observers thought Georgia Tech was heading to the Orange Bowl for a return engagement. However, Fred Digby made a trip to Atlanta and on November 4, an unusually early signing date, Tech surprisingly committed to the Sugar Bowl. Bobby Dodd's Engineers were ranked third in the United Press poll at the time, 6-0-0 with four games remaining.

Dodd, it seems, grabbed the Sugar because of an offer of 14,000 tickets (1,500 more than the SEC requirement) for Tech supporters. That story was printed and denied by both parties. Before the denial, however, Dodd was quoted as saying, "I wanted as many tickets as I could get because I don't want Tech fans saying we let them down. We want as many fans as can go with us."

For an opponent, the Sugar waited for either Maryland or Oklahoma to indicate an interest, despite their respective conference stands. Another possibility was Mississippi, tied twice in early season games but undefeated since then.

Ole Miss took matters into its hands and forced the bowl to make a decision. Coach Johnny Vaught's Rebels pulled off what was acknowledged to be 1952's college upset of the year by beating Maryland, 21-14. The victory, probably the most important in Ole Miss history, jumped the Rebs to No. 7 in the national polls. It was the school's first Top 10 ranking, and it earned them a Sugar Bowl berth. This was Ole Miss' first major bowl invitation since a 1936 Orange Bowl appearance.

"Bowl fever killed us," said Coach Jim Tatum of Maryland. "We wanted to go to the Sugar badly."

So did Ole Miss, who after its ticket allotment was gone was left with 65,000 supporters still trying to get in. It wouldn't be quite as trying for these fans as it was for those who didn't get tickets in past years, though. For the first time, the Sugar, Cotton, and Orange Bowls would be telecast nationally. The Rose Bowl, in populous southern California, a media center, had already gone national the year before.

Television depended then on coaxial cable, but it didn't yet reach New Orleans. Sugar Bowl President Irwin Poche had a friend, Basil O'Connor, who was president of the national March of Dimes. Porche suggested to O'Connor early in 1952 that a large portion of the proceeds be donated to the March of Dimes when the Sugar Bowl was carried on national TV. O'Connor hit on the idea of asking AT&T to extend the coaxial cable to New Orleans as its donation to the March of Dimes. It may have been a coincidence, but the cable was in place for the 1953 Sugar Bowl.

The Sugar Bowl had received $50,000 for its 1952 telecast, which was carried locally on WDSU-TV and then sent to other cities. On December 10, 1952, the Sugar Bowl and ABC completed arrangements for its national coverage. "That made us nationwide," said Charles Zatarain. "That was the difference between national television and the radio." The network paid $100,000 ($25,000 of which was earmarked for the March of Dimes for the length of the contract) for a combined TV-radio package.

It was a huge step forward, but it was not without additional headaches. ABC was the new network and, because of limited outlets in comparison to NBC and CBS, its largest sponsor withdrew. ABC had to depend on local sponsorship in the cities where the Sugar Bowl was piped. But it was a start.

Coach Bobby Dodd seemed to have a lot more to worry about than mundane things like television, despite his Yellow Jackets being a 7-point favorite. Tech finished the season as undefeated SEC champion, ranked No. 2 nationally. In the last few games, however, his team had incurred numerous injuries, including those of running backs Leon Hardeman (ankle) and Bill Teas (collarbone). This threatened to curtail their playing time, if, indeed, they could play at all.

Georgia Tech 24-Mississippi 7

"I see you've still got your watch and chain."

Right off the bat, Rebel quarterback Jim "King" Lear took the proud Tech defense apart. Tech's defense was the backbone of a 25-game unbeaten string. Eight plays into the game, Lear had run the Rebel sprint-out offense 57 yards and had numbed Tech with a 7-0 lead. Wilson Dillard scored from the 1, and Lear kicked the PAT.

If the traditionally slow-starting Yellow Jackets didn't feel overly concerned at that point, Ole Miss gave every sign of going for the jugular early. Backed up to the 8, Tech's Glenn Turner gained 12 yards for some space, but Billy Teas fumbled on the next play. Rebel Jim Ingram recovered on the 19. Lear passed Ole Miss inside the 10. Another pass to

Harol Lofton put the Rebs on the 2 with two downs left.

Dick Westerman gained a yard; then Dillard crashed into the line on fourth down. Players were piled up at the edge of the goal line; when they were untangled, Dillard was ruled an inch short of a touchdown and the ball went over to Tech. Coach Johnny Vaught protested later, "That ball was over, but they pushed it back two inches!" Engineer linebacker Larry Morris thought the call could have gone either way, but his linebacker running mate George Morris remained certain Dillard didn't get in.

Ending the first quarter, Lear fumbled and Tech

Little Leon Hardeman (11) swings past Ole Miss defender in first all-SEC pairing.

gained momentum and began steaming toward the Mississippi goal 49 yards away. Teas and Leon Hardeman, both performing far better than pregame reports indicated, camped Tech on the Ole Miss 9 with a first down to begin the second period. The ball popped loose as Turner hit the line, but he caught it in midair and gained 4 yards. Bill Brigman sneaked over the goal from the 2.

Westerman busted loose for 20 yards to put the Rebels back in position near midfield. Then Lear looped a perfect pass to James Slay, who made the grab at the 25 and cruised another 20 yards before George Morris saved the touchdown.

Dillard gained 2 yards. After Lofton was stopped over center, Lear slipped for no gain at left tackle. Then Bobby Moorhead threw Lear for a yard loss—four plays, one yard, no points. "That's where we won the game," said Bobby Dodd. "Those goal line stands won the game."

Georgia Tech was beginning to control the Mississippi offense, which had started off so impressively. Frank Broyles, a Tech assistant, explained, "We changed the play of our tackles. All season long we have been crashing our tackles straight ahead on pass plays. There's not but one quarterback in 50 who can get out of the pocket we form that way. Lear was that one in 50. So we changed the angle on them. Instead of charging straight, we sent them crashing out at an angle toward the sidelines."

Hardeman and Teas began punching holes in the Rebel defense after the Ole Miss failure at the 5, and Tech drove from its 30 to the Reb 5. When Georgia Tech didn't get in, Franklin "Pepper" Rodgers kicked a 22-yard field goal to give the Engineers a 10-7 halftime lead.

"When we went into the locker room I remember Coach Dodd sitting on a table, swinging his legs and drinking a coke," said George Morris, who was recruited for Tech right out of the Rebel stronghold of Vicksburg, Mississippi. "He said, 'Well, boys, it looks like we got 'em on the run.' Our reaction was that Coach Dodd wasn't watching the same game we were." The atmosphere was much different in the Rebel locker room where Vaught was telling his team that he just wanted to find 22 players who really wanted to play football, and that his second unit would open the second half.

Bill Thaden put Ole Miss in deep trouble early in the second half by recovering a fumble on the Rebel 18. Hardeman, a 5-foot-6 bowling ball whose performance Lear said "should make medical history," fought his way through right tackle and scored from the 6, removing Tech from any immediate danger. The Rebels argued—to no avail—that Hardeman's knee had touched about the 3, and it did appear so. When Vaught sent his front liners back in, Morris yelled, "Where you been, fellas. We missed you."

A third controversial call occurred in the third period when Lear punted to Moorhead on the Tech 24. As three blue-shirted Rebels zeroed in on the re-

ceiver, he gave a last-second motion that was described as "something like a wave to his girl friend." The ball was knocked loose and Ole Miss recovered at the 21. But the officials ruled the faint fair-catch signal had given the coverage enough time to back off, a decision derided by the press.

The 15-yard penalty pushed the ball up to the 39 and Tech drove to the Rebel 2, where Ole Miss held on downs. Tech was in the van by that point, although Rodgers threw a 24-yard TD pass to Jeff Knox in the fourth quarter.

Statistically, little separated the Engineers and Rebels, but the stats were deceiving. In the first half Ole Miss gained 164 yards. In the second half the Rebels had 123 yards against the revamped Tech defense. Ninety of those second-half yards, though, came after Tech's 24th point.

Unfortunately, the officiating marred the Yellow Jacket's 24-7 victory. *Times-Picayune* sports editor Bill Keefe couldn't resist noting, "Three of the four officials who worked in the Sugar Bowl live in Georgia. Two are from Atlanta." Mississippi Governor Hugh White sent letters to George Gardner, president of the SEC Officials' Association, and to Bernie Moore, SEC commissioner, saying he had "witnessed the worst officiating I have ever seen." A Rebel fan spotted Ole Miss President Dr. John Davis Williams walking from the stadium and noted, "Well, Doc, I see you've still got your watch and chain, so maybe we're lucky."

Hardeman spins away from a Rebel lineman to score a 6-yard Georgia Tech touchdown.

Georgia Tech-West Virginia

FRIDAY, JANUARY 1, 1954

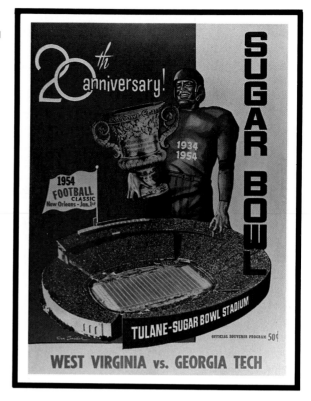

"You taught me too well."

The NCAA Extra Events Committee voted unanimously, January 9, 1953, to continue postseason bowl games that it sanctioned (the recommendation of the 10 presidents of the American Council on Education committee having fallen on deaf ears).

Maryland's acceptance to play in the 1952 Sugar Bowl and Clemson's participation in the Gator Bowl had dramatic results in the spring of 1953. Maryland and Clemson, along with North Carolina, North Carolina State, Wake Forest, Virginia, and South Carolina, broke from the Southern Conference and formed a new league, the Atlantic Coast Conference.

The ACC first approached the Sugar Bowl on the feasibility of a tie-up. The Sugar Bowl would not commit to a tie-up, but assured the ACC if it produced a good team they would receive an invitation. The fledgling conference wanted more, and secured an Orange Bowl tie-up several months later. Miami also tied up the Big Seven, which rescinded its bowl ban. This meant that five of the eight berths in the major bowls were filled automatically. It also meant that the choice of quality football teams for New Orleans had diminished greatly, considering that most of the conference-bowl agreements allowed only the designated representative (not necessarily the champion) to participate.

General Manager Fred Digby wrote that the Sugar Bowl and the Southeastern Conference unsuccessfully discussed a tie-up on several occasions. The Sugar Bowlers were reluctant to tie up because they

had been successful without such an agreement.

In 1954, the Sugar Bowl openly wooed unbeaten West Virginia and the Southern Conference. The conference's executive committee was empowered to lift its bowl ban for one year, but only if a member received a bid.

Several attractive Southwest teams were available, including Texas, Baylor, and high-scoring, colorful Texas Tech. With the SEC championship up for grabs, Alabama, Georgia Tech, Auburn, and Ole Miss all looked promising. At breakfast in Birmingham the morning of the Tech-Alabama game, Irvin Poche, the president of the Sugar Bowl committee, extended an invitation to Engineer Coach Bobby Dodd. With three games remaining and not wishing to put a bowl in a difficult position, Dodd declined, saying he was uncertain about the outcomes of the 'Bama and Duke games. He did promise to contact the Sugar Bowl before accepting another bid.

Alabama defeated Tech, but the colorful Yellow Jackets were still a prime contender. The Cotton Bowl put out a feeler and the 'Jackets voted to go to Dallas; however, this was with the stipulation that if they were invited to the Sugar Bowl, the team could vote again. Poche told the press November 24 that the Sugar Bowl would wait until that weekend's games were completed before making its selection. Then Dodd called saying he had a Cotton Bowl invitation. An emergency meeting was hurriedly called. Tech players revoted for the Sugar, and Georgia Tech was extended an invitation.

West Virginia's stock had slipped considerably with a 12-7 squeaker against VPI and a 14-20 loss to South Carolina, but the Sugar Bowl chose them to play Georgia Tech. Many thought this was a mismatch, one made because Dodd was allowed to handpick his opponent and the Sugar Bowl didn't want to disappoint the Southern Conference it had been playing to most of the season.

Clark Nealon, sports editor of The *Houston Post,* blistered the Sugar saying, it buttered Texas and Baylor "on a contingency basis, then forgot it all and made its mind (up) in one session. The question is: Did Bobby Dodd operate with the "ax" of having the Cotton Bowl bid in his pocket when he started negotiations with the Sugar Bowl? And did he close with the Sugar Bowl with the understanding he would play West Virginia? . . . From what we have cause to believe Dodd dealt within a finger snap of final closing with the Cotton Bowl, then, when news leaked out in the Southeastern area and the Sugar Bowl beckoned, closed with the Sugar Bowl with the understanding he name his own opponent."

Everyone connected agreed the story was too ridiculous to comment on and most of the New Orleans press sugarcoated the situation.

Fred Digby's protégé, Hap Glaudi, refused to drop the matter and unrelentingly mocked the selection, referring to the game as the "Lemon Bowl." The situation caused a breach between Digby and Glaudi, who tried to explain to his old mentor, "I only did what you would have done. You taught me too well."

Georgia Tech, 8th-ranked and weighing an average of 12 pounds less than the ponderous 10th-ranked Mountaineers, was made a 12½-point favorite.

Georgia Tech 42- West Virginia 19

Pepper Rodgers directs devastating attack against West Virginia.

"It got them off to a bad start."

West Virginia hoped that the 8-3 defense Art Lewis employed would shut off Georgia Tech's wide plays and force the Yellow Jackets into the Mountaineer line, which averaged 228 pounds— and that the scorn the team had incurred would inflame it to action. The Mountaineers' defense shut down the running game but opened the airways for quarterback Franklin "Pepper" Rodgers, who hit on passes of 20, 15, 9, 11, and 21 yards and a touchdown on Tech's first possession.

Mountaineer Tommy Allman fired right back on a pitch-out sweep that went 60 yards into the end zone. West Virginia was penalized for holding, and the touchdown was called back. Rodgers moved his team back downfield and threw a 1-yard pass to Jimmy Durham to push Tech to a 14-0 lead.

At the start of the second quarter, Danny Williams capped a 70-yard Mountaineer drive with a 5-yard touchdown run around right end. Larry Morris blocked Jack Stone's PAT. After the kickoff, Wil-

West Virginia tackle Sam Huff.

liams put West Virginia back in the thick of it with an interception and runback to the 'Jacket 34. Tech held for downs, but Billy Teas fumbled and Phil Canton recovered on the 25. West Virginia powered its way to the 5, but end Cecil Trainer threw quarterback Freddie Wyant for a 16-yard loss. An opportunity to climb within a point of Georgia Tech was lost on the fourth down when Joe Marconi dropped a Wyant pass in the end zone.

"Won't say it demoralized them," Coach Art Lewis said of Allman's called-back run and Marconi's drop, "but it got them off to a bad start."

After taking over on its 23, Rodgers passed the 'Jackets downfield again and Henry Hair caught a 2-yarder to inflate the halftime score to 20-6. At intermission Tech had a record 233 yards passing to 13 for West Virginia and the outcome was sealed, leaving announcers Bill Stern and Johnny Lujack little but prattle to transmit to listeners over the airways.

Shortly after the second-half kickoff, Dave Davis recovered a poor handoff on the West Virginia 8

and, eventually, Rodgers kicked an 18-yard field goal. That was followed in quick order by a burst up the middle by Leon Hardeman which extended the lead to 29-6.

West Virginia drove against the Tech reserves and Marconi scored from the 1, but Larry Ruffin made a spectacular sideline run and fell over the corner end zone flag to make the margin 35-13.

Allman finished off an 84-yard West Virginia march by diving over from the 1. Late in the game Wyant was rushed and fumbled on his 9. Jake Shoemaker recovered for Tech, and Teas hit left tackle for the last merciful touchdown of the day.

Rodgers, who finished with 16 completions in 26 attempts for 195 yards, was clearly the dominant player and was named recipient of the Miller Memorial Trophy.

The West Virginia locker room was numb. Lewis said, with eyes glistening, "We thought we'd get beat, but not by that much." Guard Sam Huff couldn't express himself, at least not with the emotion of Wyant who spat out, "They ain't so good!"

Navy-Mississippi

SATURDAY, JANUARY 1, 1955

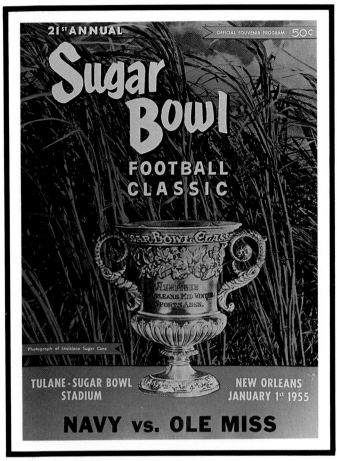

"That streetcar down in New Orleans."

After the debacle of the 1954 game, the Mid-Winter Sports Association felt obligated to reestablish itself as the premier bowl. The Sugar went hunting in new territory: the service academies. Army and Navy still had college football glitter, and both were excellent football teams. Either one would be a bowl coup.

In the Deep South, fate played a hand in the Sugar Bowl's 1955 pairing. Ole Miss ran away from the SEC field with a 9-1-0 record. The Rebels led the country in total defense and were fifth in offense, although some critics pointed to a "patty-cake" schedule. Arkansas, the only nationally ranked team Ole Miss played, defeated the Rebs, 6-0. However, Mississippi played exciting football and won the SEC championship.

Coach Johnny Vaught was asked how a Sugar Bowl invitation would be received in Oxford after his squad whipped LSU. Vaught replied he would like to return "because I'm still unhappy over the thing that happened down there two years ago (Georgia Tech's 1953 victory)." Rebel players weren't concerned about a game played two years ago. They wanted a Cotton Bowl invitation for another shot at Arkansas. Razorback Coach Bowden Wyatt slammed that door in Ole Miss' face by telling Dallas officials he saw no reason why he should give a regular season opponent a repeat game.

Army wasn't interested in Sugar Bowl "feelers." However, Navy was, and the Cotton Bowl also moved into the picture. Navy had lost two close games to Pittsburgh (19-21) and Notre Dame (0-6) but was a colorful and courageous squad. Coach Eddie Erdelatz, after a particularly satisfying win, likened his team "to that streetcar down in New Orleans, the one they call Desire." Thus, Navy became the "Team Named Desire."

Fullback Joe Gattuso felt certain, because of the rumors swirling around the Naval Academy during the week, that if the Midshipmen could defeat Army they would be allowed to participate in a bowl. End Ron Beagle, the Player of the Year, didn't believe it. But at halftime of a dogfight with the favored Cadets, it was confirmed. "At the half of our game with Army—we were leading 21-20, you know—Coach Erdelatz asked for our attention," said

Beagle. "He told us, 'Go out and finish the job. Beat Army today and you're in the Sugar Bowl game!' That's all we wanted to know. We wanted to beat Army real bad, and we wanted to go to the Sugar Bowl, too. We went out and got both."

After beating Army, 27-20, Navy was selected as the first service academy to play in a bowl since the 1924 Rose Bowl. Navy's bowl opponent was Mississippi, who beat Mississippi State 14-0 in its last season game.

According to Sugar Bowl mythology the nation applauded Navy, but realistic odds-makers looked upon the Middies as lambs about to be sacrificed to the lordly Rebels. Before the game opened, Navy was picked as a three-point favorite, a fact that irritated Vaught. "It makes no difference if Navy is the favorite," said a miffed Vaught. "I saw pictures of Navy's games with Notre Dame and Army and I'm sure we're going to win." But before the game started, Navy halfback Bob Craig came down with tonsillitis and tackle Jim Royer sustained a hip injury and both were unable to play. Noting those

losses against an opponent that was 15 pounds heavier, with much deeper reserve strength and more experience, Ole Miss' stock with the odds-makers climbed. By New Year's Eve, they were a point-and-a-half favorite.

A blast from the frigid winds of social change made a mark on the 1955 Sugar Bowl. Clarence Mitchell, a member of the National Association for the Advancement of Colored People in Washington, protested to Secretary Charles R. Thomas that Sugar Bowl tickets read they were for use by whites only and that others were subject to ejection. Actually, blacks had been attending the Sugar Bowl from its inception, although they were seated in segregated areas.

Secretary Thomas replied to Mitchell by telegram, stating the Navy Department had distributed its 13,000 tickets without regard to racial restrictions, "and will be so honored regardless of any printing thereon." "The Navy statement speaks for itself," said Bernie Grenrood, then Sugar Bowl president. "No other comment is necessary."

A streetcar named Desire and its namesake Navy squad before the 1955 Sugar Bowl.

Navy 21-Mississippi 0

"If you think you can make it, go for it."

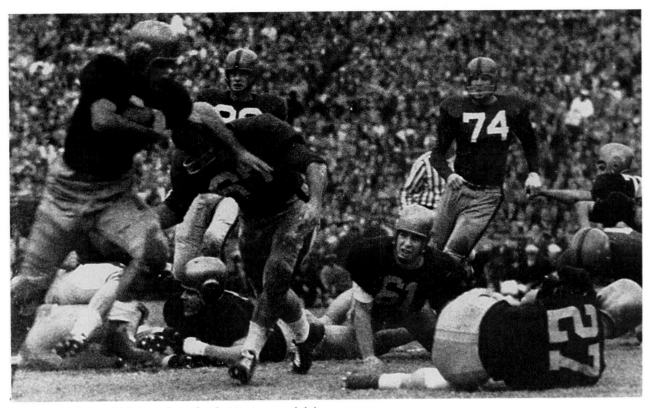

Joe Gattuso of Navy high-steps through Ole Miss' vaunted defense.

Johnny Vaught told his team to kick if Ole Miss won the toss, putting his faith in his defense, expecting it to pin Navy down and get the ball in workable field position for the offense. George Welsh took the kickoff at the 11 and returned to the Navy 30.

From there the Midshipmen, taking advantage of a flaw in the Rebel defense that Eddie Erdelatz spotted on film, began working painstakingly upfield. A third-down play had left the Sailors short of a first down at the 39. "When I got back to the huddle," related quarterback Welsh, "the fellows all said, 'C'mon, George, we can make it. Let's try it.' So we had (Joe) Gattuso slant off tackle."

Gattuso gained 4 yards. Contrary to legend, Ole Miss was offsides on the play and, in fact, Navy accepted the 5-yard penalty. But the play seemed to prick the poise and pride of the Rebels. "The coach tells us only one thing," explained Navy second-string quarterback Dick Echard. "If you think you can make it, go for it. Because if you believe you can, then you will." "When I saw them do that," said Erdelatz, "I knew we were going to play a whale of a game."

Navy Coach Eddie Erdelatz pensively watches his 'Team Named Desire' shock Ole Miss, 21-0.

Middie bench in a brief moment of concern during Navy's 21-0 cruise over Ole Miss.

Welsh continued running options for short, but surprisingly consistent, gains. "We sent a flanker out on one end, and then ran the option to the opposite end," Welsh said of Erdelatz's plan. "They would put one or two men out to cover the flanker, leaving them short on the other end. We don't block their end, so that gave us two men out for blocking in the secondary. The end played me halfy-halfy, letting me get in good position before pitching out."

The strategy worked all the way until Navy reached the Rebel 12. A 15-yard penalty pushed the Middies back to the 27. Then John Weaver ran out of the backfield around end, a run paved by Gattuso's block, and made his way to the 3 where Eagle Day stopped him. On the next play, Gattuso scored off right tackle against an eight-man line. Weaver kicked the extra point.

Navy's bug-sized defense (using 14 looks) played head-to-head with the Rebs for the remainder of the quarter. In the second period, Welsh moved the Middies into a threatening position again. Navy went from its 40 to the Rebel 8 where three line plays produced nothing. On fourth down Welsh threw a pass to Ron Beagle, who made a flying catch right on the goal line. It was called a touchdown, but head linesman Charles Wood, who was in

better position, overruled it. Wood said that while Beagle's feet were in the end zone he fell just outside when he made the catch. Film revealed it to be a highly controversial call.

Back Allen Muirhead eased into the Navy secondary just before the half and was open to the goal at the Middie 35 when Day's pass missed him by 10 yards. Defensive back Echard said he would have been at fault had the play worked.

"I went up to cover the short man," he admitted, "and let Muirhead get behind me." He also added he was the reason the play didn't connect. "I bumped him off stride as he went by," Echard grinned.

Jack Garrow gave the Navy offense breathing room by returning the kickoff to the Midshipmen 44. Three plays later Navy was on the Ole Miss 34.

Gattuso roared through right tackle on the ensuing play, tearing down to the 17. He then picked up another yard, and Weaver got another. Welsh overshot Weaver, but on fourth down Weaver flared into the end zone and Welch threw straight into the Ole Miss coverage. Weaver, with Billy Kinard's arms around his neck and Day practically inside his jersey, went up and made a miraculous catch. Weaver also added the PAT.

Things were well in hand for Navy. Ole Miss

continued to be held at arm's length by the Middies until Day, one of the nation's outstanding quarterbacks, gave the Rebs an opening. He got off a 72-yard punt to the Navy 7. If Ole Miss could hold them, or force Navy to make a mistake, the Rebels might turn the tide. Instead, Navy gained four first downs in succession, one a 22-yard run by Gattuso and another on a Gattuso fumble that bounced 14 yards upfield to be recovered by teammate Wilson Whitmire. Then Weaver raced 21 yards around right end. Gattuso scored from two yards out on his third consecutive carry from the 5.

Gattuso (111 yards) and Weaver (106 yards) each outrushed the Ole Miss offense, which had only 78 total yards rushing and 43 passing.

"The difference," Erdelatz told the press, "was desire." The coach asked the media to move away from the center of the locker room, saying he wished to speak to his team. "Men," he said simply, "you were terrific today. Let's get down on our knees and thank God." A moment of silence was offered by the grateful Midshipmen who knew full well what they had accomplished. Then Erdelatz leaped up, fist in air, and shouted, "Now let's go raise hell in Noo Awleans."

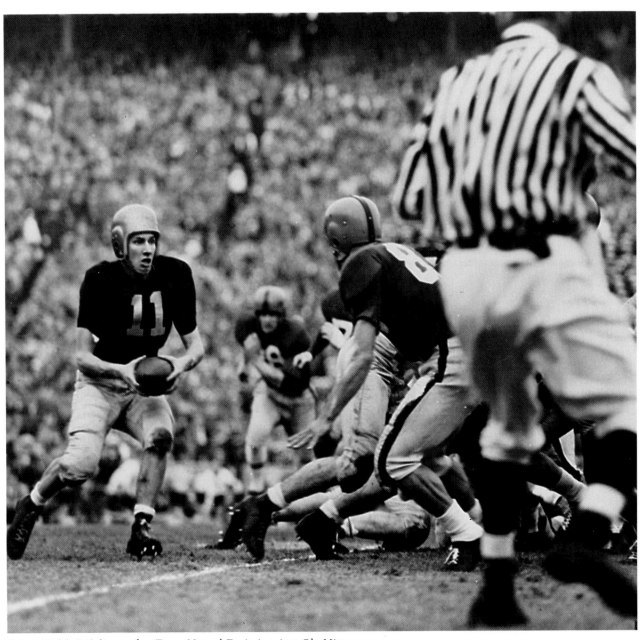

George Welsh (11) directs the 'Team Named Desire' against Ole Miss.

Georgia Tech-Pittsburgh

MONDAY, JANUARY 2, 1956

Fred Digby points to a dream come true.

"The South stands at Armageddon."

Something was amiss. As fine as the Ole Miss-Navy pairing was, something of the old Sugar Bowl matchmaking magic was gone. Not since the 1951 Kentucky-Oklahoma game had a Sugar Bowl been close, and this from an organization which took extraordinary pride in its thrillers. To be sure, the task was more difficult because of all the tie-ups by the other major bowls: the Orange with the Big Seven and the Atlantic Coast Conferences, the Cotton with the Southwest, and the Rose with the Big Ten and Pacific Coast Conferences.

The Mid-Winter Sports Association still felt it could get the best game possible by remaining "open," but it was also feeling a certain amount of self-imposed pressure to produce the kind of exciting, close games that had become a Sugar Bowl hallmark.

West Virginia, despite the debacle in New Orleans two years before, and Navy were high on the Sugar's checklist for the 1956 game. Mississippi and Georgia Tech were the most desirable Southeastern Conference teams. Paul DeBlanc and Claude Simons scouted the West Virginia-Pittsburgh game for the Sugar Bowl. The 6th-ranked Mountaineers had an 11-game winning streak broken, 26-7. Although it had lost three games, two to highly ranked Oklahoma and Navy, Pitt greatly impressed the scouts and newsmen Hap Glaudi and Steve Perkins.

An invitation was extended to Pittsburgh with the worst record (7-3) of a Sugar Bowl team since 1945—and it was accepted. Georgia Tech would be the opponent.

Then began a period of stormy controversy. Fif-

teen years after Louis Montgomery watched from the press box as his Boston College teammates achieved one of their school's most stirring moments, a Sugar Bowl team's roster (Pittsburgh) again included the name of a black player, fullback Bobby Grier.

Georgia Governor Marvin Griffin focused a spotlight on Grier and the Sugar Bowl, and the national press made the game a cause célèbre. New Orleans was caught in a no-win situation, although mixed athletics were not new to the city. Loyola University competed against blacks in basketball and, indeed, days before Grier would set foot in Tulane Stadium, a 6-foot black sophomore named Al Avant would play for Marquette in the Sugar Bowl basketball tournament.

The flap roared across national front pages when Griffin said in a telegram to Regent Chairman Robert O. Arnold, "It is my request that athletic teams of units of the university system of Georgia not be permitted to engage in contests with other teams where the races are mixed on such teams or where segregation is not required at such games . . . The South stands at Armageddon."

Arnold indicated the board had no control over university athletic policies, and Pittsburgh announced that Grier would be on the Sugar Bowl squad and he would "travel, eat, live, practice, and play with the team." A school spokesman added, "If Grier regains his midseason form he will be our starting fullback. Heck, he intercepted the pass (against Penn State) that put us in the Sugar Bowl."

In Atlanta, Tech was mightily trying to ignore the

Pete Neft (18) shows air-arm while on the run behind blocker Bobby Grier (38) in the Pitt-Georgia Tech war.

governor. A Georgia Tech spokesman said, "Our boys voted to play in the Sugar Bowl, and we will not break our contract, especially since Georgia and Tech have played against Negroes before and there has been no criticism."

Security around the governor's mansion had to be increased at night as it became a rallying area for torch-carrying throngs of protesting Tech students. The Southern press, for the most part, joined Georgia Tech professors, students, alumni, and players in the disagreement with Griffin.

The individuals whose opinions on the matter should have counted most, the Georgia Tech athletes, were finally asked what their thoughts were. Quarterback Wade Mitchell said he considered the entire situation "silly." Mitchell went on, "I personally have no objection to playing a team with a Negro member on it, and, as far as I know, the rest of the boys feel the same way."

The Georgia Board of Regents voted 10-1 to allow the team to participate, although there was a soothing rider attached for the segregationists. It barred future games in the state of Georgia between Georgia colleges and integrated teams.

Georgia Tech 7-Pittsburgh 0

"You don't really believe that, do you?"

The Pittsburgh players, realizing a teammate was going to be under a tremendous strain, tried to keep things light. "At first, we were offended," said guard Hal Hunter, one of the Panther co-captains. "Then, to loosen him up and try to take the pressure off him, we played some practical jokes on Bobby during practice for the Sugar Bowl. One night some of the players dressed with white sheets over their heads, and we burned a circle outside our dorm."

As the game began, the Tulane Stadium clock malfunctioned, and an immediate controversy involving Bobby Grier occurred.

Allen Ecker recovered Lou Cimarolli's fumble at the Pitt 32. Quarterback Wade Mitchell called one of Coach Bobby Dodd's favorite plays, "the Kingsport Special," designed to hit the opposition when they were down.

Mitchell faked to left halfback Paul Rotenberry, who hit left tackle as the fullback and right half took off for the sidelines to the left. Mitchell hid the ball on his hip and started to follow the other two backs around left end. Suddenly, he wheeled and made a 180-degree turn and raced for the right sideline, took the ball off his hip, and lofted a soft pitch to right end Don Ellis.

"I was outside in what we called an 'Eagle' defense," said Grier. "I went back with the player and when I turned to look up and see where the ball was, I got pushed in the back. The ball was over his head and I was lying on the ground, then the official (back judge Frank Lowry) threw a flag and said I pushed him . . . with me lying on the ground, looking up and the ball over both our heads."

Don Ellis reaches for the ball as Bobby Grier goes down in the biggest, and most controversial, play of 1956.

Ellis said, "I got behind him. Then, when I turned around to look for the pass, he shoved me in the stomach, knocking me off stride. It was a fine pass, and I think I could have caught it."

The film was inconclusive but indicated Grier may have been out of position, stumbled, and fell a few yards in front of Ellis. A roar of protest erupted from the stands as the ball was placed on the 1-yard line. Immediately the reporter sitting next to Buddy Diliberto began typing a bulletin that read, "Bobby Grier, the first Negro to play in the Sugar Bowl, was roundly booed by a crowd of 80,175 spectators today in Tulane Stadium."

"You don't really believe that, do you?" shouted the incredulous Diliberto. "They're booing the call, not Grier!"

After Pitt was penalized a half-yard for offsides, Mitchell followed the surge of his line and made it into the end zone by inches. He then added the extra point.

Pitt and Georgia Tech sparred the remainder of the quarter, but the Panthers took complete control in the second period, allowing the Yellow Jackets only five plays. A 79-yard drive put Pitt at the Tech 1 with time running out in the first half. Franklin Brooks and Allen Ecker stopped what appeared to be a hurried quarterback sneak on fourth-and-goal. 'Corny' Salvaterra, the Pitt quarterback, said, "I thought time was running out on us, so I got 'em out of the huddle in a hurry with the instruction that we were to move on the center snap. I didn't know there was time left to play." The time was being kept by the officials due to the stadium's malfunctioning clock.

Pitt had two opportunities in the third quarter, once driving to the Tech 16, with a 26-yard crowd-pleasing run by Grier that almost went all the way. But Ecker intercepted to end the threat. The other was a 76-yard drive to the Tech 7, where Ken Thrash recovered a fumble for the Engineers at the 10.

Georgia Tech put together its only concerted drive of the day at that point, pushing to the Pitt 7. Dodd's team only put the ball in the air 3 times against Pittsburgh, with no completions (the interference call was ruled a penalty). "We didn't want to pass because we didn't want to stop the clock and give it (Pitt) any more time later when it got the ball," explained Dodd. Then Dodd gave quarterback Toppy Vann the green light to pass with cautionary instructions not to throw an interception. But Ray DiPasquale did intercept the third down pass with over eight minutes left to play.

Toward the end of the game, Coach Johnny Michelosen sent in third-string quarterback Darrell Lewis to try to get Pitt on the scoreboard. The left-hander almost did. He whipped a pass to Fred Glatz to the Tech 30 for a 23-yard gain. Rushed heavily on the next play, Lewis tucked the ball under his arm and sailed around left end. Only a last minute

Pan American Films sequence of controversial play between Bobby Grier and Don Ellis.

flying tackle, sending Lewis pinwheeling out-of-bounds at the 10, prevented a touchdown.

Before going to the huddle, Lewis asked an official how much time remained and he was told 2 minutes and 39 seconds. Pitt's Hunter asked and was told only 39 seconds remained. In either case, there was enough time for several plays. Ralph Jelic was sent on a power play that carried inside the 5. As Pitt lined up again, the officials began waving their arms, signalling the game's end. "I thought we could get off another play easily," protested Lewis.

A despondent Grier tearfully told reporters afterward, "I didn't push that man. I was in front of him, how could I have pushed him?"

Grier says that call, shattering as it was, was one of several remembrances of that trip he would rather not have. The others were not being allowed to attend a Sugar Bowl party afterward ("Nobody said anything," he said. "It was just understood. I went to another function at Dillard University.") and not being permitted to stay with his teammates at a downtown hotel when Pitt left the Tulane dorms after the Sugar Bowl.

"I don't blame the city," Grier said. "New Orleans really went out of its way for me in many ways. My arguments were with the governor of Georgia and a game official."

Time has a way of affecting memory, particularly in a game like this where Pitt had all the stats and Georgia Tech had the scoreboard. Both Hunter and Lewis felt the loss was racially motivated, pointing to a "crew of southern officials." It may or may not have been competent, but it was not a crew of southern officials. It was a split crew, and one agreed to beforehand by Pittsburgh authorities.

The game was a distinct landmark in Sugar Bowl history. From its inception the Mid-Winter Sports Association looked for intersectional matches. But after the 1956 game, the Sugar Bowl was forced to retrench because of the climate of the times and the Louisiana legislature. For the next decade the Sugar Bowl would have great teams and great games. But not a single representative would come from outside the Southeastern, Southwest, or Atlantic Coast Conferences.

Bobby Dodd on the sideline during the controversial Georgia Tech-Pittsburgh game.

Baylor-Tennessee

TUESDAY, JANUARY 1, 1957

"Some kind of Dixie championship only."

In the mid 1950s, the federal government began moving in earnest to guarantee equality in all phases of American life, but southern state governments began passing segregation laws as restrictive as any before. Louisiana passed more than a dozen segregation laws in 1956, some designed to limit interracial social and athletic activity. The crux of Act No. 579, vigorously fought by the Mid-Winter Sports Association but signed into law by Governor Earl K. Long, was a prohibition of racially mixed athletic events.

The Sugar Bowl, well aware that such a law could make its events backyard triflings, voiced the only opposition to the legislation. Noticeably silent were Tulane, LSU, and Loyola, all of which had games scheduled with integrated teams.

Long signed the law and three of the teams—Notre Dame, Dayton, and St. Louis—scheduled for the basketball tournament withdrew. The Sugar then fought for a plan to exempt cities over 100,000 from the legislation. If passed, the bowl planned to work around the segregated stands problem by having no restrictions on the tickets sent to visiting schools, but every other section would be segregated. It was a well-thought-out plan, designed to please every faction. But the bill did not pass.

Most felt like Shirley Povich of the *Washington Post*, who wrote, "For the Sugar Bowl, the upshot is that it will be known henceforth merely as a sectional contest to settle some kind of a Dixie championship only." DeBlanc said wearily, "That's the law and we will try to live under it."

It was a law that obviously couldn't stay on the books for long, but the Sugar was apprehensive about becoming a small regional contest before the prohibition was rescinded. Already there were problems with television. The contract with ABC was up and the network had reservations about renewing because the newly enacted law (Act 579) bothered prospective national sponsors.

With its boundaries greatly diminished, the Sugar Bowl went looking in 1957 for the best game possible. As it happened, the most desirable non-SEC teams were also ineligible. Oklahoma, the nation's No. 1 squad, couldn't participate in the Orange Bowl because of the Big Seven's no-return rule;

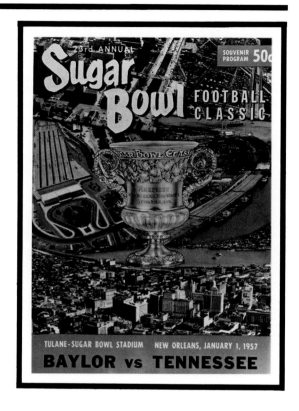

Texas A&M, the champion of the Southwest Conference, wouldn't be able to play in the Cotton Bowl because it was on NCAA probation, as was 6th-ranked Miami—the Sugar's favorite.

The spot usually reserved for a Southeastern Conference team figured to be no problem because 2nd-ranked Tennessee and Georgia Tech were both exceptional teams.

Digby was still working miracles. His deep friendship with Athletic Director Bob Neyland helped land Tennessee. Then Baylor became Digby's focal point. The Bears were a good, solid football team (although unranked) that wasn't going to a major bowl because of midseason losses to Texas A&M and Texas Christian by a total of seven points. The Sugar must have looked pretty good to Baylor, too. The match was made.

A coast-to-coast television and radio coverage agreement finally was made between the Sugar Bowl and ABC when General Motor's Oldsmobile Division consented to sponsorship.

With the 3rd- (Iowa) and 10th- (Oregon State) ranked teams, the Rose Bowl drew the quality New Year's pairing of 1957. Considering the circumstances, the Sugar didn't do badly with 2nd-ranked Tennessee.

Baylor 13-Tennessee 7

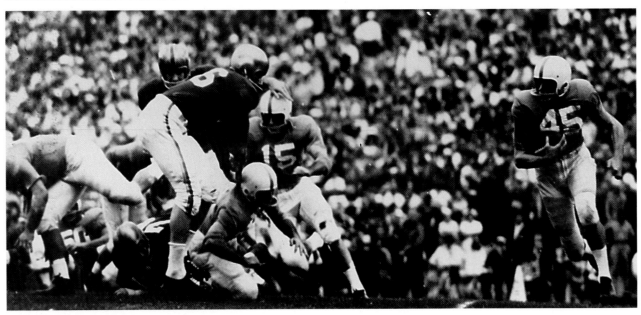

Johnny Majors (45) sweeping Baylor line.

"Mister."

Behind tailback Johnny Majors, Tennessee was a quick, opportunistic offensive team. It was also, in accordance with tradition, a fundamentally sound defensive team. Straightening out after a shaky 1956 start, Bowden Wyatt's Vols toyed with their regular season opposition. But Sam Boyd's Baylor Bears gained confidence from watching Tennessee game films. "Tennessee, with its single wing offense, is going to get about as far as our ends let 'em," crowed right end Jerry Marcontell.

Tackle John Gordy (whose father was a musician who formerly played in New Orleans with the legendary Papa Celestin) was the mainstay in the precise Tennessee line, a line that was outweighed by 14 pounds. "We knew they were good," recalled Baylor second-team fullback Larry Hickman, "but we also knew we could muscle with them. We knew we could win."

Bobby Peters lit a Baylor charge by returning the kickoff 52 yards to the Tennessee 44. While an Elvis Presley imitator, in a cerise jacket and swinging a guitar, directed the Tennessee band in a rendition of "Hound Dog" and pointed to the Bears, quarterback Bobby Jones' offensive unit was pushing the Vols on their heels. As the Bears reached the 4, the band quietened. Baylor couldn't penetrate any further, and Donnel Berry came in to attempt a field goal. Berry's kick swerved to the side as "Hound Dog" blared from the Tennessee side again.

In the second quarter, Baylor kept the pressure on but couldn't score until, ironically, Vol kicker Bobby Gordon got off a 67-yard punt that bounced into the end zone by a foot. Del Shofner then swept right end. Hickman took out the outside defender, kept his footing, and provided Shofner with another key block downfield. Gordon and Shofner's lone remaining blocker fenced until the kicker was able to get behind the runner and make the tackle. "I didn't realize we were traveling so slow," said Shofner. "The first I knew was when someone caught me from behind." Hickman shot through the defense 8 yards to the 14 for a first down, then picked up 2 yards more. Jones threw two incompletions, but then took advantage of a Tennessee mistake. Shofner, flanked to the right, went down and in on a pass pattern, taking the defensive back with him. Marcontell went down and out, found himself open, grabbed the ball on the end zone line, and fell in for the touchdown. Berry's conversion was wide to the right. At the half, Baylor appeared in complete command. The Bears had 186 rushing yards to Tennessee's 82.

Majors had the Vols smokin' when they answered the third quarter bell. He returned the Bears' first punt of the second half to the Tennessee 46. A roughing penalty put the Vols on the Baylor 39. From there Majors ran nine of 11 plays, overcoming a 15-yard penalty in the process, and scored around end from the 1. Sammy Burklow kicked the PAT and Tennessee took a 7-6 lead.

That lapse aside, Baylor linemen Bill Glass, Bobby Oliver, Dave Lunceford, and Lee Harrington seemed to have the Vol offense caged. Before Baylor could score again, Hickman took some of the gusto out of the game. Tennessee guard Bruce Burnham and Baylor guard Charley Horton got into a scuffle on the ground. Burnham got in a couple of quick punches. Seeing that, Hickman rushed in and kicked Burnham in the face.

The defenseless Vol lay sprawled on the field quivering, ribbons of blood covering his features. "I thought the boy would be gone before we got him off the field," commented a physician on the scene. "There's no way anyone could excuse what I did," reflected Hickman. "I think I was so keyed up . . . In my mind I saw him doing something he shouldn't, and I guess I just flashed temper."

Hickman was banished from the game and Burnham was taken to Touro Infirmary. For the remainder of the Sugar Bowl, Hickman sat on the Baylor bench, head in palms, sobbing.

Baylor, playing with considerably less enthusiasm, turned a fourth-quarter opportunity into go-ahead points. Majors took a Shofner punt at the Vol 6, raced out to the 15, was smacked by Glass, and the ball popped up. Ruben Saage recovered for Baylor.

Quarterback Buddy Humphrey sneaked over for the touchdown six plays later, and Berry converted to make the score 13-7.

Unbelievably, Baylor gave Tennessee one last chance by going for the yard on fourth down and one with 4:44 left. A fourth-down pass by Majors just brushed the fingertips of a streaking Tommy Bronson in the Baylor end zone.

Most of the postgame talk centered not on a magnificent upset but on the kicking incident. Burnham had a concussion and broken nose, but it seemed he wasn't in nearly as much pain as Hickman, who stood in a corner of the Baylor locker room still crying. When approached by Tom Fox of the *Item*, Hickman again buried his head in hands and "quivered like a child. Once he raised his head and again tried to speak. 'Mister' was all he was able to say before he burst into tears again."

Coach Boyd, who admitted the incident had dulled the victory for him, said simply his team outguessed Tennessee in passing situations. "Our two lines outcharged Tennessee. We simply lined up our guard opposite their guard, our tackle opposite their tackle, and our end opposite their end. We just blocked straight ahead. But we told our men to just make sure they carried those other fellows with them." That bit of stategy represented the third Sugar Bowl loss in 16 years for a Tennessee team that entered the game undefeated and untied.

Hickman visited the recovering Burnham the next day at the hospital to apologize personally. New Year's night at the Sugar Bowl party, the 20-year-old stood before the Volunteer football team and softly said, "I hope someday that boy and you Tennessee players can find it in your hearts to forgive me for what I've done. I'm sorry, truly sorry."

Del Shofner (27) sweeps behind the blocking of Larry Hickman (38) and quarterback Bobby Jones (12) in Baylor's 13-7 upset of Tennessee.

Volunteer do-it-all back Majors.

Mississippi-Texas

WEDNESDAY, JANUARY 1, 1958

Coach Darrell Royal knew his Longhorns were in over their heads.

"We weren't that good of a football team."

Even the Southeastern Conference began putting the squeeze on the Sugar Bowl. With northern and western teams virtually unobtainable for New Orleans, Auburn emerged in 1957 as the New Year's most desirable trophy. The undefeated, untied War Eagles were the season's national champion but were ineligible for bowl competition because of NCAA probation. Mississippi, which missed a share of the SEC title because of a final game tie with Mississippi State, was a solid second choice. Ole Miss was still embarrassed over its previous Sugar Bowl appearances against Georgia Tech and Navy, and wanted a New Orleans stage again.

"Jimmie-nee! I have a special desire to win this one. That's what we're going down there for—to try to win," said Rebel Coach Johnny Vaught.

Getting a suitable opponent was a man-sized job. From the season's beginning, Texas A&M was in the corner of every bowl's eye. Bear Bryant's Aggies started fast and finished slow while young Darrell Royal's Texas Longhorns came off a disastrous 1956 and a slow 1957. The Longhorns rode a season-ending surge that battered A&M on national television, as well as Cotton Bowl-bound Rice and TCU. The Sugar then took Texas, which finished 6-3-1 and wasn't in the Top 10.

Royal later said, "We shouldn't have been in a bowl to begin with. We were kind of a Cinderella team even with that record. The year before we were 1-9, so we received a lot of notoriety. But the truth of the matter is we weren't that good of a football team."

Ray Brown, who quarterbacked the 6th-ranked Rebels and led the team with a better than 5-yard-per-carry average, was the story of the 1958 Sugar Bowl. Ole Miss had a superb defense, headed by Gene Hickerson, and a top-ranked offense. But it was Brown who was the team's soul.

When Brown was a child, a small friend pulled a wagon from under him. "We thought it was just another fall," said his mother, "but Ray ran a high fever . . ." Doctors in Memphis diagnosed osteomyelitis; they had to operate and scrape the bone. It looked doubtful that he would walk again.

"They used tractions on my right leg . . ." said Ray. ". . . saved me from being crippled . . . after I showed doctors I could walk, well, then I started running . . . and then I went out for high school football . . ." He kept going until he became the ignition of Vaught's high-octane offense.

Ole Miss' Ray Brown (15) wiggles free against Texas.

Mississippi 39-Texas 7

"Lateral, Ray, lateral."

Things were never hard for Ole Miss that chilly, 47-degree day. Ken Kirk recovered a Rene Ramirez fumble at the Texas 33, which, coupled with a 15-yard penalty, gave the Longhorns a shooting-gallery look. Ray Brown scored from the 1. Bobby Khayat missed the conversion.

Later in the first quarter, Brown's offensive unit steamrolled to three successive first downs from the Rebel 45. A 12-yard run by Brown and a 17-yard pass from Brown to Don Williams put the ball on the 5 as the second period opened. Williams caught a 2-yard pass from Brown for the touchdown.

After Brown shoved the Longhorns in a hole with a punt that went out-of-bounds on the Texas 7, Bob Lackey, the quarterback, passed. Brown intercepted on the 20. This play led to an 8-yard TD run by Kent Lovelace. It was 19-0 at the halftime, and things seemed to get worse for Texas. Longhorn Walt Fondren, Texas' millionaire quarterback, fumbled on the Rebel 47 and Larry Grantham recovered. Bobby Franklin scored on a 2-yard run. Khayat's PAT gave Ole Miss a 26-0 lead.

As the game wound down, ballots were passed out in the press box for the selection of the Most Valuable Player. All 116 media voters placed Brown as their choice for his quadruple-threat performance. Raoul Carlisle, an Arkansas newspaperman who had covered every Sugar Bowl, commented to Pie Dufour as Brown dropped into the end zone to punt, "He's the greatest performer in Sugar Bowl history." Pie noncommittally answered, "He certainly is one of the best."

As they talked, Brown took a high snap and, before he could boot the ball, noticed a Texas end boring in unopposed. He bolted, circled right end, and began steaming for the Texas goal, 103 yards from where he had been standing. "I was weary, so weary that I thought about asking for a replacement to do the punting," Brown said. "I told the fellows,

'I don't know if I can kick that ball 20 yards I'm so tired. You'll have to get downfield in a hurry . . .' I didn't plan to run with the ball. I was going to kick it. But I saw this Texas tackle charging at me and I told myself I'd never get the kick away. So I just tucked it under my arm and ran. The Texas end hit me a few yards out, but not enough to knock me off stride.

"I didn't know I was in the clear till I looked back near midfield and saw all those blue shirts around me. And I kept hearing Jackie Simpson yelling, 'Lateral, Ray, lateral.' I knew if he wanted the ball there wasn't anyone else around me but us Rebels."

"That proves Brown's the best," Carlisle screamed in Dufour's ear to make himself heard over the din of the crowd. Ole Miss scored another touchdown after a Texas fumble in the final 12 seconds. Everyone, Rebel and Longhorn alike, was aware they had witnessed a special individual performance. Brown's 92-yard run from scrimmage had pushed his rushing figures to 157 yards in 15 carries, a 10.5-yard average. Several of his passes were dropped in the cold, but he completed three of eight for 24 more yards. He averaged 34.7 yards on four punts, specializing in out-of-bounds rolls. Brown scored two touchdowns, passed for a third, and was brilliant on defense, intercepting three passes. He also saved a touchdown early by bringing down George Blanch after the Longhorn had galloped 46 yards.

Coach Johnny Vaught chuckled about the run and insisted, "We called that one from the bench." The 6-foot-1, 190-pound Brown was elated when he was awarded the Miller Memorial Trophy and then was informed he was the first unanimous selection. "Say, if nobody has ever won it that way before, that means I have a chance to make the all-time Sugar Bowl team. Oh, man, I'd like that."

LSU-Clemson

THURSDAY, JANUARY 1, 1959

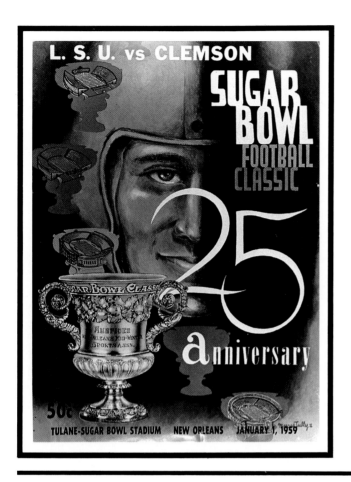

"I'd like to see once more."

Fate occasionally takes strange twists. It was a little unbelievable to those who built it, but the Sugar Bowl would be celebrating its silver anniversary game on New Year's Day, 1959. Twenty-five years had passed since Warren Miller and the Cooperative Club had initiated a bold plan to make a New Orleans-postseason football game a reality. The current Sugar Bowl's president was Claude "Monk" Simons, whose football exploits made Tulane the winner of the inaugural game. After a quarter of a century, the Sugar Bowl exceeded the stature and prominence that even Fred Digby envisioned.

Time brought other changes. Miller and nine original members of the Mid-Winter Sports Association were deceased. The *Item*, which had been the project's incubator, was sold to the Times-Picayune Publishing Co. and merged with the *States*.

On September 12, 1958, two days before the *Item* slipped under the waves, sports editor Hap Glaudi reprinted Digby's column of October 31, 1947 (the last day he served as the paper's sports editor). Two days later, in the final *Item* editions, Digby's byline again appeared on the *Item*'s sports pages, along with that of his protégé and that of his staff, each in his own way saying good-by. Digby recounted some of the most memorable events and people he had covered in a piece headlined "I'd Like To See Once More . . ." Less than two months after the *Item* died, and less than a month before the Sugar's silver anniversary game, Fred Digby passed away.

"We knew he was ill," said Mary Frances Digby, "but we didn't know he was as sick as he was. He was on a fishing trip with A.B. Nicholas in August when he took sick. He looked like death then. I called our doctor, a longtime friend, and he told me to get him to the hospital as fast as I could. After he took X rays he called us in and told us this was the hardest thing he ever had to do, as much as he thought of Fred. But he had cancer of the liver, that he could operate but he didn't hold much hope."

Digby was allowed to go home where he continued to work with the Mid-Winter Sports Association on plans for the festivities of the 25th game and on his piece for the *Item*. He had to return to the hospital on October 21.

The evening of the November 2, 1958, he listened from his hospital bed to the broadcast of the LSU-Mississippi football game. Both teams were high on the Sugar Bowl checklist. Digby was visibly moved when announcer J.C. Politz passed along the good wishes of himself and of the schools. The next day, with his wife at his bedside, Fred Digby died. An outpouring from the high and mighty as well as the humble of collegiate sports, and from newspapermen far and near, engulfed the Digby family and his monument, the Sugar Bowl.

Joe Carter, who had covered every Sugar Bowl as sports editor of the *Shreveport Times*, summed up the feelings of those involved with the Mid-Winter Sports Association in a touching piece just before the 1959 game. "They are going to stage the 25th annual Sugar Bowl football classic in the Tulane University stadium this Thursday afternoon, New Year's Day," Carter wrote. His words conveyed the riot of color, the carnival atmosphere and hysteria of 80,000-plus football-frenzied fans—the parade of bands, the dancing and prancing of beautiful cheerleaders, and the color-bearers.

"Even the familiar cry of the hucksters as they ply their trade both on the inside and the outside of the huge stadium will be there," Carter wrote, "but in the press box far above the maddened crowd will be a vacancy. It will be the spot where Fred Digby, general manager of the Mid-Winter Sports Association, sat every New Year's Day game and watched the dream of a lifetime unfurled. A spot from where he saw his master handwork put into reality . . . ."

Lawrence diBenedetto, another original Sugar Bowl member and the person who coordinated the Association-sponsored track meets, died several days after Digby. Adding to the melancholy circumstances,

James M. Thomson, the former *Item* publisher and the man who offhandedly made the first suggestion of a New Year's Day game in New Orleans, died in September of 1959.

LSU, en route to the national championship, was obviously the first choice of the Mid-Winter Sports Association. After a late-season squeeze past Mississippi State, the eventual signing of the Tigers was a simple formality.

When young Coach Paul Dietzel took the LSU job some years before, he suggested to Digby he match his team and Army in the 1958 Sugar Bowl. Army, of course, was out in 1959 because of the segregation problem, but Dietzel would later leave LSU to coach the Army team.

Most New Orleans fans preferred to match LSU with SMU, with its spectacular quarterback Don Meredith.

From the available teams of Clemson, North Carolina, SMU, Southern Mississippi, and Air Force, Clemson was picked for two reasons: The Tigers were champions of the Atlantic Coast Conference with an 8-2 record; also, Dietzel, LSU's Coach, thought his lightning-quick team could easily handle them.

Clemson Coach Frank Howard realized he was sitting in a gap with practically all the New Orleans sports pages centering on the home-state Tigers and the lukewarm sentiment for Clemson's selection. "The fans can think what they want," snapped Howard, before adding to the overconfidence of LSU supporters. "My boys play like a bunch of one-armed bandits," Howard said in comparison to the LSU defensive team, the Chinese Bandits.

LSU was a 14-point favorite. Howard was privately confident his Tigers could blow holes in the light LSU line and that no third-string unit like the Chinese Bandits could stop his offense. Howard commented, "You can tell them for me, they're gonna have to be No. 1 to beat us . . . that's the way our boys feel about this game."

LSU 7-Clemson 0

"It went off with a prayer."

Howard was riled, and so was most of the South Carolina contingent on the chilly, overcast New Year's Day, 1959. "They (the press) keep telling us we're not worth a darn," drawled the tobacco-chewing coach of the 11th-ranked Carolina Tigers. "I don't know, maybe we're not. But you keep telling a feller that long enough and it begins to get under his hide."

Clemson had decided to train its offensive weap-

ons on LSU sophomore guard Charlie Strange. But it was the quicksilver Bayou Bengals that put in the early bid for points, driving to the Clemson 22 late in the first quarter before a fumble thwarted the march. Clemson then gained 9 yards on three carries, and Charlie Horne dropped back to punt. He got a bad snap and, under a strong rush by Max Fugler, hooked the ball straight up and out-of-bounds for a minus 2-yard punt at the 29. "When

'The pass the Lord threw' from Billy Cannon, far right, to Mickey Mangham (88).

he saw me coming in, he tried to kick it off to the side," said Fugler. Fullback Red Brodnax gained 8 yards, and a pass in the flat from Warren Rabb to Billy Cannon put LSU on the Clemson 12. There LSU again came up empty when quarterback Rabb attempted four consecutive passes, including one on a fourth-down fake field goal, and missed his receiver each time.

Later in the second period, Rabb kicked up another drive, running for 33 yards, but suffered a broken hand on the tackle. "I didn't know it was broken until I came out before the half," he explained. "I think it got hit with a helmet." Rabb continued to pilot the drive, completing a 24-yard pass to end Mickey Mangham and directing LSU to the 1. Brodnax crashed into the end zone but fumbled, and Doug Cline recovered for the Clemson touchback. "I thought I was over," insisted Brodnax.

LSU had muffed three scoring opportunities in the first half and lost its quarterback in the process, changing the game plan. "I was glad, in a way, the first half ended the way it did . . . I felt certain they thought they had us," said Dietzel.

Clemson, which posed no serious threat in the first half, quickly jumped into contention the second half. Rudy Hayes, Horne, and George Usry did the carrying as the Clemson Tigers moved from their 28 to the LSU 30 on suddenly devastating off-tackle slants. Then Usry sliced through to the 20 where he was hit by Red Hendrix and fumbled. "I hit the football squarely when I brought my arm around to tackle him," said Hendrix. Strange, fighting off every Clemson thrust, recovered for LSU on the play.

Tommy Davis boomed out a 52-yard punt and when Clemson failed to move again it appeared the two sets of Tigers were settling down into trench warfare. A reserve center, Paul Snyder, was in during this series. As it happened, Synder's snap went

Billy Cannon releasing the touchdown pass.

awry and bounced off the leg of Doug Cline. LSU tackle Duane Leopard fell on the loose ball at the Clemson 11.

End Ray Masneri threw Cannon for a yard loss, but the spearhead of the LSU offense gained four on second down. Cannon then took a pitch-out, rolled to his right, and shot a pass to Mangham, who was clear in the end zone. The play was not run as diagrammed. "I didn't throw it, the Lord did," said Cannon. "I looked for (halfback) Johnny Robinson and they had him covered . . . then I spied Mickey

and let go . . . I wasn't sure it would get to him until he grabbed it . . . It went off with a prayer." Cannon also kicked the extra point.

Behind, and against the third string, the Chinese Bandits' quarterback Harvey White started a drive from the Clemson 17. White completed two passes, both 12-yard gains, to ends Wyatt Cox and Sam Anderson. Clemson then returned successfully to the run until Clemson was in sight of the Bengal goal.

At the 25 the Bandits threw up one of their patented stands. Two running plays gained a yard, and

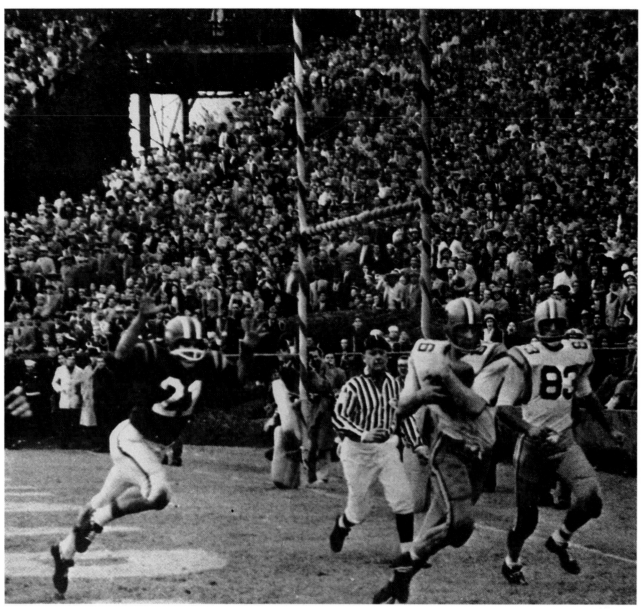
Mickey Mangham clutching the pass that allowed LSU a 7-0 victory.

a third-down pass went incomplete. On fourth-and-nine, White flipped a screen pass to Usry who appeared to have running room. The left halfback started to run before he had complete possession and dropped the pass. Howard was certain Usry "would have gone all the way" had the pass been complete. "It was perfect play," he said. "All the downfield blockers were in position to clear the road to the goal." Less than two minutes to play remained.

Howard admitted his strategy didn't work out the way he figured and said in his opinion Strange, not Cannon, deserved the MVP award. "We figured we could drive Strange back 10 yards at a crack—and planned our offense to run right over him," said Howard. "But as it turned out, he was the toughest man on the field." Because he was, LSU finally won a Sugar Bowl game—the first national champion to do so since 1940.

Mississippi-LSU

"The game would be a natural again."

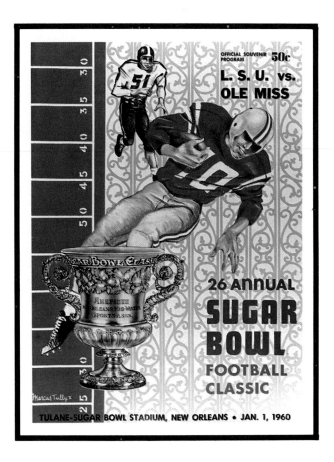

Jim Cartwright, a Tennessee player, proved to be the most influential figure in the bowl makeup of 1960. But before Mr. Cartwright stepped into the picture, LSU and Mississippi played the season's "Game of the Century" on Halloween night, 1959. The Tigers, still unbeaten and No. 1-ranked, were losing a game of field position and defense to the No. 3-ranked Rebels until Billy Cannon cut loose with a fourth-quarter superhuman 89-yard punt return for a touchdown. LSU prevailed, 7-3.

It was a Southeastern Conference classic. Fred Russell of the *Nashville Banner* wrote, "For its suspense, and competitive team performance, Louisiana State's 7-3 throbber over Ole Miss was the fullest and finest football game I've witnessed in 31 years of sports reporting." Mercer Bailey of the Associated Press wrote two days after the game, "Maybe the Sugar Bowl folks should go ahead and invite Louisiana State and Mississippi for its New Year's Day extravaganza. If tense, exciting football is what they want, they could hardly improve on a rematch of the national champion Tigers and those classy Rebels."

The wheels were set in motion for the rematch the following weekend by Tennessee's Jim Cartwright. LSU was running wild against the Vols, but had scored only one touchdown by the third quarter. Quarterback Warren Rabb threw to wide-open halfback Johnny Robinson; and Cartwright, who had been blocked from Rabb's line of vision, made a leaping interception and ran unmolested 59 yards for the tying touchdown. Cartwright became the first man to cross the Tiger goal line in 40 quarters and changed the entire complexion of the game. LSU, which had three backs individually out-rush the entire Volunteer team, lost 14-13 and dropped from its No. 1 perch.

Within seven days, Ole Miss tore apart the same Tennessee team 37-7 and moved to No. 2 in the national polls, one spot ahead of LSU. The Rebels were considered the SEC's "Team of the Decade" and were leaning toward the Cotton Bowl until the Sugar promised to help bring about Mercer Bailey's

dream game, a rematch with LSU. Coach Johnny Vaught unofficially committed to the Sugar Bowl right after the Tennessee victory.

However, some felt a rematch would be too sectional to suit the taste of television. "Not so," said Tom Gallery, NBC's sports director. "NBC would be most happy if the Sugar Bowl was able to land LSU and Ole Miss. The game would be a natural again, as it was the first time."

LSU was not as enthusiastic. The Tigers would be placed at a severe psychological disadvantage playing a team they had already defeated. Also, LSU was a weary, wounded football team at season's end.

The other bowls were rapidly filling. Syracuse, which took over the No. 1 position after LSU's loss to Tennessee, was paired with Texas in the Cotton; fifth-ranked Georgia, which won the SEC championship after the LSU-Tennessee-Ole Miss round robin, was matched with Missouri in the Orange. If the Tigers wanted a bowl game, it would have to be either in the Sugar against Ole Miss or in Houston's Bluebonnet in another rematch with a defeated opponent, Texas Christian.

Dietzel polled the team informally and a full third voted to sit out the bowls altogether. Dietzel and the Tigers wanted to choose a bowl after a December 5 game between Syracuse and UCLA. If Syracuse lost the game, it would mean LSU could be playing for at least the Football Writers of America's version of the national championship, which was awarded after the bowl games. If Syracuse won, then LSU would stay home. Dietzel said, "If an honor (a bowl invitation) becomes a chore, then perhaps it is best left undone."

The Tigers took an official team vote, considering both the Sugar and Bluebonnet invitations as well as sitting out the bowls, on November 23 with a battalion of newspapermen sitting outside. Tension began to mount as the session stretched into a half hour and then an hour. Seventy minutes after the voting started, Carl Higgins, LSU's sports information director, burst into the waiting room and announced, "They voted to play." Billy Cannon walked in with a slight grin and said, "It was a unanimous vote. So I guess it will be Ole Miss again." Dietzel described his reaction as "shell-shocked"; he thought the team would call it a year.

As it happened, Syracuse walloped UCLA 36-8. Then on December 22 at practice, halfback Johnny Robinson broke a hand. Things were definitely not going well for LSU.

It didn't matter to the fans. The game, of course, would be televised, the first bowl to be telecast in color from coast-to-coast, but tickets were being swapped for used cars and refrigerator repairs. Four tickets went for a 14-foot fiberglass boat; 60 tickets went for a 1952 Cadillac and 4 new tires. The sizzle of the rematch had the fans steaming. It was estimated the Sugar Bowl had over a quarter of a million requests for tickets.

Ole Miss had given up only 21 points during the entire season, the lowest for a major college in 20 years—since the 1939 Tennessee Vols went undefeated, untied, and unscored upon. LSU gave up only 29 points. The rivals were ranked one-two nationally on defense. LSU allowed an average of 2.5 yards per play to the opposition; Ole Miss gave up an average of 2.8 yards.

Mississippi 21-LSU 0

"Go everywhere he went."

An Ole Miss fan said unsmilingly to a newsman before the rematch, "We'd rather beat LSU than be president." Coach Johnny Vaught gave his constituency a victory in a landslide. Vaught, criticized for his conservative approach in the 7-3 regular season Tiger win, gave the Rebels the green light to "go for broke." He wasn't going to hold anything back.

Warren Rabb, the LSU quarterback, was not an outstanding passer and his knee strain from the Tennessee game had not completely healed. Further complicating matters for LSU was halfback Johnny Robinson, who started with a protective covering over his fractured hand. He would not carry a single

time during the Sugar Bowl, meaning the Ole Miss defense could zero in on LSU's only threat, Billy Cannon. "We did something I don't think we had ever done before," said Billy Brewer, a Rebel safety. "We went to a man defense in the secondary because we knew LSU wouldn't be a passing threat. My assignment was to stay with Cannon, go everywhere he went."

Murky, damp weather made the field muddy in spots, and a cold wind lowered the temperature to 49 degrees for the kickoff. The revenge-bent, 7-point favorite Rebels wasted little time in warming things up on the floor of Tulane Stadium, however. LSU couldn't move on its first possession, and Cannon

Rebel quarterback Bobby Franklin looks for a receiver in 1960 rematch with arch-rival LSU.

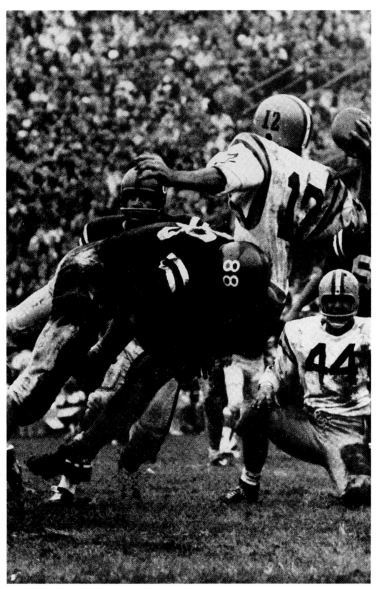

Larry Grantham (88) brings down Warren Rabb (12) in the 21-0 avenging of regular season defeat to LSU.

punted to the Mississippi 44. Bobby Franklin immediately began probing the Tiger perimeter, throwing a 12-yard strike to fullback Charlie Flowers. In short order the Rebels were camped on the LSU 33 with a first down. But the threat ended a few plays later when Rabb intercepted Franklin at the 5, slipping on the soft turf.

Another first-quarter Rebel march pushed down to the Tiger 18, where the LSU defense held again. Vaught sent in field goal specialist Bob Khayat. On the first play of the second period, the kick was wide. Ole Miss got the ball back on its 41 and again methodically set sail toward the LSU goal. After a 7-yard loss, a pass had the Rebs camped on the Tiger 33. Flowers gained 9, 3, and 9 yards to the 11. This put the teams directly between the stands holding the student bodies, and the din from LSU's side became so great the Rebels couldn't get

off a play. The LSU band rhythmically played "Hold That Tiger" while Vaught fumed on the sidelines, pointing to the stands while arguing with officials. Flowers hit the line twice in the midst of the clatter and gained nothing.

As LSU took over, the Ole Miss side opened up with a deafening roar and drum beating. There was an offensive mix-up on the first play; Cannon and Rabb bumped each other and the halfback was thrown for a 5-yard loss. Rabb then punted.

Despite its problems, the LSU defense was keeping the game even on the scoreboard. Then with 43 seconds left and Mississippi on its 42, the Tigers were assessed a 15-yard personal foul penalty. Ole Miss' Jake Gibbs, who led the SEC in total offense, received instructions from the bench. He took the snap, started to roll out, and pulled up behind tackle for the kill. Right end Johnny Brewer went

Billy Cannon (20) and Tiger Coach Paul Dietzel look on in dismay as Rebels completely dominate LSU.

Chinese Bandit quarterback Darryl Jenkins (10) has no protection against the rampaging Rebels.

straight down and deep, taking Cannon with him; halfback Bobby Crespino flared to the sideline; and left end Larry Grantham went down deep and out, taking Rabb. Delaying an instant, halfback James "Cowboy" Woodruff raced downfield behind Grantham and cut slightly to the center where Gibbs' pass was arching down. A Tiger wasn't within 15 yards of the receiver, and Woodruff, following the same route run in the first quarter when Rabb intercepted, went for a 43-yard touchdown.

"I don't think there's any question that the touchdown pass just before the end of the half broke our backs," said Dietzel. "It might have been a different game if we had gone into halftime 0-0."

Franklin returned the second-half kickoff 20 yards to the Rebel 37 and then engineered a second touchdown drive, the score coming on a 19-yard pass from Franklin to Grantham. The TD just before

the half was the first passing score the Tiger defense had given up in 14 games. A second in a matter of a few playing minutes illustrates just how dominant Ole Miss was. A fourth-quarter Rebel touchdown, an 8-yard pass to Dewey Partridge, was only window dressing.

Ole Miss held an awesome edge in statistics, 373 yards to 74; the Tigers gained 49 yards rushing but lost 64 for a net gain of minus 15 yards. The longest Tiger gain of the day was 8 yards by Darryl Jenkins of the Chinese Bandits—the defensive unit. It had taken LSU more than 25 minutes to get its initial first down, and that was the only one the Tigers were credited with in the first half. Cannon made 8 yards in six carries.

In the satisfied Rebel dressing room, Cowboy Woodruff sighed, "I always thought we had a better one (team), and I kind of feel we proved it today."

Mississippi-Rice

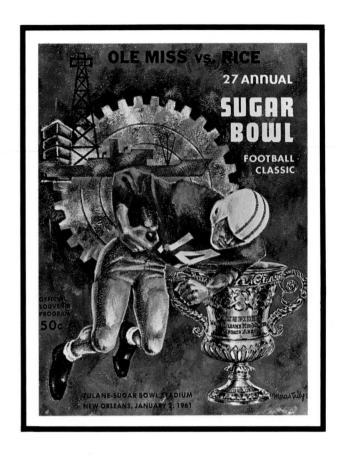

"You are going too, aren't you?"

From the beginning the Mid-Winter Sports Association seemed to have been conceived under a providential star. Even the strangulation of the segregation law hadn't damaged its string of successes.

A young New Orleans state legislator, Maurice 'Moon' Landrieu, believing the race laws clearly put the Sugar Bowl in jeopardy, tried to convince Louisiana Governor Jimmie Davis. Davis listened and never got back to Landrieu. Landrieu tried to buttonhole members of the Sugar Bowl for a plan to fight the legislation, but by then the Association was unwilling to take on both state government and public opinion.

The air began seeping from the balloon with the 1961 Sugar Bowl. It wasn't a dramatic occurrence perhaps, but in looking back, it seems obvious that the Sugar Bowl's fortunes altered slightly.

Mississippi, which had participated in two of the last three Sugar Bowls, was head and shoulders above the rest of the Southeastern Conference. Because there was no championship berth attached to a New Orleans invitation, the No. 2-ranked Rebels understandably wanted to play elsewhere during the holiday season. It would have been pleasing to New Orleans fans, too, because they wanted new blood in the game. But Ole Miss was the best team in the area, and the Sugar Bowl really didn't want to take a hand-me-down.

The Rebels, who were prohibited by Mississippi state law from competing against teams with black athletes, were coveted desperately by the Sugar, Gator, and Bluebonnet Bowls. Reports filtered out of Houston that Ole Miss had unofficially accepted an invitation to play in that game. Coach Johnny Vaught and Lou Hassell of the Bluebonnet selection committee both denied a deal had been struck.

Ole Miss eventually signed to play in the Sugar Bowl again. Apparently the Rebels gave the Bluebonnet an indication that they were interested. When the Sugar realized it was losing the No. 2 nationally ranked team, it went to work on the warm friendship the bowl and school had enjoyed for years.

To its credit, the Sugar Bowl didn't have only Mississippi in its sights. It made long-shot attempts at No. 1-ranked Minnesota (the Big Ten contract with the Rose Bowl had lapsed), and was briefly interested in No. 4-ranked Navy, although it is hard to see how a service academy could have gotten around the segregation issue. Sugar Bowl President George Schneider told the New Orleans Quarterback Club that the Association had tried to get Minnesota. "It's our understanding that although the Big Ten pact with the Rose Bowl has been concluded, a Big Ten team can only play in the Rose Bowl this year." It was reassuring to realize that the Sugar Bowl would still reach out.

For whatever reasons, the Sugar Bowl was far more serious about Duke, Baylor, and Rice. After a 7-6 Duke loss to North Carolina, New Orleans eyed the season-ending Baylor-Rice game. Baylor dropped out of the picture before the game was played by accepting a Gator Bowl invitation. So the Sugar Bowl more or less pinned its hopes on the Owls, who could move into a tie with Arkansas with a win. An 8-2 co-champion would have suited New Orleans just fine. Instead, the Bears won 12-7 in the fading minutes, a finish that would characterize future Sugar Bowl selections. Rice dropped into a second-place SWC tie and put an unranked team with three losses in the Sugar Bowl.

Thrice-beaten or not, Rice was no pushover. It had an excellent pass defense, intercepting 17 passes over the course of the season and holding its opponents to a 44 percent completion average. Its defensive middle was good; offensively it ran a sound attack that boasted of 10 backs who carried at least 25 times each, nine gaining 100 yards or more over the course of the season. Its 74 pass receptions were spread over 14 receivers. All Rice lacked was a little luck.

Ole Miss could be awesome. Jake Gibbs, by consensus the finest quarterback in the country, com-

pleted passes at a 60.6 ratio and directed his offense to a perfectly balanced 18 rushing touchdowns and 18 passing touchdowns. Another was added by an interception return. Rice Coach Jess Neely assessed, "They tell me Ole Miss can beat you up the middle, but humiliate you outside." He had heard right, and the Owls were immediately made a 10-point underdog—biggest of the major bowls.

The only thing that appeared to concern Ole Miss was the rankings. The final Associated Press and United Press International polls came out, placing the Rebels second and third respectively. Students made "AP" and "UPI" dummies, hung them from the Union Building, and burned them while chanting, "We're No. 1, to hell with AP and UPI."

Times-Picayune columnist Buddy Diliberto noticed how unconcerned the Rebs seemed about Rice and wrote the game would be closer than the betting line. Ole Miss, he analyzed, was in the same position LSU was in for the 1959 Sugar Bowl against Clemson. It had no reason to get 'steamed up.' "The Rebs can't prove anything by winning," said Diliberto.

Vaught had a very difficult time turning his team's thoughts to the capable Owls. While the Rebels prepared in Oxford, one of his reserve backs, Frank Halbert, asked Vaught if he knew what time the team would arrive in New Orleans. The boy's family wanted to greet the squad and the anxious sub inquired, "so what time are we going to get there?" The traveling squad hadn't yet been made up, and Vaught responded with, "What do you mean, 'we?'" Halbert was taken aback. He hesitated, then innocently asked, "Well, coach, you are going too, aren't you?"

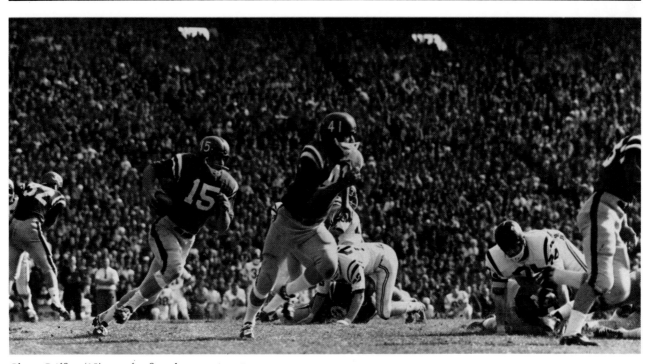

Glynn Griffing (15) runs for first down against Rice.

Mississippi 14-Rice 6

'The Rifleman,' Ole Miss' Jake Gibbs, runs for a first down against Rice.

"Once I straightened up I had blockers in front of me."

Buddy Diliberto was right. Mississippi wasn't ready for Rice, though not a person in the crowd of 82,851 would have believed it during the opening 3 minutes and 20 seconds.

Jake Gibbs, Ole Miss' "Rifleman," put up the first points of the game in that span. Jim Anderson returned a short kickoff from the Rebel 27 to the 48. Gibbs and Anderson picked up a first down before Bobby Crespino shook loose off left tackle for a 27-yard gain to the Owl 15. George Blair caught a pass to the 8. Then Gibbs, faking a pass, rolled out around end and scored.

It was an awesome, effortless drive that darkened the festive mood in the Rice stands. Rufus King, an Owl guard, said, "I think we were trying too hard the first time they had the football. We were a little tense . . . " Coach Jess Neely found a remedy for the tenseness; he took out most of his starters. So did Rebel Coach Johnny Vaught, although Vaught

made his move to give his regulars a little rest after the shakedown.

From then until the fading minutes, Rice starters and subs played Ole Miss on better than even terms. It was tentative at first, but the Owls received impetus when the Rebels moved back downfield to threaten at the 25. On fourth and three the Rebels disdained a field goal attempt that could have made the score a discouraging 10-0 for the Rice defense. When the Owls broke through and tossed Gibbs back to the 32, Rice began playing with sureness and certainty.

A 78-yard Rice drive ended in frustration. Six inches in another direction on one play on this drive might have changed the outcome. Randy Kerbow pushed Rice to the Ole Miss 27 where, on a fourth and one, he crossed up the Rebels by sending 163-pound junior halfback Butch Blume wide on a power sweep to the right. "I got some good blocks and made the turn," Blume (son of an orchestra leader) explained while demonstrating with a two-step. "I was moving down the sidelines when my foot went out by no more than six inches. If I had just a little more running room I could have walked in."

Blume's run gave Rice a first down at the 10, but two plays later Allen Green intercepted another Kerbow pass at the Rebel 9.

Gibbs punted and Rice started back toward the Rebel goal, a threat ignited by a 16-yard run by Blume. But Johnny Robinson intercepted Blume's halfback pass at the 17 and the score remained 7-0 at the half.

Later in the second half, Billy Cox got Rice pumping again, moving from the Owl 23. In 18 plays—the most important a 30-yard pass to Dan Brast at the Rebel 26—Rice was on the boards. Cox got the ball to within 2½ yards of the end zone. It took four downs to get in from there, but Blume went in around end carrying three Mississippians on his back. Max Webb missed the extra point, leaving Ole Miss with a precarious 7-6 lead. "I simply hurried my kick," the downhearted Webb said.

The teams seesawed for most of the second half. Things heated up again as the fourth quarter was running out. Kerbow, attempting to put his team in position for a field goal attempt, went to the air. Reggie Robertson intercepted on the Owl 30 and returned it to the 11. The Rice defense shoved Ole Miss back to the 17 where, almost unbelievably, the Rebels again passed up a field-goal attempt that could have cinched the game. Ole Miss was stopped on a running play and Rice took over.

Gibbs, who obviously was not having his typical day, finally put the Rebels in gear in the last few minutes. Reminiscent of the opening offensive display, Ole Miss pulled itself together after taking possession at the Rebel 43. In 10 plays, primarily on the strength of runners Anderson and Art Doty,

Mississippi was camped on the Rice 3. There the Owls fought the Rebs to a standoff for three downs.

Gibbs lined up his teammates—who hadn't gained a foot since reaching the 3—took the snap, stumbled, then raced wide behind rattling blocks. He was hit at the goal line by two defenders, barely slipping in and losing the ball in the process. It was ruled he had already crossed the line before he fumbled on his sterling effort.

"I almost fouled up on that last touchdown—and we needed it," Gibbs said. "I came out too fast and slipped. But once I straightened up I had blockers in front of me and knew I'd go in for six." Ole Miss held a 14-6 advantage with 5 minutes and 16 seconds left to play.

Rice out-first-downed and out-gained Ole Miss in a fine ball-control exhibition that allowed the Owls to run 81 plays to the Rebels' 60. But Ole Miss got two touchdowns to Rice's one because, as Pie Dufour wrote, "Rice left too many men on base." Although the Owls held Gibbs to 15 yards rushing, 11 of those yards accounted for both Rebel touchdowns.

Probably the most memorable part of the game for gallant Rice, after the defeat wore off, was sophomore lineman Ray Alborn wobbling off the field after being cracked in the fury of the pit. He walked on legs of jello to the Ole Miss bench to have a seat. "I don't remember any of it," said Alborn, "but some teammates came to get me and bring me over to our side of the field. They knew they couldn't win without me . . . We did win, didn't we?"

No, and to point up how important that fact was, Minnesota didn't win either. Wisconsin beat the Gophers 17-7 in the Rose Bowl. Because of it, Ole Miss, who won in less than impressive fashion, found a poll that agreed the Rebels were No. 1.

The Football Writers of America, who vote after the bowls, ranked Mississippi at the top of its final poll.

Alabama-Arkansas

MONDAY, JANUARY 1, 1962

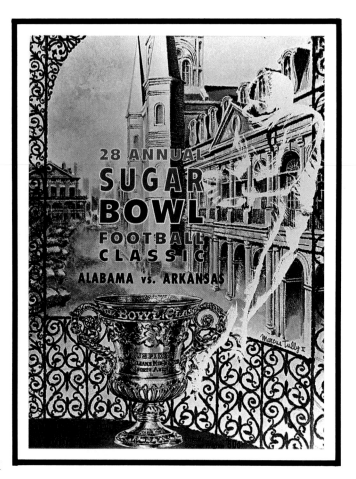

"The boys voted to go to the Sugar Bowl."

Since 1956, when the segregation edict went into effect and as civil rights became the overriding domestic political issue, the Sugar Bowl was fighting a war with one arm tied. It was winning the war, but only because two backyard schools, LSU and Ole Miss, were enjoying some of their finest seasons. One or the other had participated in four consecutive Sugar Bowls. It was fortunate that those teams were available at the time, but the feeling began to grow that LSU and Ole Miss were becoming crutches for the Sugar Bowl.

It was an ideal situation for New Orleans: Pencil in one of those popular teams and automatically fill one berth with a high national contender. Then all the Mid-Winter Sports Association had to do was look for another team that wouldn't be offended by segregated seating.

Both schools were in their accustomed elite positions in the 1961 national rankings, along with a newcomer, Alabama, ranked second behind Texas. The crutch was rudely knocked from under the Sugar when in mid-November Tiger Coach Paul Dietzel informed the Mid-Winter Sports Association that under no circumstances would the Tigers accept a Sugar Bowl invitation. Although LSU came under some heat from home-state fans, the Tiger position had some merit. An 80-mile bus trip from Baton Rouge to New Orleans the day of the game wasn't a big reward for a job well done—particularly since, unlike the Cotton, Orange, and Rose Bowls, participation didn't automatically establish championship status of the "home" team. Also, Dietzel was still irritated by the corner he was painted into for the 1960 rematch with Ole Miss, when the Sugar Bowl insisted he make a decision before the LSU hierarchy really wanted to.

For the 1962 game, the Sugar Bowl wanted a match between No. 2 Alabama and the No. 4 Tigers, two SEC schools who had not played in the regular season. A committee from the Mid-Winter Sports Association visited Baton Rouge to meet with

Athletic Director Jim Corbett and Dietzel and offer an invitation. Corbett met with the committee. Dietzel refused, telling Corbett in effect, "If you want this team to play in the Sugar Bowl, you'll have to take 'em."

Ole Miss was already unofficially committed to the Cotton Bowl, and Alabama was no guarantee either. The Big Ten contract with the Rose Bowl had still not been renewed, and Pasadena was flirting with Alabama and LSU. Alabama had far more tradition in Pasadena than in New Orleans, winning five of six California appearances before the Rose Bowl closed on both ends. Tide Coach Paul "Bear" Bryant saw a Rose Bowl invitation as a dramatic way of reasserting Alabama football, which had fallen on desperate times before he returned in 1958.

A poll of Southern California sportswriters favored Alabama and LSU in that order for the 1962 game. Fred Neil of the Los Angeles *Herald Express* wrote, "The sportswriters' No. 1 choice is Alabama because everyone thinks they have a better team. I think they (the Rose Bowl) will look favorably on LSU. The Big Ten teams under consideration are dull, and there's a little reaction to our going to the Big Ten with hat in hand and begging them to play us."

LSU took itself out of the California picture by accepting an Orange Bowl invitation to play Colorado, but 'Bama continued to wait. There was some sentiment on the West Coast against a southern team because of the segregation issue, although Alabama obviously had no qualms about playing an integrated team.

Ohio State, the Big Ten champion, was tentatively offered the Rose Bowl bid November 28. Shockingly, the school's faculty council rejected it. Reporters quickly got in touch with Dr. Frank Rose, president of the University of Alabama, who said his school should not be considered a Rose Bowl candidate. "If we win Saturday (the season finale against cross-state rival Auburn) our team is to go to the Sugar Bowl," said Dr. Rose. "The boys voted to go to the Sugar Bowl if invited, and I think they will be invited."

During the bowl chess match, Texas Christian had upset Texas and Alabama had moved up to No. 1. A 34-0 victory over Auburn solidified Bryant's first national championship.

The Sugar Bowl then grabbed the next most attractive team available, No. 9 Arkansas, the Southwest Conference co-champion. New Orleans had somehow come up with a stellar attraction . . . again.

Alabama 10-Arkansas 3

"It might have been my praying."

Almost a month before the Sugar Bowl game, Paul "Bear" Bryant was in New York at the Hall of Fame dinner to accept the MacArthur Trophy from the general for whom it was named, to shake hands with President John F. Kennedy, and to listen to the president talk to a pep rally in Tuscaloosa by telephone and extend congratulations on a championship year.

Later in December, with his team having pitched camp in Biloxi, Mississippi, Bryant reflected on the road that had taken him from Arkansas to the halls of the mighty. He remembered leaving his home in Moro Bottom with "ten little pigs my dad had given me to sell. If I could get a dollar each, he said I could keep half." Well, on the way, little Paul Bryant, one of 12 children, got his wagon stuck in the Arkansas mud. "I must have been there almost all day," he said, "when someone came by and pulled the wagon out."

He went on to Fordyce and sold his pigs. "It wouldn't have happened if I hadn't been lucky," he said, pointing to the element he credits with a family move to Fordyce. If that hadn't happened, he said, "I wouldn't have played football, and I never would have gotten to the University of Alabama. If I hadn't been lucky, I'd still be out there somewhere plowing."

As it was, Bryant's Crimson Tide was plowing through southern football fields. His first national champion gave up a total of 22 points in 10 games, none in its last 5 games ("They played like it was a sin to give up a point," Bryant assessed); they led the NCAA in three defensive categories and set 10 school defensive records. Arkansas Coach Frank Broyles felt his team could move on anybody, although he admitted Alabama presented more problems than most. He did have a weapon no one had been able to neutralize: halfback Lance Alworth, who led the nation in running.

The Razorbacks, unaccountably jittery throughout the first 30 minutes, punted after three plays. In six more plays, the Crimson Tide had covered the 79 yards necessary for the first points.

"We noticed something a little different in their defensive alignment," said tackle Billy Neighbors, "so we made a slight adjustment." The adjustment

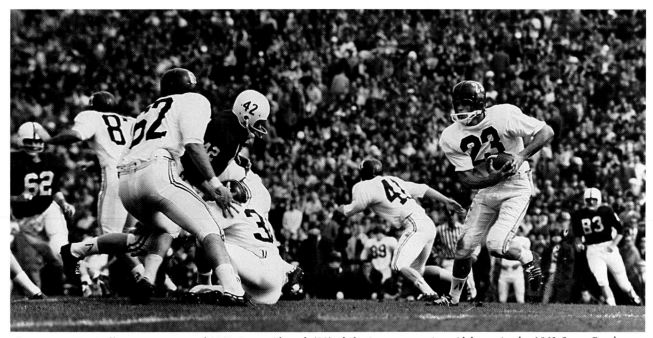

The nation's No. 1 all-purpose runner of 1961, Lance Alworth (23), shifts into gear against Alabama in the 1962 Sugar Bowl.

sent running back Mike Fracchia firing past a defender who penetrated into the backfield, past another just beyond the line, and wheeling down the sideline 43 yards to the Arkansas 12. On the next play, quarterback Pat Trammell faked a pass and then ran it in from left end. Neighbors said later, "We ran that doggone play about six more times and never did do anything with it again."

The defense took over at that early stage; Arkansas continued to hold back the ever-menacing Tide, and 'Bama held almost complete sway over the Hog offense. Alabama went to the Razorback 36, then to the 40 before the quarter was over. In the second period, Trammell drove the Tide from its 37 to the Arkansas 22, but Fracchia fumbled and George McKinney came up with the ball. Coming right back after a Razorback punt, Alabama stepped from its 48 to a fourth-and-two at the 18. Tim Davis attempted a field goal, but he missed.

Butch Wilson intercepted a McKinney pass at the Hog 37 and ran it back to the 20. Three plays netted 3 yards and Davis came back. This time he kicked true and, with four minutes to go until the half, Alabama led, 10-0.

Paul Dudley almost matched Fracchia's run late in the half, and nearly allowed Arkansas to go to the dressing room just a field goal back. The Hogs, with good field position after Alworth returned the kickoff to the Arkansas 40, nudged down to the Tide 48. The thrust of the Razorback offense had been inside. But Dudley swung out to the short side of the field and, as his blockers mowed down defenders, made his way to the 10 where Tommy Brooker collared the runner.

"I should have gone the distance," said Dudley. "Billy Moore threw the key block that got me past the line, and Jim Collier cleared part of the path downfield. After Collier threw his block, I cut to the inside . . . I could see daylight, but before I could resume my regular course down the sideline I was hit from the side."

Lee Roy Jordan stopped two running plays, and a pass was off target. Mickey Cissell attempted a field goal with 28 seconds left in the first half; it wasn't close.

A third quarter fumbled punt by Billy Richardson at the Alabama 32 put Arkansas in business again. Cissell returned after three plays had produced two yards. Richardson made up for his lapse when he flashed in from the flank, blocked the kick, and recovered on the 38.

Late in the third period, Jim Grizzle recovered still another Alabama fumble, this one by Trammell on the Tide 45. Alworth caught a McKinney pass on the 23. The quarterback and Jesse Branch had the ball on the 10 in 2 plays. A pair of passes and an Alworth carry surrendered 2 yards. Cissell came on to record the first points against Alabama since October. Now at 10-3, Arkansas was back in the game.

Tim Davis kicked a 47-yard field goal in the opening minutes of the fourth quarter—points Bryant felt would have taken 'Bama off the hook. A holding penalty took them off the boards, however. "If we would have gotten those three points we would have been home free," said Bryant. "But, as it was, it was anybody's game."

McKinney began opening up in the final minutes.

Pat Trammel (12) dives for a touchdown in 1962's Alabama-Arkansas Sugar Bowl.

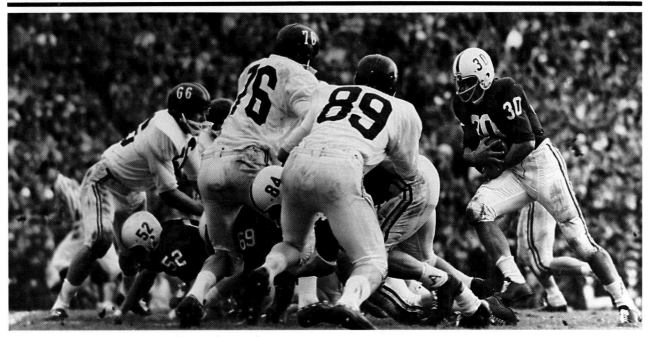

Mike Fracchia hammers Arkansas line with MVP form.

Alworth caught a 31-yard pass at the Alabama 43 that would have put the Razorbacks at least in position to make a late run, except it was fumbled when Darwin Holt and others jarred the receiver. "I didn't have the ball tucked away," Alworth said, "when 'Bama's defense nailed me from all sides . . . before I knew what happened I was empty-handed." Bryant wondered if "it might have been my praying that caused the fumble."

Still, Arkansas kept coming. McKinney got the ball again and a 37-yard attempt to Collier was allowed for interference at the Tide 40. Alworth grazed a tantalizing shot with his fingertips in the end zone; Wilson deflected another before intercepting and stepping out-of-bounds no more than four inches from the Alabama goal. Trammell ran three

plays into the line and the game was over. Bryant, who said he had "nine heart attacks out there," revealed he was prepared to give Arkansas a safety on fourth down if time had not run out. "We were in it on the scoreboard, but were never in it on the field," assessed Broyles glumly.

Alabama had won its first Sugar Bowl by allowing the Razorbacks only four chances at the goal and holding Alworth to 15 yards rushing. As the coaches met at midfield, Broyles had to cut short his congratulations because his players were trying to claim the game ball. "Give them the ball," he yelled at his squad. "They won it, it belongs to them." Bryant rumbled at his own players, "Let 'em have it." It was the only thing Alabama gave up all day.

Mississippi-Arkansas

TUESDAY, JANUARY 1, 1963

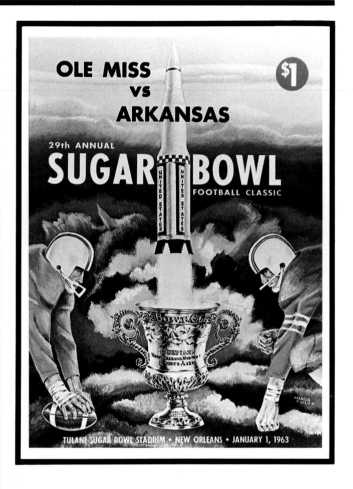

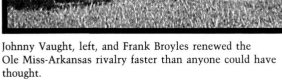

Johnny Vaught, left, and Frank Broyles renewed the
Ole Miss-Arkansas rivalry faster than anyone could have
thought.

"The number is listed."

Johnny Vaught's Mississippi Rebels, in those halcyon days of Southeastern Conference football, appeared to be suffering a bit of an identity crisis. Over the course of a decade, the Rebels were consistently the SEC's premier team. Yet since 1951, Tennessee, Auburn, LSU, and Alabama had all won consensus national championships. Ole Miss had only been presented the Grantland Rice Award by the Football Writers of America as the country's No. 1 team after its 1961 Sugar Bowl victory, though that did not carry the weight of the wire service voting.

Vaught seemed determined to show the doubters just how good his program was during the 1963 bowls. On the eve of the LSU-Mississippi football game, the Sugar Bowl tendered an invitation to Vaught, contingent upon a victory over the Tigers. The Rebels were on their way to the school's first unbeaten, untied season. At the same time the Sugar Bowl extended an invitation to Alabama, 3rd-ranked and unbeaten in 25 games.

The South was anxious for a match-up between two SEC teams which had not played each other during the season. 'Bama Coach Paul "Bear" Bryant, because he had played in the Sugar Bowl the year before and then returned to New Orleans to play Tulane in September, wasn't interested.

Quoting unnamed sources almost daily, a few New Orleans writers kept the Ole Miss-Alabama brew stirred, but nothing substantial materialized. Then Vaught, in a telephone interview with Associated Press reporter Ben Thomas, seemed to try to challenge Alabama in the same manner in which LSU had been pressured into the 1960 game. Thomas asked Vaught if he had a bowl preference. The Rebel coach laughed and replied, "Yeah, but I can't say it." Thomas asked specifically if Ole Miss wanted to play Alabama. Vaught answered that it would be the best of the bowls. "It would match two of the finest teams in college football," he said. "We'll play anybody, I don't care who they are."

Bryant responded, "We've got three more teams licking their chops to get at us, starting with Miami. When they get through with us, if they (Ole Miss) still want us, the number is listed." That

week, after a game in Florida with the University of Miami, Bryant, who saw no logic in risking his national ranking against a team from his own conference, committed to the Orange Bowl.

This all meant the Sugar Bowl was sent scrambling for the next best match-up it could find. Frank Broyles' Arkansas Razorbacks, with a loss only in the final 36 seconds to Texas, was a strong prospect with the Gator, Bluebonnet, and Liberty Bowls. Broyles wanted a quick answer from the Sugar Bowl or he would commit to another bowl. The Sugar answered with an invitation to play Ole Miss. He accepted—contingent upon Texas winning the Southwest Conference title and the Cotton Bowl berth.

Mississippi and Arkansas had been longtime rivals whose series had been terminated by Broyles in 1962. Since Broyles took over in 1958, Arkansas enjoyed its finest football moments. But he was unable to beat the Rebels in four tries. "It's easier to change coaches than change teams," said Broyles at the announcement of the series termination.

"You know," Broyles said after accepting the conditional invitation, "when people chided me about canceling the series, I told them that we'd play Mississippi in a bowl game. Now look. And here we are again."

Third-ranked Mississippi, 27-1-1 over the last three seasons, won its Southeastern Conference championship with the league's best offense, the nation's best defense, and a versatile quarterback named Glynn Griffing. Sixth-ranked Arkansas led the Southwest Conference in rushing and total defense in going unbeaten for nine games.

The game didn't have the lure of the Rose Bowl, which for the first time in bowl history had a No. 1 (Southern Cal) and a No. 2 (Wisconsin) team, but it was a good selection.

Texas upheld its end by beating Texas A&M 13-3 on Thanksgiving Day to take its SWC title. That score held Sugar Bowl interest as much as any during the 1962 season, because if Texas had lost, Arkansas would have been the SWC champion and in Dallas on New Year's Day. But Texas would not have turned to New Orleans. It would have been in the Bluebonnet Bowl.

Mississippi 17-Arkansas 13

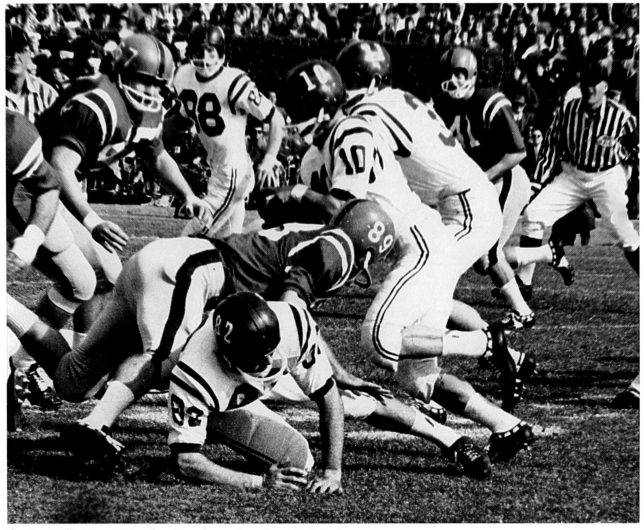

The Hogs' Billy Moore (10) rushes for a short gain against Mississippi.

"I wanted to kiss him."

Every one of the 82,900 spectators at the 29th Sugar Bowl probably would have agreed with Frank Broyles' assessment. "The difference," said the Arkansas coach afterward, "was Glynn Griffing." Griffing had an outstanding day, completing 14 of 23 passes for 242 yards, and breaking two records (passing yardage and total yardage). Somewhat overshadowed by Griffing's performance was a herculean operation by the Ole Miss line, which constantly flushed the Razorback quarterbacks from their nest and into the unprotected open field.

Arkansas got first shot when a weak punt gave the Razorbacks possession at the Rebel 27. Ole Miss turned on its viselike defense and didn't allow an inch. Tom McKnelly then attempted a 43-yard field goal which fell short.

Griffing began chopping up the Hog defense, moving the Rebels 67 yards in 19 plays. The drive was effective and time-consuming. It died at the 13, though, when Billy Carl Irwin missed a field goal.

After Arkansas punted to its 49, Coach Johnny Vaught inserted quarterback Jim Weatherly to begin the opening minutes of the second period. Mississippi was quickly back at the 13. Griffing came back in, but the Razorbacks held as Jesse Branch broke up a pass to Larry Johnson on the goal line. On fourth down, Irwin kicked a 32-yard field goal.

With six minutes left in the half, on third-and-nine from the Arkansas 19, sophomore reserve quarterback Billy Gray dropped back and spotted wingback Jerry Lamb 10 yards behind the Rebel secondary. Lamb slowed to catch the arching pass near midfield, then stumbled as he turned for the unguarded end zone. Lamb fought to keep his balance for 10, 20, 30 yards more when Buck Randall came flying out of the afternoon sun in a desperate dive. He just grazed Lamb's back and heel. It was enough to cause the staggering receiver to fall at the 13.

"I don't know how I caught him . . . I wanted to kiss him for falling down," said Randall. The play covered a Sugar Bowl record 68 yards. In three plays, Arkansas gained 3 yards and McKnelly kicked a 30-yard field goal to tie the game.

For an instant it appeared that Arkansas would get more points anyway. Dave Jennings fielded the kickoff in the Ole Miss end zone, started to run it out, couldn't make up his mind whether that was the wise move, appeared to step back into the end zone, and went down to one knee. "The official signalled it was a safety," said Broyles. "I thought we had two points . . . the official quickly reversed his decision, so I guess Jennings didn't step out of the end zone."

Weatherly immediately started up another Rebel drive, hitting on passes to Jennings for 2 yards and Randall for 14 to place the ball at midfield. Griffing replaced Weatherly, missed on two pass attempts, then found Chuck Morris at the Hog 33. On the following play, Louis Guy shook off two Razorbacks, turned, and took in a pass over his shoulder for a touchdown.

Three plays into the third quarter, Randall had his team in trouble again. He fumbled and Ray Trail recovered at the Ole Miss 18. Branch swept left to the 5. Billy Moore then rolled to the same side, saw Branch only partially covered, and dropped a soft pass into his cradled arms. McKnelly's PAT tied the score at 10.

The stung Rebels were jockeyed 80 yards in 10 plays by Griffing, who rocketed 23- and 35-yard pass completions to Guy. Ole Miss nudged out again to a 17-10 lead on a 1-yard sneak by Griffing.

A 33-yard pass from Moore to Lamb was the polish on an arduous short-gain push that placed Arkansas on the Rebel 10. Two passes went incomplete. On third down, Moore pulled on a sweep, following what appeared to be precision blocking. Randall sliced through the interference and tackled the quarterback at the 4. Moore had to leave the game, and Arkansas kicked a field goal.

McKnelly cut the score to 17-13, and Broyles was second-guessed for deciding to go for the three points. Vaught agreed with his rival. "If it had been my decision," the Rebel coach said, "I would have done the same thing. The way the teams were moving the ball in the second half, I think Broyles was correct. He thought he'd have another chance." Vaught did not give Broyles another chance.

Ole Miss threatened three times in the fourth quarter; Arkansas didn't get close again. The Rebels drove to the Arkansas 3 (where Mike Parker batted down two passes), to the 8 (where Tom Moore intercepted Griffing), and to the 9 (where the game ended).

The Rebels had been only a slight favorite, and the score indicated the odds-makers were right. But Arkansas, which averaged 241.2 yards rushing during the season, had 47 yards against Ole Miss; and Arkansas, which led the Southwest Conference by giving up an average of only 200.1 yards of total defense, surrendered 429 yards to the Rebs. Ole Miss had three times as many first downs and two-and-a-half times as much yardage as its opponent. Arkansas had stayed in the game with a superior opponent about as well as anyone ever had.

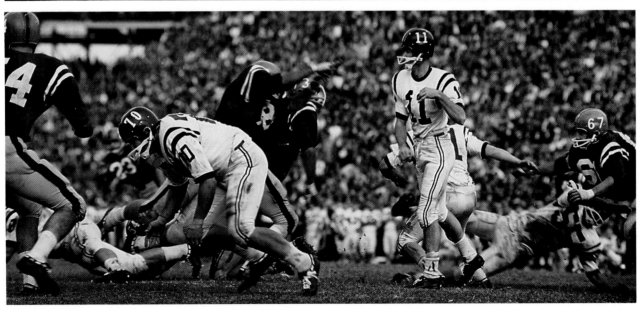

Billy Gray (11) goes over the top against onrushing Ole Miss.

Alabama-Mississippi

WEDNESDAY, JANUARY 1, 1964

"I remember a time like this."

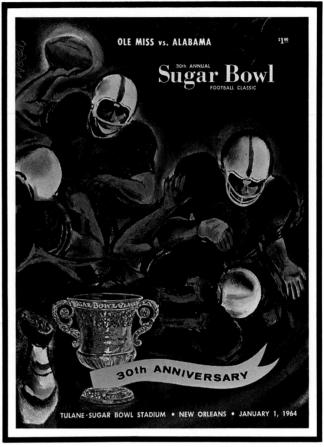

Seven Sugar Bowls had been played since the segregation issue had encased the Mid-Winter Sports Association in an insular, provincial cocoon. Almost miraculously, the damage was minimal because 1) Many Southern schools followed similar policy and law, and the Southeastern Conference was then the finest collegiate football league in America, and 2) Sheer good fortune. The situation was bound to change.

The segregation obstacle began to dissolve, although few realized it in June of 1963 when a suit seeking integration of seating arrangements and other facilities at New Orleans' Municipal Auditorium was taken under advisement by a special three-judge federal court. Horace Bynum, vice-president of the New Orleans chapter of the National Association for the Advancement of Colored People, filed the suit after the city denied it use of the building for a 1962 rally featuring such speakers as Thurgood Marshall.

According to Assistant City Attorney Ernest Salatich, closed meetings and religious assemblies could be held on a desegregated basis. Open meetings were segregated under Louisiana law. The court was asked to declare unconstitutional the state's statute requiring segregation at entertainment and athletic events.

It would take time for the court to reach a decision, but on the football front things were unraveling. In 1964, the Sugar Bowl wanted Navy and Mississippi. Roger Staubach had transformed Navy from an Eastern also-ran into a glamorous, exciting, and undefeated football team. Whether the segregation issue would have been an insurmountable barrier will never be known because No. 2-ranked Navy only had eyes for Dallas, where No. 1-ranked Texas was scheduled for a New Year's bout.

Other than Texas, the Southwest Conference did not have a strong team; there was not one in the Atlantic Coast Conference; and because of the conference contract with the Orange Bowl, the Big Eight runner-up was not allowed to play in another bowl.

The third and only alternative was an all-SEC game between Mississippi and the winner of the Alabama-Auburn game. It looked feasible because this year—unlike the previous—Ole Miss was the higher ranked team. Bryant, with two strong teams left to play, wanted a no-strings-attached invitation. He received one from the Bluebonnet Bowl in Houston and tried to use it as a lever with the Orange Bowl. Miami, who could use backups in Pitt, Syracuse, and Penn State, wouldn't bite.

When the Sugar tested the waters, Bryant laid it on the line: Either he would get a no-strings invitation, or he would accept the bid from the Bluebonnet Bowl. Auburn appeared willing to wait, but the Plainsmen seemed a longer shot than the Tide. Bryant got his invitation on his terms. Auburn accepted an Orange Bowl bid. So for the first time, when Auburn and Alabama met, two teams already committed to rival New Year's Day bowls met in the regular season. Auburn won 10-8.

Joe Namath, a young quarterback whose rubber-band right arm had the South buzzing, directed the Tide offense. It was Alabama's 17th bowl game, pushing it ahead of Georgia Tech as the all-time bowl entrant.

Despite a season-ending 10-10 tie with Mississippi

Paul 'Bear' Bryant is surrounded by his Crimson Tide before doing battle with Ole Miss in the snow.

State, 7th-ranked and unbeaten (7-0-2) Mississippi appeared as formidable as ever to Bryant.

Eighth-ranked Alabama and the Rebels hadn't played since 1944. The Crimson Tide hadn't been an underdog since 1960, but Ole Miss opened a 7½-point favorite. Then in early December, Namath was suspended for the remainder of the season (including the Sugar Bowl), because of a team infraction. The Sugar was turning sour . . .

Bryant couldn't have known it but his first recruiting trip in 1936 as an Alabama assistant would play a role in the 1964 Sugar Bowl. He signed Alvin Davis from Arkansas, who later became a prep coach in Tifton, Georgia. His son Tim was a quarterback but hurt a leg. Tim remembered his dad said, "Son, there's no reason you can't be a college kicker. But be sure to go to a school that always has a strong line." At first, Tim's knee didn't respond, but ". . . my dad kept Coach Bryant informed on my progress and he stuck with me." When the time came to choose a college, Tim chose Alabama over Georgia Tech. "Coach Bryant's colorful personality swung me," he said. Thus, Alabama acquired a talented athlete who was to determine the 1964 Sugar Bowl.

Nothing matched the snowfall of New Year's Eve, 1963. More than three inches of snow fluttered down on New Orleans, the most snow in the city since 1895. A crew of 25 workers from the police department's House of Detention worked with Tulane Stadium Superintendent Nolan Chaix until midnight clearing the tarpaulin and the seats. The crew was brought back at 5 A.M. "It looked pretty hopeless," said Chaix. "We just weren't prepared to cope with anything like we got Tuesday. The snow was still coming down when we started about 3 P.M. (Tuesday), but we had to go to work."

It seemed much more hopeless to Bryant. Alabama had given up more points (88) and more yardage (216.5 yards per game) and had been victimized with more long-scoring plays than any team Bryant coached since 1958.

"This is not the best time for us to be catching Mississippi," assessed the Bear. "They come at you in a big wave, all of them. And if we can't block Miami, and we didn't, how in the world can we block Ole Miss?" Reflecting, he added, "I remember a time like this—in 1958. We'd scratch and claw and quick-kick . . . and we won games we had no right winning."

Alabama 12-Mississippi 7

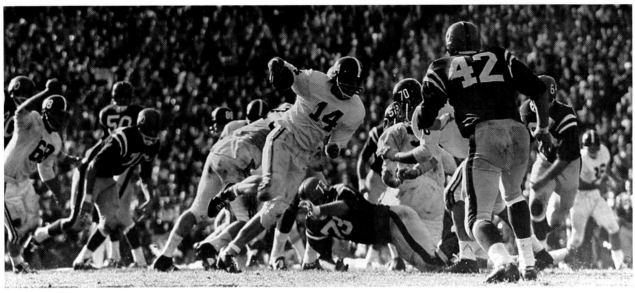

Steve Sloan (14), subbing for Joe Namath, hits Ole Miss line.

"I saw you take your eyes off the ball."

Tulane Stadium actually did resemble a huge sugar bowl on the first day of 1964, with snowbanks flanking the field. The clear 45-degree weather produced what appeared to be ideal conditions, but the New Year's Eve snow may have been the biggest factor in the game.

After Ole Miss punted to Alabama on its first possession, eighteen-year-old sophomore Steve Sloan took the Crimson Tide on a quick-hitting, tackle-to-tackle drive that netted five first downs. The Rebels, who led the nation in rushing defense, finally were able to stop Alabama at the Ole Miss 15. Tim Davis entered the fray on fourth-and-one and kicked a 31-yard field goal.

Following the kickoff, quarterback Jim Weatherly, in for Perry Lee Dunn, set the tone for a frustrating Rebel day by losing the ball with no one around him as he attempted a pass. Butch Henry recovered for 'Bama at the Mississippi 31. Ole Miss braced, and Davis came in again and kicked a 46-yard field goal to open the second quarter. The 32-yarder Davis had kicked against Arkansas in 1962 was a Sugar Bowl record, and Tim broke his own record with this one.

On the first play after Alabama kicked off, Mike Dennis fumbled and Billy Piper recovered at the Rebel 37. Davis, in for his third play of the game after Ole Miss' defense gave up nothing, attempted a 50-yard field goal, but it was wide to the right. "I ought to beat you with a stick, you rascal," Bear Bryant admonished with a smile. "You should have

had that other one, too. I saw you take your eye off the ball." Davis felt he had kicked the ball well. "My foot caught the stitches on the ball . . . it started out good and just went dead," he said.

He would get another chance. Just before the half, Dunn swung a short pass out to Larry Smith, who was hit immediately by Al Lewis. Smith dropped the ball and Ed Versprille covered it at the Rebel 16. Alabama gained 4 yards, and on fourth down with 16 seconds remaining, Davis kicked a 22-yard field goal. Alabama led 9-0 at the break.

"I'm not taking anything away from Alabama," reflected Rebel end Joe Wilkins. "We played under the same conditions. Our game, though, I feel, was much more affected by the weather than theirs. We had a much more open offense, handled the ball more than Alabama, which ran basically a simple quick-hitting offense. The main thing was the snow put more moisture in the air, and we were using much larger amounts of stick 'em to keep our hands dry. I even had to change my stance from three fingers to four to compensate because the field was slick as glass. So, our routine was hurt somewhat. With our roll-out offense, it just seemed a little more difficult for us."

Dennis picked up 11 yards on the first play of the second half, registering Ole Miss' initial first down. Two plays later, Frank Kinard dropped the Rebels' eighth fumble, bringing Mississippi Governor Ross Barnett to his feet with, "Why is it the boys can't hold onto the football?" Jack Hurlbut recovered at the Tide 49; 'Bama returned the favor by fumbling at the Ole Miss 37. Then Piper intercepted Weatherly in a game that began to take on the complexion of a tennis match.

From the Tide 41, Sloan wormed Alabama back into position for points. When the Tide stalled at the Rebel 31, Davis kicked a 48-yard field goal, the longest kicked in any bowl. Tim now practically owned the Sugar Bowl's kicking section in the record book. He had the most Sugar Bowl field goals by a single player (5, including one in 1962) and the longest field goal (48 yards, breaking his earlier record of 46 yards). He also tied the scoring record (12) and established Alabama as the team with the most field goals in a single bowl game (4).

The devastating Ole Miss offense awoke in the fourth quarter. On the third play of the period,

Dunn rolled out and cut loose to wingback Dave Wells on the Alabama 35. Wells appeared clear, but a spectacular diving tackle by Gary Martin at the 13 prevented a Rebel touchdown. The 42-yard play allowed Mississippi to cross the 50 for the first time. Dunn pushed the Rebs to the 5 where he flipped a touchdown pass to Smith. Irwin kicked the PAT and, almost unbelievably, Ole Miss was in position to win.

Dunn, who was hot now, got an opportunity to move ahead two plays after the kickoff when Sloan fumbled at the Alabama 33 and Bobby Robinson recovered for Ole Miss. Fred Roberts caught a Dunn pass just inside the 10. The Rebels were at the 4 in two plays, then Dunn shot a pass to Allen Brown, who caught the ball just out of the end zone and fell in a snowbank. Dunn attempted a left sweep on

The snow gives Tulane Stadium the look of a real sugar bowl as the Apache Belles entertain.

Rebelettes entertain Sugar Bowl crowd at the Alabama-Ole Miss game.

'Bama boosters frolic in the snow before the 1964 kicking clinic by Tim Davis.

Rebelettes perform in the snowy, sunny South on January 1, 1964.

fourth down, but Martin and Jimmy Dill stopped him at the 2. Bryant would say later, "If I remember right, we (Kentucky) stopped Oklahoma in almost exactly the same spot in the '51 game."

Mississippi wasn't done yet. Buddy French punted to the Tide 40, and immediately Dunn put Rebel fans in a frenzy by hitting Dennis with a 21-yard pass. End Joe Pettey caught another pass in the numbers, 11 yards down and near the sideline. Pettey couldn't hold the ball as he was tackled and Versprille recovered it at the 9. "I just happened to be in the right spot at the right time," he said. "Someone else hit Pettey and jarred the ball loose . . . it was rolling toward the sidelines when I fell on it."

It was difficult to realize that a game with 17 fumbles, 11 by Ole Miss, (all-time bowl records) could be as exciting at the finish. Davis, of course, was the postgame story. He credited the snow with his performance. "I think being off the day before the game was the answer," Tim explained. "I just had more zip in my kicks. I could see it when I was warming up before the game. If the snow hadn't forced us indoors Tuesday, I probably would not have been so strong and accurate."

New Orleans sportswriter Buddy Diliberto and Atlanta reporter Jim Minter somehow got into the Alabama dressing room before the press was to be admitted. The pair watched Bryant quiet his players, then kneel in their midst to offer thanks. Then Bryant let out a war whoop, jumped on a trunk, and began doing a jig while singing "Yea, Alabama" with team and staff.

Diliberto leaned over to Minter and asked, "Do you think the players heard that prayer?" "I don't know whether they did," answered Minter, "but I know God didn't." The two mulled that for a while and wondered.

Bear Bryant offers thanks with his Crimson Tide after the 1964 Sugar Bowl.

136

LSU-Syracuse

FRIDAY, JANUARY 1, 1965

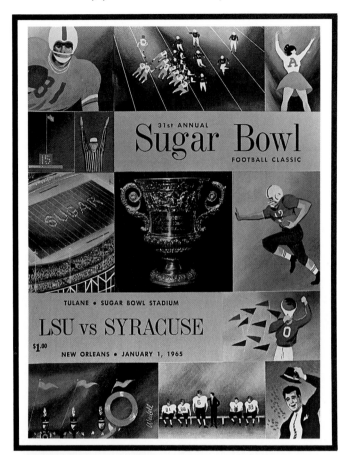

Syracuse Coach Ben
Schwartzwalder
gives instructions to
quarterback Walley Mahle.

"Attractiveness and individual stars."

Seven days after the Alabama-Ole Miss football game, the United States Supreme Court ruled that the Louisiana statute requiring racial segregation of public entertainment and athletic events was unconstitutional. Ernest N. Morial and A.P. Tureaud, who argued the case for Horace Bynum, were the winning attorneys. Both were trailblazers in the civil rights' years and Morial, 14 years later, would become the first black mayor of New Orleans.

That decision removed a barrier that had hindered the Sugar Bowl from being the national game it had been before 1957. There was no reason New Orleans shouldn't pick up the bowl tempo again.

Meanwhile, the Orange Bowl, in one of the most farsighted moves any postseason game ever took, changed its kickoff from early afternoon to prime television time—in the evening. The Rose Bowl, because of the time difference, had always started later than the other three bowls. That, combined with the tie-up between two of the country's most populous areas, had given Pasadena control of the ratings and a much larger TV contract than the others. Miami, no longer bound to the Big Eight, would now also be unopposed. Eventually, the money would be an inducement to help the Orange Bowl get the games it most desired. This was the real start of the television age for the bowls.

Hearts across the nation quickened when it was rumored Notre Dame might break its long-standing bowl ban. Irish Athletic Director Ed "Moose" Krause ended such banter by stating, "We're not going to any bowl game." He couldn't have been more definitive. Alabama, who would finish as the national champion, had no-strings-attached invitations from the Sugar, Cotton, and Orange Bowls. Coach Bear Bryant said he wouldn't consider any of them until after his Georgia Tech game.

It was known, however, that he favored the Cotton Bowl, a game he had not been to since his coaching years at the University of Kentucky. But the Orange Bowl lured Bryant from Dallas to Miami for a titanic confrontation with 5th-ranked Texas. Undefeated Southwest Conference champion Arkansas was scheduled against Nebraska in the Cotton. Both were excellent pairings. The Sugar was left with a solid, if not quite as flashy, hand.

Sam Corenswet, Sr., of the Mid-Winter Sports Association was asked what he looked for in bowl matches. "Attractiveness and individual stars," he said.

That left a great deal of leeway in the 1964 season. *States-Item* columnist Peter Finney and his *Times-Picayune* counterpart Buddy Diliberto felt one team filled both bills for the Sugar Bowl: Syracuse—the East's best team—featured an incredible running tandem in fullback Jim Nance and halfback Floyd Little. The two accounted for 1,779 yards and 25 touchdowns.

The problem was the Orangemen had two defeats and one game to go before the Bowl invitations would be extended. Finney and Diliberto continued to plug for Syracuse. "For one thing," said Diliberto, "we thought it would be a dramatic way to end the segregation thing. Secondly, there was talk beginning then that New Orleans might be in line for a National Football League franchise. If there was any doubt about racial problems in the city, it could have endangered that move."

"The East vs. the South competition," wrote Finney, "as far as I'm concerned has more postseason appeal than the SWC vs. SEC or all-SEC matches we've been getting."

Louisiana State University had an iron defense and an exceptional flanker-kicker. The kicker had tied a national record with 13 field goals during the regular season. LSU was a logical SEC choice since Alabama was going to the Orange Bowl. Seventh-ranked LSU, however, also had a loss and a tie with a game with Florida remaining.

The Sugar took a chance and invited both. Ninth-ranked Syracuse lost its last game to West Virginia. LSU was beaten by Florida, setting up a New Orleans match with the most combined losses since 1945.

"Finney and I were sitting in the press box when the results of the Syracuse-West Virginia game began coming in by quarters," laughed Diliberto. "Man, you should've seen the looks the Sugar Bowl people were giving us. We just kind of ducked our heads and talked to each other. No one else would. But, considering everything, it was still the right choice."

Doug Moreau stretches for a reception as LSU catches Syracuse 13-10 in 1965.

Floyd Little, one of Syracuse's most exciting runners.

Joe Labruzzo (22) of LSU is wrapped up by the Orange defense.

LSU 13-Syracuse 10

Doug Moreau (80) of LSU makes another miracle catch on an unbelieving Syracuse secondary.

"I-26-wide-and-go."

The last time Syracuse played a Southeastern Conference team was in the 1953 Orange Bowl. "Alabama nosed us out that day," Coach Ben Schwartzwalder chuckled, "61-6, a game which set Eastern football back at least 10 years."

He didn't have to worry about such jokes from the Sugar Bowl pairing. It was a game that matched the nation's best rushing offense against the nation's third best defense. More than that, the match of Syracuse and LSU was tailor-made. The main weakness of the Orange was pass defense. LSU entered the Sugar Bowl with two completions and three interceptions in its last 22 pass attempts over two games.

If East vs. SEC was a perfect vehicle for ending the segregation years, it was not a good way to fill the stadium. A crowd of 65,000, the smallest Sugar Bowl audience since 1939, sat in the stands. The teams' records and the smallest school ticket sale (1,300 by Syracuse), more than any political considerations, kept the crowd down.

Floyd Little, Jim Nance, and Walt Mahle, who was moved from quarterback to halfback for this game, steadily probed the Tiger defense for three first downs. Dick King then hit Bradlee Clarke for 12 yards and a first down at the LSU 8. Mahle carried to the 3, but Syracuse was set back with its first crucial mistake. The Orangemen were penalized

140

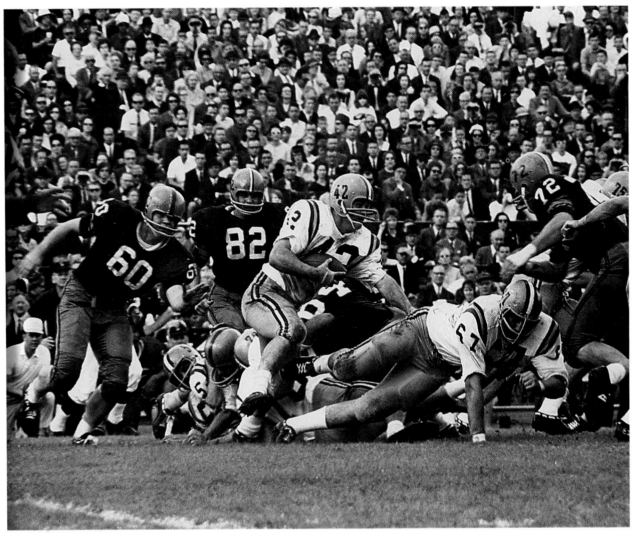

Don Scwab (42) of LSU picks his way through the Syracuse defense.

for holding to the 19. Roger Smith kicked a 23-yard field goal, the first he had made all season and only the second Syracuse had attempted.

LSU was stopped by a 15-yard penalty, and Buster Brown punted to the Orange 42. Charley Brown fumbled, and Richard Granier recovered. LSU again couldn't move and Buster Brown punted to the Orange 3. George Rice bolted into the end zone to wrap up Little on the first play of the series, giving LSU its first points. "That guy must've come out of the ground," said Little. "I think the man responsbile for me thought I was coming to the inside," said Rice. "At least, he was leaning that way . . . so I went outside and had a good shot at him before he could get going."

Dennis Reilly, a 205-pound guard, seemingly put Syracuse out of immediate danger before the first quarter came to an end. The Tigers, again unable to penetrate the Orange defense appreciably, sent Brown in to punt from the LSU 40. Reilly broke through and blocked the kick, which bounced at the 30. Reilly and Clarke took off after the ball. Reilly motioned for Clarke to pick it up and Clarke ran it in from 28 yards out. "LSU's guard and tackle were split wide," said Reilly. "I almost got my hands on the first two Brown kicked. The guard was supposed to block me. So I moved closer to the tackle . . . this meant the guard had to come out too far to do any blocking," Brown explained. "The snap was a

Moreau kicks a 28-yard field goal to beat Syracuse in final minutes.

little high and I had to reach for it. I don't remember even seeing the man until he blocked it."

Smith's conversion made the score 10-2 and the embarrassed Tigers, 5½-point favorites, obviously were in a game that wasn't going to be handed to them.

On its first possession of the second half, after a holding penalty pushed LSU back to its 43, substitute quarterback Billy Ezell stepped into the huddle and called, "I-26-wide-and-go." The play would send flanker Doug Moreau out as a lone receiver. He would run downfield, fake a cut to the sideline, and then head for the end zone. In the first quarter, Moreau had cleanly beaten defensive back Will Hunter by 15 yards on the same play, but Ezell overthrew him. Hunter went for the fake again. Ezell pumped once and lofted the ball to the flanker at the 25. Moreau said of the second-and-16 play, "When I broke straight, there was the ball." The touchdown covered 57 yards.

LSU went for a two-point conversion, the first in Sugar Bowl history, and Ezell shot an arrow a second time, hitting halfback Joe Labruzzo.

Starting from its 22, Syracuse began shaking the rust from its offense, too. Nance and Nathanial Duckett began powdering the defensive line to the Tiger 45. In succession, Duckett gained 5 yards, Nance 3, and Mahle 2 to place the ball at the 34. Little was thrown for a 6-yard loss. Mahle completed a pass to Jim Cripps at the 19 for a first down. Syracuse forced its luck and went to the air again. Tiger White Graves intercepted at the 1.

Midway through the final period, with the out-come looking like the Sugar Bowl's first tie, LSU's Pat Screen was substituted at quarterback. Two plays lost 2 yards at the Tiger 26. Then Screen rolled out and twisted through the Orange secondary for a 23-yard gain. "I saw the goal line and headed for it," said Screen, "but I couldn't get into high gear after getting free. On the previous play, I pitched to (fullback) Gawain DiBetta going left and their end was looking for it. We lost two yards. The next time I went right, faked a pitch, and saw daylight."

Two plays after that, Screen threw to Labruzzo on the Syracuse 19. The Tigers nudged down to the 8. There was 3:48 left in the game when Coach Charlie McClendon called on Moreau for a field goal.

The field goal was good from 28 yards away. "The kick felt good when it left my shoe," said Moreau, "then before I looked up to see, Billy (Ezell, the holder) screamed, 'It's good!'"

Moreau's father, Al, a former LSU world record high hurdler, said, "I told Doug that after doing so well this year on field goals the fans probably would have shot him if he had missed it . . . or maybe I would have."

Nance gained 70 yards and Little gained 40 in a bit of a collapse of the Syracuse offense. LSU Coach Charlie McClendon became the first former Sugar Bowl player ever to come back and coach a team to a victory. It was the city of New Orleans that was the big winner, though. Jim Nance exuded without solicitation, "I'm going to tell everyone about the splendid treatment we received down there."

Missouri-Florida

SATURDAY, JANUARY 1, 1966

Steve Spurrier (11) throws into the teeth of the Missouri defense during an awesome fourth-quarter performance.

"You find another ginmill."

Less than two weeks after Jim Nance endorsed New Orleans, an American Football League All-Star game was moved from the city to Houston because of discrimination charges. This civic embarrassment stemmed from black players being refused cab service and admittance to French Quarter nightclubs.

There was no problem whatsoever with the better establishments. Indeed, the New Orleans hotel, restaurant, and motion picture associations agreed to accommodate all citizens and visitors. Players were welcomed into places like Al Hirt's, where Buffalo end Ernie Warlick was introduced and applauded. It was some less-fashionable spots that were in question, a detail that steamed the ire of Orleanians. The black professionals voted 13-8 to pull out, and AFL Commissioner Joe Foss complied.

New Orleans suffered a huge black eye, one that would affect the next Sugar Bowl, and one that the northern press predictably emphasized. Only Dick Young, the respected sportswriter of the *New York Daily News*, peeked beyond the obvious for eastern readers. Young wrote: "... What I mean is, you don't judge an entire town by some slob cab driver because there are a lot of good cabbies, and you don't say an entire city stinks just because some guys in a lousy ginmill insult you, because there is something about a ginmill that makes it very easy to be insulted, whether you're black or white, and when that happens you either fight your way out of the joint or you find another ginmill . . ."

"There were many fine places in New Orleans willing . . . Some AFL Negroes stayed away from Bourbon Street. They ate in the Blue Room of the Roosevelt Hotel, and in Antoine's, and in other swank, respectable places, and apparently they were well-treated . . ."

The walkout was to play a role in the 1966 bowls, and New Orleans was made to pay further. The rules were changed in the 1966 postseason jousting tournament. Because so many outstanding teams were still in the running, the Associated Press decided to name its national champion after the bowls so the top teams were looking for the match that would best help their chances. Alabama-Nebraska was the match-up for which both of the "open" bowls (Orange and Sugar) were angling. The Cotton Bowl, with No. 2-ranked Arkansas, had the highest-rated team either 'Bama or the Cornhuskers could play in their quests for the national championship. Razorback Coach Frank Broyles, however, wasn't interested in putting his team's long winning streak on the line against either one.

Largely due to the effect of the AFL walkout, Nebraska wasn't coming to New Orleans.

Intrigue characterized the bowl cast after it became apparent Alabama and Nebraska were to play in Miami. Southeastern Conference Commissioner

Bernie Moore became the middle man in providing SEC teams for the Sugar and Cotton Bowls. Missouri, who lost a 16-14 heartbreaker to Nebraska and held only a 5-2-1 record with Oklahoma and Kansas remaining to be played, had moved into the Sugar Bowl picture.

It appeared that Kentucky would host the Sugar Bowl, and Florida was headed for the Cotton. But Kentucky had beaten Missouri and agreed to accept a Cotton Bowl bid if it defeated Houston. (It did not.) Florida, meanwhile, agreed to take the Sugar Bowl bid if it beat Tulane (which the Gators did).

LSU, with a 7-3 record, eventually filled the spot for the desperate Cotton Bowl. And Florida later lost to Miami, also falling to an unexciting 7-3 record. Florida under Graves, who had played for Tennessee in Boston College's monumental 1941 upset, had a spectacular passing combination in quarterback Steve Spurrier and receiver Charlie Casey. Missouri, with a horde of pro prospects, was a more conservative but very steady team offensively and defensively. But in some ways the 1966 Sugar Bowl was the low point of the Mid-Winter Sports Association.

Missouri 20-Florida 18

"Yep, it was pretty impressive all right."

Conquering Florida's offense and defense must have looked relatively simple to Coach Dan Devine on the blackboard. The Tigers used a wide tackle six, or eight-man line, in an effort to put more pressure on quarterback Steve Spurrier. Should the Gators withstand the Missouri rush, the task would fall to secondary Coach Clay Cooper's unit, which was formidable with safety Johnny Roland slicing up the passing lanes.

The Tigers felt that eventually the Gator line would give under the hammering Missouri offensive assault. "It couldn't have worked better," reflected Spurrier. "For a while, I couldn't breathe out there."

Gary Lane moved the Tigers 71 yards with the opening kickoff, but the Gators finally stopped Missouri at the 9 by limiting Reese and Charlie Brown to 1 yard in two attempts. The 17-play drive used 8 minutes and 45 seconds of playing time. Spurrier completed a 9-yard pass to Jack Harper, but after two plays lost 3 yards, the Gators had to punt. That was Florida's offense for the first quarter.

Lane, a methodical craftsman, took over at the Missouri 41 and immediately started another Tiger drive. Brown, a 5-foot-8, 185-pound halfback who looked more like a professor than a student, made a diving catch of a pass at the Florida 45. Then from the 33, Lane picked his way on the option to the 20. After three consecutive plays, the Tiger quarterback gained a first down at the 9 as the first quarter ended.

Brown lost a yard, then swept left, got a block from Butch Allison, split a pair of defenders, and dove into the end zone just inside the flag. Bill Bates kicked the extra point, and it appeared Devine was writing a textbook on the game.

Missouri took definite command after a punt ex-change. Harper lost a Tiger kick in the sun and Ray Thorpe recovered it on the Florida 11 for Missouri. Devine rushed in Roland who executed a perfect halfback pass to Earl Denny who was open at the goal.

"It wasn't an unusual play," said Cooper. "Roland had been an offensive back until that year, and we had used the play during the regular season. We just caught 'em asleep, I guess."

Lane then directed Missouri unerringly to more points. A 15-yard burst by Brown put the ball on the 25; but after three plays netted 5 yards, Bates kicked a 37-yard field goal.

That was how the half ended, but even with a 17-0 lead Devine sensed his team may have been weakening, both from following the game plan so well and from the 78-degree heat.

Florida was changing things at halftime. The offense was modified by placing a halfback wide as a receiver. Spurrier was ordered to roll away from the pressure and to look for targets in the flat. At first it didn't work.

"I hit one of our lineman and it kind of knocked me off stride," said Barry Brown, who was brought down near the goal. ". . . maybe I would have gone all the way. I'll never know now."

Missouri inched inside the 10, but a holding penalty placed the Tigers back at the 18. Bates came in later and kicked a 34-yard field goal.

"We figured," said Spurrier, "we could only score three times in the last quarter. What we had to do was keep Missouri from getting a touchdown. But they might have gotten close enough for a field goal, which would have given them 23 points. So, to win, we would have needed 24 points."

Scrambling away from the Tiger points of pres-

Missouri's Earl Denny (45) swoops down on the Gators.

sure, Spurrier completed passes for 17 yards and 4 yards to tight end Brown. Then he went to Harper for 19 and 16 yards, and Dick Trapp ran over the middle for 9 more, putting the ball at the Tiger 22. Harper worked his way behind the secondary, just inbounds of the end zone, and Spurrier laid the pass into his cradled arms. Six passes, six points—Coach Graves sent in instructions to go for two points on the conversion, but the pass was off target.

Florida kicked off, and on the second play, Denny took a pitchout from Lane and was rattled by Steve Heidt's tackle. The ball fell loose and George Grandy recovered for Florida at the 10. "That looked like manna from heaven," remembered Spurrier. Alan Poe caught a pass over the middle for 7 yards, Harper ran for another yard, and Spurrier snuck in for the touchdown. Florida lined up with its kicking unit, but the ball went to Harper in an effort to catch Missouri unguarded. Harper threw a halfback pass into the end zone, but it was incomplete. The simple extra point would have put the Gators only seven points back. "Looking back on it," reflected Spurrier, "I wish we had done something different."

The Tigers took the kickoff, made one first down, and had to punt. Spurrier ran for 7 yards from the Florida 19, hit Brown for 18 yards and then Poe for 10. Poe grabbed another for 10 yards, and Brown had 4- and 9-yard grabs to put the ball at the 21. Under tremendous rush, Spurrier threw the ball in

the ground twice. On third down, Spurrier saw Casey in the end zone and tried to float a pass to the receiver. Gary Grossnickle came up and covered Casey perfectly, deflecting the ball. But Charlie Casey, in an awesome second effort, dove headlong into the end zone and caught the ball just off the ground. For the third consecutive two-point attempt, a pass (this time Spurrier's) went astray. Florida, given up for dead at the start of the fourth quarter, trailed 20-18 with 2:08 remaining.

Florida didn't get the ball back until there were 50 seconds left, and that was at its 3. The game ended with Florida 68 yards from the Missouri end zone.

Spurrier and his teammates were as valiant in defeat as any team ever was. In the fourth quarter the junior quarterback swept his team to three touchdowns in barely 11 minutes of play. He completed 16 of 23 passes for 198 yards and two touchdowns, and scored another himself within that 15-minute frame. To put it in perspective, the Sugar Bowl pass completion record for an entire game had been 17, set by Davey O'Brien in 1939.

"Yep, it was pretty impressive all right, said Clay Cooper. "They were a real good team, and we knew that sooner or later they would hit a couple on us. They hit more than a couple, but you noticed who won the game? . . . Missouri."

Alabama-Nebraska

MONDAY, JANUARY 2, 1967

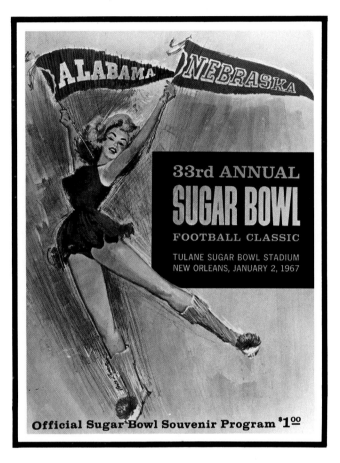

Paul 'Bear' Bryant, the Sugar Bowl's winningest coach and its patron.

"This is the only time I feel like a success."

As an artistic endeavor, the 1966 Sugar Bowl was a smashing success. But by other measures it served only to show how far behind the other major bowls the Sugar had fallen. It attracted 67,421 fans, only a couple of thousand more than the dismal attendance of the 1965 game. And with the Associated Press balloting coming after the bowls, the Sugar Bowl was the only New Year's Day game that had no direct bearing on the national championship. LSU defeated No. 2 Arkansas in the Cotton, UCLA upset No. 1 Michigan State in the Rose, leaving Alabama to outslug Nebraska 38-28 in the Orange and take its long-shot national crown. The almost unbelievable domino effect made for excellent reading the following week in *Sports Illustrated*, the foremost sports magazine in the country. No one would read about Missouri-Florida, though. It wasn't covered.

The Sugar Bowl appeared to be on a merry-go-round it couldn't control. As good as its luck was in earlier days, the reverse seemed to be true in the mid 1960s. LSU-Syracuse was a good match for the 1965 game—until both lost their last games. Florida-Missouri was blemished by a late Gator loss.

States-Item columnist Peter Finney correctly wrote, "Check these Sugar figures (national rankings) for the last 10 games and you'll probably come to the same conclusion I did. You can't beat national ratings or a match between Southern teams when it comes to putting people in the ball park."

Among other problems the Sugar Bowl now confronted was the growing feeling that its membership was too restrictive. When no one else stepped forward in 1934 to help launch the project, the Mid-Winter Sports Association limited the organization to the founders, their offspring, close relatives, and special, sponsored individuals. Thirty-three years later, the founders were getting old and many of their sons simply weren't as interested—or as capable—as the fathers. The image of the Sugar Bowl had become one of a snobbish exclusive fraternity, which didn't matter much as long as its product remained one of quality. But it was plain the product had slipped.

The Sugar Bowl's Executive Committee began mulling over possible candidates to join the Association. They wanted people who were hardworking and upstanding, had made a positive mark on the community, and had the ability to get things done.

New associate members selected were John U. Barr, Aruns Callery, Henry Zac Carter, William J. Childress, Harry M. England, Robert J. Fabacher, Charles G. Glueck, Richard L. Hindermann, and Richard H. Nelson.

In other business the Sugar finally saw the wisdom in an Orange Bowl move—a local television blackout should the attraction not sell out.

Nineteen sixty-six was a wondrous year for college football. Three exceptional teams dominated the sports pages: Notre Dame, Michigan State, and Alabama. All had legitimate claims to the national championship, but the Irish were proclaimed No. 1 even after a 10-10 tie with the Spartans. Undefeated, untied Alabama was insulted, and Coach Paul Bryant maintained for years afterward that this was the best team he'd ever coached.

Notre Dame did not compete in bowl games, and Michigan State could not go to the Rose Bowl because of the no-repeat rule, leaving Alabama the highest-ranked team in postseason competition.

Bryant and Bob Devaney, coach of the 4th-ranked, undefeated Nebraska Cornhuskers, had decided to try to play each other in an "open" bowl. This would be the Sugar, because Alabama had played in Miami two consecutive years and Bryant liked to have his teams enjoy all the postseason sites. Both coaches also knew a victory over the other would give either of them a slight chance to win the MacArthur Bowl, the National Football Foundation's version of the national championship.

Alabama and Nebraska signed for the Sugar Bowl; then the Cornhuskers, in what was becoming a Sugar Bowl tradition, lost its last game to Oklahoma. Alabama upheld its end, coming in unblemished in a 10-game schedule and providing a rare glimpse of the soul of the man who would rule the Southeastern Conference with a crimson-colored fist. "This is the only time I feel like a success," Bear Bryant said of the undefeated season.

Devaney's team was formidable, built along the lines of the other Midwest giants, Notre Dame and Michigan State. It was very big but also slow. Alabama, which would be outweighed by 35 pounds a man, was a remarkable team—one known for its defense but which featured notables like quarterback Ken Stabler and receivers Ray Perkins and Dennis Homan.

Perkins, however, had pulled a hamstring and wasn't expected to play. "Nothing was going to keep me out," said Perkins. "That game meant everything to us. We felt we had to win, and win convincingly. Coach Bryant felt sure we'd win the MacArthur Bowl with a big win. I even told Stabler I was going to beat him out of the MVP trophy."

Devaney didn't count on playing Alabama without Perkins either. He said he wouldn't be surprised if Stabler didn't throw to Perkins on the first play of the game. Then Devaney, noting 'Bama's eight-point favoritism and the huge weight advantage his team enjoyed, said he was going to pray for rain.

Alabama 34-Nebraska 7

Quarterback Ken Stabler (12) fires into the heart of the Cornhusker secondary.

"They even knew our hometowns!"

Bob Devaney, outstanding coach that he was, batted a thousand in prayers and predictions. Rain swept the city for two days before the game. A steady, light shower finally stopped an hour and a half before the kickoff, but the field remained in good condition—with the exception of one spot at the 10-yard line on the north side.

As Devaney had predicted, on the game's first play from scrimmage, at the Alabama 28, Ken Stabler faked fullback Les Kelley into the line, stepped back, and lofted a pass to Ray Perkins at the 49. Perkins made the catch and slithered down to the Nebraska 27 for a 45-yard gain. "We intended to give them a set we would use the first time we got the ball," said Coach Bear Bryant. "We wanted to throw long to Perkins and see what defense they were in. If Ray was covered, Kenny Stabler was to overthrow him. Perkins got behind his man, though, and that really gave us a big lift."

Perkins, who in 1983 succeeded Bryant as the Alabama coach, said the completion didn't surprise

Alabama at all. "We felt it would work because we were pretty certain our receivers could get open on their defensive backs. They were kind of slow."

Seven plays afterward, Kelley scored from the 1. That, for all practical purposes, ended the game. The Cornhuskers couldn't move on their first possession and punted; then Stabler led the relentless Crimson Tide downfield again. The 71-yard drive was highlighted by a 42-yard completion to Perkins at the Nebraska 20. Stabler took the ball in on a run around left end from the 14 as the 'Huskers appeared to be grabbing at ghosts. Steve Davis' PAT made the score 14-0 with 7:28 remaining in the first quarter.

The weight advantage which Devaney expected to be one of his chief allies wasn't working out. "We couldn't do the things against them we did against other teams," Davaney offered.

Harry Wilson fumbled at the 'Husker 39 and Charlie Harris recovered for the Tide. Stabler, seemingly trapped, somehow slipped through a Nebraska

Ray Perkins (88) breaks free against Nebraska.

rush and, aided by a block from David Chatwood, ran to the 12. Three plays lost 1 yard and Davis (brother of Tim Davis, the kicking machine of the 1964 Sugar Bowl) came on to boot a 30-yard field goal with 28 seconds left in the opening period. Bryant used 35 players in digging Nebraska's football grave in that 15-minute whirl of offense. Surprisingly, Alabama wasn't just using its speed to the flanks or for its passing game. Alabama was also butting heads successfully with the Nebraska middle, which few thought they could.

"Our game plan was to go wide," said Stabler, "but we discovered we could run up the middle and I think we got most of our rushing yardage doing that." Tackle Cecil Dowdy said, "They were reading our backs on the option 28 play. They were taking the fakes real well and we started running off the cross buck in our line play."

Quarterback Wayne Trimble came in for Stabler in the second quarter, and immediately picked up where Ken left off. Trimble completed a 9-yard pass

to Dennis Homan. Then halfback Ed Morgan gained 13 yards to place the ball at the Nebraska 49. In deep trouble on the following play and severely harassed by three defenders, Trimble managed to get off a pass to John Reitz. Reitz slipped away from a tackler and broke to the 'Husker 18. Alabama inched it in from there as Trimble, six plays later, slid to left end, stiff-armed a charging Cornhusker, and went into the end zone standing.

Only the score was in question by this time. Bryant, using 43 players, had his team gobbling up real estate at a 295-yard to 112-yard advantage for the first 30 minutes. "Well, we were pretty confident at the half," admitted Perkins, "but we felt we had to win convincingly."

Davis kicked a 40-yard field goal in the third quarter, though late in that period Bob Churchich started hitting effectively. A series of shots carried Nebraska to the Tide 15, and Nebraska finally got on the boards with a touchdown throw to Dick Davis seconds into the fourth quarter. The game's

The Bear has a few choice instructions from the bench.

Kenny Stabler takes a breather.

last points came when Stabler, shaking off defenders at the Alabama 45, threw to Perkins at the Nebraska 30. Perkins broke the grip of one tackler, eased past another, then outran two more.

"I was afraid Nebraska might control the ball and just wear us out," said Bryant afterward, "particularly on the slippery field. I just didn't know my own kids well enough." A Nebraska player paid tribute to the Tide coaches for preparation. "They even knew our hometowns!" he exclaimed.

The victory extended a remarkable record. It was Alabama's 23rd consecutive game without a holding penalty called on it. But the 34-7 blowout also made the results of the MacArthur Bowl presentation even more disappointing. Notre Dame won that, too.

"The hardest part about that whole season," said Perkins, "is that we were never recognized. They gave us the national championship the year before, and we probably didn't deserve it with a loss and a tie. But in 1966, with an 11-0 record and beating a good team soundly in a bowl game, I think we did deserve some recognition. It was disappointing."

Devaney also was disappointed, although he immediately knew where his mistake was made. "Sure, I prayed for rain. But that was a mistake," he admitted. "I should've prayed for a driving rain!"

LSU-Wyoming

MONDAY, JANUARY 1, 1968

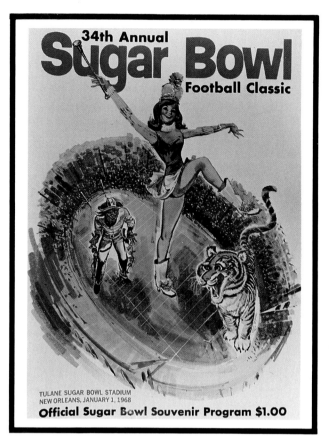

"It's the biggest thing since statehood."

The Sugar Bowl, still basking in the glory of 1967's outstanding bowl game, felt it could get one of football's storied names into the 1968 classic. Army, 5-1 at the time, had indicated an interest in breaking its bowl ban in either the Sugar or the Gator Bowl. New Orleans would have loved it, even taking into account that Army was more of a curiosity piece than a proven commodity. Army hadn't beaten a single winning team and lost 10-7 to five times beaten Duke.

If West Point had any such notion, it disappeared as soon as the story came out in the open. Secretary of the Army Stanley Resor stated officially, "It is concluded that accepting any invitation to play in a postseason game would tend to emphasize football to an extent not consistent with the basic mission of the academy, which is to produce career Army officers."

The host spot would also be hard to fill because Tennessee, the Southeastern Conference champion, let it be known early that its first preference was Miami, and Bear Bryant was guiding his 8-1-1 Alabama team to Dallas for the first time since 1954.

Circumstances painted the Sugar into what was becoming its usual wait-and-see position. On the second-to-last weekend of the regular season, it was decided that 1) If Ole Miss beat Tennessee, the Rebels would be invited; 2) If Ole Miss lost and Auburn beat Georgia, Auburn would be invited; 3) If both Ole Miss and Auburn lost and North Carolina State beat Clemson, North Carolina State would receive the invitation; 4) If all three lost, Penn State would be considered the visitor; 5) In case Ole Miss lost, an alternate possibility was LSU, then a precarious 4-3-1 but impressive enough in its final two games to merit a bid. Wyoming, then 9-0-0 and 7th-ranked, but like Army somewhat of a curiosity, couldn't be counted out of the visitor's corner because of its impressive record. However, the Western Athletic Conference was an unknown quantity, and the Sugar Bowl had not scouted the Cowboys. The results rolled in: Tennessee 20, Ole Miss 7; Georgia 17, Auburn 0; Clemson 14, N.C. State 6.

Penn State defeated Ohio University 35-14 to save what appeared to be a snakebitten Sugar Saturday. That night LSU waxed Mississippi State 55-0, and Wyoming completed a perfect season with a 21-19 edging of Texas Western. The Sugar jumped at an LSU-Penn State match, but the Nittany Lions wanted to hold off any firm decision until after their game with Pittsburgh the following week. Sight unseen and reminiscent of the early days, the Cowboys were contacted and asked if they'd be interested. Wyoming most certainly was.

The Cowboys led the nation in rushing defense (42.3 yards) and total defense (185.2 yards) and was 10th in passing offense (207.7 yards). It had not lost in 14 consecutive games and was unbeaten in one Gator and three Sun Bowl appearances. According to one fan, the reaction to the Sugar Bowl invitation by Wyoming's 330,000 inhabitants was, "It's the biggest thing since statehood."

LSU, an old bowl hand, took things as a matter of course. Despite its 5-3-1 record and unranked standing, LSU was an excellent football team and one that stood only 10 points away from a perfect season. Each of its losses and the tie could be traced to its placekicking game. "I've never seen more losses in one season stemming from the place-kick," said Tiger Coach Charlie McClendon. "If we would have made all our placekicks, we'd be on top."

With only arch-rival Tulane left to play, LSU looked like a shoo-in for a 6-3-1 record. At the half the Tigers were ahead 28-0. In the second half Tulane picked up the fight and cut the difference to 34-27 in the fourth quarter. With Tulane driving for a possible tying or winning touchdown, an ill-looking Sugar Bowl President Sam Corenswet, Jr., forced himself to his feet and told *States-Item* columnist Peter Finney he was going to search for a place to jump out of the stadium. "Try the press box window," advised Finney. "That's high enough so that if they go for two and miss you'll have enough time to pull the rip-cord."

Fortunately for Corenswet, matters didn't come to that. LSU won, 41-27.

LSU 20-Wyoming 13

"I don't know if I can run that fast again."

It was unfortunate for Lloyd Eaton, but the 34th Sugar Bowl lasted only the regulation 60 minutes. The Wyoming coach said he would have given half a year's salary to have stretched the game to 60 minutes and 10 seconds. But he sensed early what kind of day it would be for his 6th-ranked Cowboys.

New Year's Eve had again been cold, damp, and rainy. The Sugar Bowl field on New Year's Day was cold, damp, and soggy under a drizzle. "The dadgum tarpaulin had been taken up at 9 A.M.," recalled Eaton. "That was the time, by its agreement with the Sugar Bowl, it normally should have been lifted. If it could have been left alone for three or four more hours, I would have paid them myself."

"I believe the weather could be an important factor," Eaton said New Year's Eve. "The team with the best runners and pass receivers, and the heaviest linemen, would have the advantage on a wet field." Everyone agreed that on all counts those conditions favored LSU. "We were limited in that we had a sparse club," said Eaton, whose 47-man team was a 6-point underdog. "Charlie McClendon would use 55-60 players routinely. We just didn't have that kind of depth, and I knew by the fourth quarter our boys would be leg-weary."

Obviously, the best thing Eaton could hope for was to be far enough ahead after three quarters to withstand a fourth-period assault.

Quarterback Paul Toscano put Wyoming in good position on the Cowboys' first possession. Interspersing runs at the Tiger middle by Tom Williams and Jim Kiick and passes to Gene Huey and Hub Lindsey, Wyoming pushed from its 45 to the LSU 21. There, on fourth-and-four, kicker Jerry DePoyster attempted a 37-yard field goal. Tiger safety Sammy Grezaffi sliced through and blocked the kick. "He came left of center," said DePoyster. "I don't know whether he came through a hole or just jumped over his man."

LSU, which hadn't played particularly well in any of its previous seven Sugar Bowl appearances, showed early signs of that again. The Tigers recovered the blocked field goal at the Wyoming 46 but could gain only 2 yards. Mitch Worley punted out-of-bounds at the Cowboy 11.

A 31-yard pass from Toscano to tight end George Anderson placed the Cowboys on the LSU 47. Then Kiick wheeled through left tackle for another 13. Wyoming dug out another first down in three plays; then Toscano swept left and cut upfield through the

The chase is on after LSU's Sammy Grezaffi blocks Wyoming's Jerry DePoyster's field goal attempt.

Jim Kiick (21) evades Johnny Garlington (89) behind a block.

Nelson Stokley flings a pass over Wyoming's Jack Bowen to Tommy Morel for a touchdown.

Tiger defense for 19 yards to the 1. Kiick, on second-and-one, took the handoff, slipped behind the line, and scored on the first play of the second quarter. DePoyster kicked the PAT.

Toscano persistently probed and found soft spots with a consistently mixed offense before completing a 15-yard pass to Anderson at the LSU 13. The Cowboys went to the 6, but a pass for Lindsey into the end zone on third down was broken up by Gerry Kent. DePoyster kicked a 24-yard field goal with 2:58 remaining in the half.

LSU couldn't move and punted to midfield with a minute and a half to go. Wyoming maneuvered itself into DePoyster's range—which seemed limitless—and he kicked a Sugar Bowl record 49-yard field goal with one second left.

Eaton's troops not only had a 13-0 lead but had 11 first downs to LSU's 1. They had outrushed the Tigers 130 to 33 and had outgained LSU passing 85 to 5. Everything looked fine for the Cowboys except for the loss of tackle Larry Nels, who injured an ankle and couldn't return. "I didn't think the 13-0 lead would hold up," said Eaton, "but we were in

pretty good shape at that point." "We were very worried by the half," explained Tiger center Barry Wilson. "Despite what the coaches told us, I think we underestimated Wyoming." Wilson added, "We had not played on slippery footing once during the season. The field turned up a little sloppy, and it upset our plans to block Wyoming low. Because we weren't able to get solid footing, they merely pushed us off and got to the ballcarrier. They were also able to put a lot of pressure on (quarterback) Nelson (Stokley). At halftime, we decided to hit 'em higher, and we decided to take advantage of their pursuit by starting to the outside and then running back against the grain."

Wyoming then started a drive which ended when DePoyster barely missed a 46-yard field goal attempt.

Finally, LSU seized the momentum. Tommy "Trigger" Allen gained 3 yards and Stokley overthrew Tommy Morel before third-team tailback Glenn Smith flew out of the backfield, grabbed a pass over his shoulder down the middle, and sloshed for a 39-yard gain. A 14-yard pass to Jim West and an 11-yard keeper by Stokley to the 1 were the highlights of the ensuing eight plays as LSU covered the remaining distance to get back in it. Smith went in from the 1, and Roy Hurd's PAT cut the score to 13-7.

Grezaffi returned DePoyster's next kick 13 yards to the LSU 48, and the suddenly smokin' Stokley alternated hitting medium passes, running the option, and handing off to Smith as LSU swooshed downfield. "It's a draw-action pitch off the sprint-out pass," Tiger assistant Charlie Pevey said of the play that suddenly had Wyoming on its heels. "Usually the play is to the outside, but Smith had the option of picking his hole and slicing in against the grain behind cross blocking," said the coach. "In other words, cut back against their pursuit and run to daylight," added Wilson. "Glenn was great at doing that, too." Smith gained 17 yards, Stokley 14 yards, and Morel caught two passes totalling 19 yards in a 52-yard drive. Morel outjumped two defenders for the 8-yard touchdown pass. Hurd missed the PAT, leaving the score tied at 13 with 11:39 to go.

Vic Washington returned the kickoff 29 yards to the Wyoming 32. In two plays the Cowboys picked up 9 yards, but on third-and-one Toscano fooled the defense by falling into the pocket and searching for his best receiver, Huey. The split end was open briefly, but the pass was short.

With 5:53 to go and under heavy pressure, Toscano got away a shaky pass to Lindsey, but Benny Griffin intercepted on the LSU 45 and returned it to the Wyoming 31. Smith barrelled through the Cowboy middle for 16, then 1 more. On the third play of the drive, Stokley rolled out, spotted a wide-open Morel at the 1, and threw for LSU's go-ahead points. "The defender (Washington) must have

Stokley (14) finally lights LSU's fire against Wyoming.

LSU tailback Glenn Smith (26) breaks away from the Cowboy defense in key play of Tiger comeback.

thought I was going to go to the middle again," said Morel, "so I faked that way and when he went flying by, I cut to the side. All I had to do was step into the end zone."

Hurd's PAT put LSU ahead 20-13 with 4:18 remaining. But the remaining minutes would be wild.

Wyoming moved, somewhat cautiously but steadily, from its 14 to the Tiger 46 before Johnny Garlington sacked Toscano, then recovered his fumble 11 yards behind the line. There was 1:37 remaining, but the Tigers could run only 58 seconds off before Wyoming got its last shot, taking possession at its 18. A pass to Kiick gained 10 yards. Toscano dropped and threw to a more than adequately covered Anderson. One of the three Tigers converging on the ball reached up and tipped it—right into the tight end's hands. Anderson was suddenly racing, alone, for points. Cornerback Barton Frye somehow was able to catch up and bring Anderson down—54 yards from the line of scrimmage at the LSU 18. "When I saw Anderson take off with the football," said Frye, "I started running for my life. I don't know if I can run that fast again."

Toscano, with no time-outs left, lined his team up without a huddle and threw a pass out-of-bounds.

The play drew an illegal procedure penalty, costing five yards but saving one second on the clock. Huey cut across the secondary from left to right on the game's final snap. Toscano went to him at the 5 where Huey made the grab but was immediately stopped by Kent.

"LSU was in a prevent defense," the receiver said. "I never really saw daylight—they were all coming up when I caught the pass." "I would have given half a year's salary for 10 more seconds," said Eaton, "just 10 more seconds."

Depth, the very factor Eaton most feared, was the difference. Smith, with little more than a quarter's playing time, finished with 74 yards rushing and caught one pass for 39 yards to be named the game's MVP. "There were just more than we could keep track of," Eaton said of the Tiger reserves. "I conceded all along that depth could be a big factor, and the game bore me out."

Smith, a sophomore from New Orleans, had a different perspective on the biggest Sugar Bowl comeback since Tulane fell behind Temple 14-0 in 1935. "If Wyoming had beaten us," Smith said, "I wouldn't have been able to go home."

Arkansas-Georgia

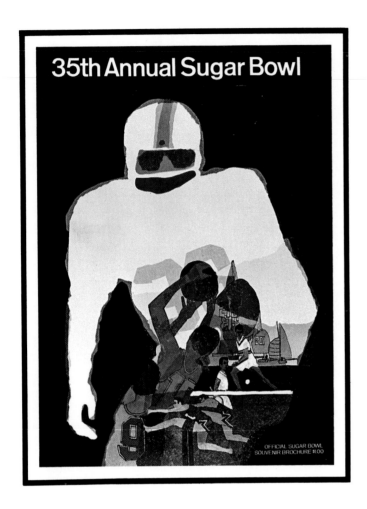

35th Annual Sugar Bowl

OFFICIAL SUGAR BOWL
SOUVENIR BROCHURE $1.00

"Someday I will!"

North Carolina lost a heartbreaker to Georgia in the 1947 Sugar Bowl. It's doubtful, though, that the game meant any more to the participants than to 14-year-old Vince Dooley from Mobile, Alabama. A neighborhood friend and his father asked him to accompany them to the game. Young Dooley received his year's allowance, one dollar, from his father and was permitted to go. "I thought I could buy a ticket," Dooley recalled, "but when we got there, all I could see was people holding tickets up and offering two for $100. It was harder to get in than now."

The boy sat on a curb outside the stadium and listened to the crowd cheer the exploits of Charley

A pair of young lions: Coach Vince Dooley of Georgia and Frank Broyles of Arkansas pose before 1969 Sugar.

Trippi and Charley Justice for a heartbreaking half. Eventually he made his way downtown and into a bar. "No one questioned my age," said Dooley, "in fact, I don't think anyone even noticed me. Everyone was involved with the game. . . . I recall a TV in the place, but I know that was before television so I guess it was a radio everyone was huddled around.

"That was my first Sugar Bowl, but I remember while I was sitting outside the stadium a policeman asked me what was the matter. I told him 'I didn't get in. But someday I will!' "

Twenty-two years later Vince Dooley did return, as head coach of Georgia's unbeaten Bulldogs. It took some doing to get Georgia in the 1969 Sugar. Early indications were that the Orange Bowl gambled and packaged a Penn State-Kansas game, which was a fine pairing. After the Jayhawks lost to Oklahoma, though, it lost some of its appeal. On the surface, Georgia was still the pick of both the Orange and Sugar. The Bulldogs, leaders in total offense and defense for the SEC, were atop the standings with an undefeated but twice-tied record.

The Sugar Bowl was not an object of Georgia affection. Bulldog officials and fans felt Georgia, not LSU, should have been asked to the 1968 game. But while the Orange Bowl said it wanted to await the outcome of the Georgia-Auburn game, the Sugar Bowl offered Georgia a no-strings-attached invitation which was accepted.

Missouri was the first choice for the visitor's berth, but a loss to Oklahoma forced the Sugar to look at the Southwest Conference. Texas and Arkansas were tied for the conference lead. An expected Longhorn victory over Texas A&M and a Razorback win over Texas Tech would put Texas in the Cotton Bowl and send Arkansas to New Orleans. The reverse would put Texas in the Crescent City. However, it worked out as planned.

The 8th-ranked Hogs had given up a very noticeable 187 points during their 9-1 season. Dooley immediately explained Arkansas' success, "Overall, I believe the Arkansas defense recovered 22 fumbles and made 20-odd interceptions. To put it simply, they did an exceptionally good job of getting the football for their offense."

Coach Frank Broyles relished the role his seven-point underdog Hogs took against the 4th-ranked Bulldogs. "You know, it's not cricket for an underdog to talk about the favorite," he grinned. "They are favored, and a year older and stronger across the board." Broyles' 80-year-old mother was going to be at the game, and even she knew not to believe everything a coach says before a game. "She hasn't missed one of our bowl games," laughed Broyles. "I remember in 1945, when we (Georgia Tech) played Tulsa in the Orange Bowl, my father couldn't make the game so mother put an ad in the paper saying, 'I'm Frank Broyles mother. I need a ride to the Orange Bowl.'" Needless to say, she got it.

Georgia's SEC-leading statistics in total offense (391.7 yards), total defense (235 yards), scoring offense (28.2 yards), and nation-leading scoring defense (9.8 yards) brought reminiscences from Broyles.

"I'd like to thank the Sugar Bowl for being so nice to us," said Broyles. "This is our third trip here. Our first two opponents were Southeastern Conference champions (Alabama in 1962, Ole Miss in 1963) and both led the nation in scoring defense. This year we're playing Georgia, another SEC champion, and they had the best defensive average this year. Why pick on us?"

Arkansas 16-Georgia 2

"I couldn't believe I was past him."

Arkansas' Bill Burnett skips past Georgia defender.

No one had to tell the Razorbacks their defense was suspect. Coach Frank Broyles had been saying it since the start of the 1968 season. A quick-on-the-draw offense, featuring linchpins quarterback Bill Montgomery and receiver Chuck Dicus, propped Arkansas' 9-1 year. The Hog defense earned its keep, as Vince Dooley had observed, by being adept at forcing turnovers.

For Arkansas to be able to stay with the formidable Georgia units, Broyles felt he had to find something to exploit in the Bulldog defense. And the Arkansas defenders would have to play a game that would ensure a couple of turnovers. After viewing Georgia films, Broyles decided to try to use one of the Bulldog strengths against them. "Jake Scott was just a great safety," explained Dicus, who was then a 171-pound sophomore. Scott normally covered the tight end in Georgia's three-deep, man-to-man secondary.

"We had noticed that when a team went to a slot

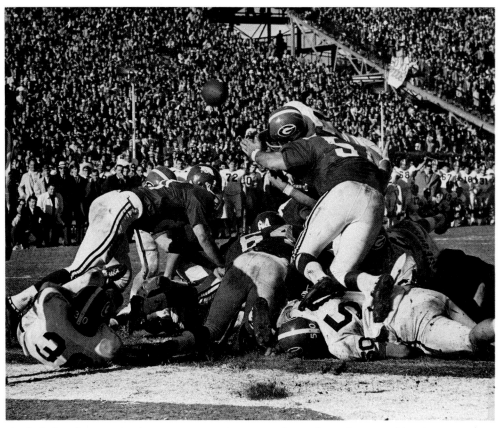

The ball flies from Brad Johnson's grasp and Vince Dooley realizes things couldn't have been nearly as bad in 1947 as in 1969.

formation, where the split end, flanker, and tight end were all lined up on the same side," Dicus added, "that Scott would cover the slot man." Montgomery said, "The idea was to get Scott one-on-one with Dicus." Broyles ordered his defensive backs to delay the Georgia receivers and installed a blitz defense. The idea was to pressure quarterback Mike Cavan into hurrying his plays, perhaps forcing turnovers, and preventing the receivers from getting deep before the pressure could be applied.

A game plan has seldom worked as successfully as this one did in the first quarter on that bright, sunny afternoon. Georgia had six possessions in the period but lost the ball four times (three fumbles and an interception). Montgomery was faring little better, though, throwing seven incompletions and one interception as well as being sacked once, before his first bull's-eye, a one yarder. The first pass to Dicus was nearly intercepted. The second one, on the next play, was.

Worse, one of the Georgia turnovers, a fumble at the Bulldog 38, netted only 14 yards and Bob White missed a 41-yard field goal. The quarter ended scoreless. Arkansas took over at its 35 in the last minutes of the period. Bill Burnett, Bruce Maxwell, and

Montgomery moved to the 49 as the first phase of Broyles' offensive blueprint fell into place. Dicus caught his first pass, a 12-yarder. Max Peacock made a 3-yard catch and Dicus caught another for 9 yards. On the first play of the second quarter Dicus faked a down-and-out, then blew downfield on a post pattern and made an arms-extended, fingertip grab of a pass at the goal line for a 27-yard touchdown.

"I had been running the down-and-out with some success," said Dicus. "I think Scott had gotten to where he was anticipating it, so we changed to the post. I couldn't believe I was past him," said Dicus of Scott.

The teams swapped possessions and a clipping penalty put Arkansas back at its 6. Tailback Burnett, on the first play, started to sweep out to his left, but end David McKnight flashed through and dropped the runner in the end zone for a safety.

Although the Razorback free kick went only to the Arkansas 44, Georgia couldn't capitalize any further. Hog hearts stopped momentarily when tackle Bill Stanfill tattered the offensive line and sent Montgomery spinning to the ground. Bob Stankovich recovered Montgomery's fumble, and Montgomery had to go to the bench for a checkup. The quarterback would need a nerve shot at the half and, late in the game, the injury would bother him.

Reserve Georgia quarterback Donnie Hampton moved the Bulldog offense from the Arkansas 47 to the 29 in a bid for the lead. On fourth-and-two at that point, perhaps the most crucial single offensive play of the afternoon for Georgia, Kent Lawrence fumbled a pitchout from Hampton for an 8-yard loss.

Montgomery returned to the game in spectacular fashion, directing a drive featuring completions of 35, 12, and 9 yards to Dicus. During that push, Montgomery tied Glenn Dobbs' 26-year-old Sugar Bowl record of nine consecutive completions. Arkansas reached the 17 and ended with a 34-yard field goal by White to make the score 10-2 with 1:59 left until the half. Then Cavan led a Bulldog raid to the Hog 26, but Jim McCullough's 36-yard field goal attempt was short.

Georgia no sooner came out for the second half than it found itself in threatening position again. John Rees fumbled Georgia's kickoff and Trav Paine recovered for the 'Dogs at the Hog 20. Cavan completed a 10-yard pass to Charles Whittemore after a yard pickup by Brad Johnson. Then Johnson gained 6 yards in two plays. Johnson tried to hurdle the Razorback line from the 3, but Dick Bumpus and Lynn Garner sandwiched the runner and the ball jetted from Johnson's arm straight out of the end zone for a touchback.

"It was about then that I realized how much better off I might have been 22 years before," said Dooley, "when I was a kid sitting on the curb outside the stadium." "You could almost feel the lift that gave us," said Broyles. "And it had to take something out of them."

An early fourth-quarter drive, again displaying the pitch-and-catch talents of Montgomery and Dicus,

produced a 24-yard field goal by White. The kickoff following that was fumbled again and recovered by Mike Boschetti at the Georgia 30. White missed a field goal try, but three plays later Chuck Powell intercepted Hampton and returned the ball 10 yards to the Bulldog 15-yard line. White put the game completely out of reach with a 31-yard field goal with 6:21 left to play.

With 40 rushing yards, it was obvious Broyles' aerial plan was essential. It produced only one touchdown, but Dicus caught a Sugar Bowl record 12 passes for 169 of Arkansas' 185 air yards and kept the Georgia defense off balance.

The Arkansas defense was just as striking, slicing Georgia's 397-yard average to less than half. Arkansas recovered five of seven Bulldog fumbles and intercepted three passes. Noting those stats and that Cliff Powell had eight unassisted tackles and was in on seven others, that Guy Parker had 10 solos, and defensive back Jerry Moore had two interceptions, broke up two passes, and was in on four tackles, Hog tackle Gordon McNulty had one question for his coach in the locker room.

"Coach, is the defense still suspect?" McNulty asked with a smile. Broyles returned the grin.

There were precious few smiles for Bulldog fans. Undefeated seasons are hard to come by and this one had slipped away. A New Orleans cab driver picking up fares outside the stadium observed the somber countenances of the Georgia faithful and was perplexed. "I can't understand what happened to that Georgia team," he said. "When I brought several of them (Bulldog fans) to the hotel at 2 A.M. this morning, they told me there was no way they could lose to Arkansas."

Mississippi-Arkansas

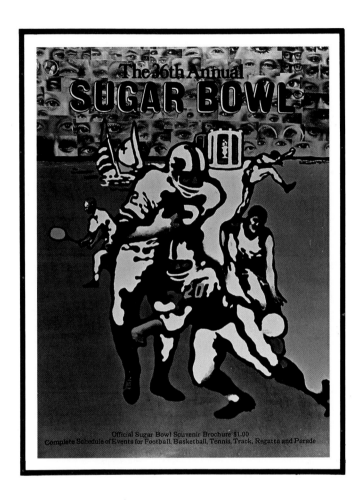

"Hee-haw, hee-haw."

In a roundabout way the seeds for the 1970 Sugar Bowl pairing were planted in a magazine article. Nineteen sixty-nine was a season that would bring one of the most dramatic changes in the bowl scene, and one in which the Mid-Winter Sports Association would deliberately select a lesser-ranked team over a stronger possibility.

Rumors began circulating in November, 1969, that Notre Dame, because of expected projects in the athletic department, would consider breaking the school's 45-year-old bowl ban. Coach Ara Parseghian told the Chicago Football Writers, "In all previous five seasons I've coached at Notre Dame, we've re-ceived a bowl invitation every year. And every year our board meets to review and consider these invitations, and every year the board turns them down. I'm sure, if we can win the rest of our games this year, we'll probably get another invitation, but I have no reason to believe the policy will change. Maybe somebody knows something that I don't know."

As the football season moved toward the middle of November the bowl scene seemed to be falling easily into line. No. 1-ranked Texas held the almost certain home spot in Dallas; Tennessee seemed headed for the Orange Bowl; the Sugar looked well-fixed with a possibility of either Auburn or LSU. Joe Paterno's excellent Penn State Nittany Lions were the top priority as the opposition for all three bowls. Texas Coach Darrell Royal tried to talk Paterno into a Dallas New Year's because this fine pairing would have given the Cotton Bowl the foremost game of the day.

Second in line for Dallas was LSU—truly an exceptional team that allowed only 38 yards a game rushing and 91 points for the season while scoring 349 points, a modern school record. It translated into a 9-1 record and an eighth place in the polls. Las Vegas odds-makers considered only Ohio State and the Longhorns better than the Tigers on a neutral field.

When Penn State declined its offer to play Texas, LSU was rarin' to prove its mettle in Dallas. With only a 3-point loss to Ole Miss on its record, the right set of circumstances and a victory over the No. 1-ranked team would catapult the Tigers very high in the final voting, which again would take place after the bowls.

But that 3-point loss would prove an insurmountable obstacle. Mississippi started the season as the odds-on choice to win the Southeastern Conference championship. Early losses to Kentucky and Alabama and a later defeat to Houston made the Rebels a disappointment. With the most exciting quarterback in the country, Archie Manning, a scrambling, tackle-slipping shadow, Ole Miss was one of the nation's most entertaining offensive shows—one that left a mark on SEC and national standings. Georgia was unbeaten and ranked 6th when it played the Rebels. Ole Miss won 26-23.

The week Mississippi was to play unbeaten and 3rd-ranked Tennessee, things started cracking. Rumors of Notre Dame breaking its bowl ban grew stronger. Then there was the matter of Tennessee linebacker Steve Kiner's quotes in *Sports Illustrated*. "I don't think they're that tough," Kiner said of the Rebels. The reporter said, "But they have a lot of horses down there." Kiner snorted, "A lot of people go down on the farm and can't tell the difference between a horse and a mule."

Ole Miss beat Tennessee, 38-0. When the score reached 31-0, Confederate flag-waving Rebel fans in Jackson's Memorial Stadium began braying at the Vols, Kiner in particular, "Hee-haw, hee-haw . . .''

Tennessee's eye-catching loss knocked it from the Orange Bowl.

Then Notre Dame agreed to meet Texas in the Cotton Bowl. The Orange Bowl quickly secured Missouri to play Penn State. The Sugar Bowl would seem to have found a diamond with LSU. A breakdown in communications, however, left the Tigers home for the holidays.

"We thought we had the Cotton Bowl locked up," said one person in the LSU athletic department. "We handled the thing all wrong. We waited all day for word from the Cotton Bowl, but they never called. LSU didn't handle it right, and neither did the Cotton Bowl for that matter."

The Sugar Bowl, miffed because its home-state team seemed far more interested in playing Texas than playing in New Orleans, bypassed what looked to be an obvious choice and selected Ole Miss. Tiger fans immediately began saying the Sugar should go for an LSU-Rebel rematch, like the 1960 game into which they felt they had been cornered. Dr. Fred Wolfe, president of the Sugar Bowl, reminded Tiger supporters, "We did invite LSU, but to my knowledge they wanted to go to the Cotton Bowl."

Arkansas, 3rd-ranked with a fiery offense featuring junior quarterback Bill Montgomery and receiver Chuck Dicus, was to be Ole Miss' opponent. The Hogs had an outside chance at winning the national championship, though the Rebels' 7-3 record took some gilt off the game.

In the final analysis the Sugar Bowl's choice of Ole Miss was a vote for the most exciting player in America—Manning. Coupled with Arkansas' firepower in a game that couldn't touch the other bowls in ranking, the Rebels would give New Orleans a game the others couldn't match in spectacle.

Mississippi 27-Arkansas 22

"We were just a hot football team."

"That was an exceptional year in college football," recalled Archie Manning. "There were a lot of real good teams all across the country. But I honestly felt, despite the loss to Texas, that we had drawn the best team anywhere in the Sugar Bowl. Arkansas was one heck of a football team."

Coach Frank Broyles won the toss but decided to kick off. Mississippi, a three-point underdog, answered the bell by being rocked on its heels.

After each team had failed to score on a possession, Manning, a mild-mannered, red-haired quarterback with volcanic ability, ran three plays to place the ball at the Ole Miss 31. Fullback Bo Bowen popped through on a simple trap, meandered away from the Hog middle, sideswiped two defenders at the Arkansas 37, picked up a block at the 10, and scored. Perry King's PAT put the Rebs ahead, 7-0.

"From that door to here," Bowen demonstrated afterward in describing six feet of wide-open space when he cracked the line. "It was the same play we used to beat Tennessee, and the hole was there because they have to respect Archie outside."

"We had a rush call on," explained defensive end Bruce James. "It was first and 10 and we weren't expecting them to run, even the linebackers were rushing."

Bruce Maxwell, the Hog fullback, almost returned the favor on the following Arkansas series. He broke loose on a 46-yard run to the Rebel 23. The threat fizzled and Bill McClard came in to attempt a 32-yard field goal that was wide. Six plays after that, Ole Miss was ahead, 14-0.

Vern Studdard took a deep pass out of the clutches of Arkansas defensive back Dennis Berner at the 40 and raced to the 27 before being brought down. Fifteen of the 57 yards gained were subtracted when Studdard received a penalty.

With a fierce Arkansas rush on in a second-and-25, Manning displayed his "hell-bent-for-leather" trademark. He scrambled away from the rush and as he was about to be sacked near midfield, he passed to Studdard for a yard gain. On third down, he cracked the heart of the secondary to Preston Carpenter for 15 yards, leaving Ole Miss a yard short

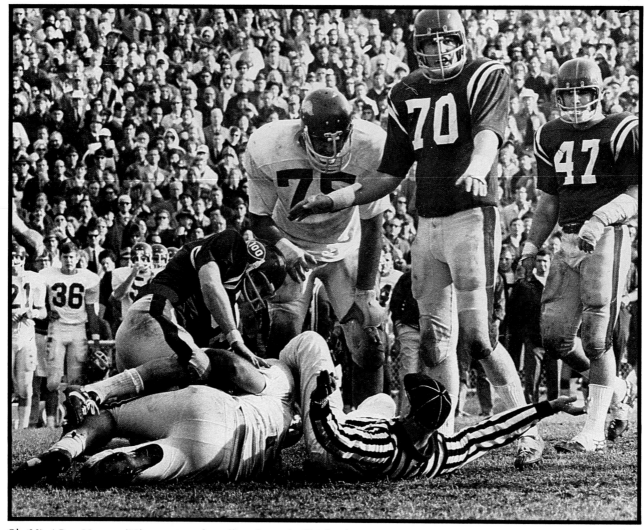

Ole Miss' Buz Morrow (70) appears to be calling downed official safe.

on fourth down. The Razorbacks braced for a shot at their middle, but Manning hightailed it around right end. He ran over two Hogs at the 15, then slashed through several more before high-stepping into the end zone.

The teams sparred for a while, then Hog quarterback Bill Montgomery, an excellent field general in his own right, took his team 81 yards in 13 plays. Using Bill Burnett and Maxwell to soften the Rebel wall, Montgomery whipped his unit to the Mississippi 12. There Burnett took a pitch, got outside the containment, split a pair of Rebs near the goal, and scored. McClard's PAT was wide, leaving the score at 14-6.

Scrambling and passing, Manning came back immediately as the Rebs drove to the Razorback 20, but an interference penalty shoved them back to the 35. Cloyce Hinton kicked a Sugar Bowl record 52-yard field goal to add to the Ole Miss tally. "I'll tell you, we were just a hot football team," said Manning. "Everything was working for us."

There were just under five minutes until the half when Hinton kicked the field goal. Arkansas

couldn't move and punted, and in four plays Ole Miss scored again.

Moving from the Rebel 45, Manning completed passes of 11 and 14 yards to Leon Felt and Randy Reed. Tight end Jim Poole then cleared across the middle from the right side and both Razorback defensive backs on that side went with him. Studdard was open at the 15. He grabbed Manning's pass and went in untouched. "Archie rolled away from the direction I took and I started downfield, stopped, and came back for the pass. The backs had gone across to stop Archie and I was all alone," said Studdard.

Montgomery put Arkansas back in the game by furiously lashing the Hogs 80 yards in the remaining 2½ minutes. Chuck Dicus glided down the sideline and cut back behind the Rebel secondary, which got caught in the switches. The quarterback threw him the ball and Dicus scored on the 47-yard hookup with 35 seconds left. Broyles elected to go for two, but Montgomery's pass was knocked down and the half ended, 24-12.

"You know, we had 260 yards offense at the

Archie Manning (18) of Ole Miss searches for a receiver.

Manning throws against Arkansas in spectacular shoot-out.

Elusive Archie Manning slips loose from Razorback defense.

half," said Montgomery, "so we couldn't be disappointed with that aspect. We just didn't score enough points."

In the third period, Bob Knight returned a punt 19 yards to the Arkansas 44. Bo Bowen gained 4 yards; then Manning, pressured out of the pocket, squeezed off left tackle and cut back toward the middle, running 31 yards before Jerry Moore caught him at the Hog 9. A pair of losses and a penalty shoved Ole Miss back to the 19 where Hinton kicked a 36-yard field goal. Montgomery retaliated with a 10-play, 80-yard drive that reached the Mississippi 6 before the Rebels braced and forced a field goal attempt. This time McClard was true and the score jumped to 27-15.

A pair of fourth-quarter interceptions put Arkansas right back in the fray. Glenn Cannon, who was having a spectacular day in the Rebel secondary, picked off a Montgomery pass in the end zone after the Hogs zipped through the airways from their 21 to

the Mississippi 11. Montgomery rolled out as if in a sweep, then reared up and fired. Cannon made a grab at a pass intended for flanker John Rees.

Three plays later, Berner intercepted Manning at the Rebel 41 and returned it 30 yards to the 11. The upshot was that Montgomery, in three plays, had Arkansas within five points of Ole Miss. Montgomery rolled right, was hit hard by Hap Farber, and still managed to get the ball to Maxwell; he went in for the touchdown. That cut it to 27-22.

As the game began winding down, it was left to Cannon to preserve the Ole Miss lead. Arkansas worked its way from its three to the Rebel 38, primarily on a 47-yard Montgomery-to-Dicus pass. On second down, Montgomery again went to Dicus over the middle but Cannon broke it up. Another jolting Cannon hit separated Dicus from the ball on third down. Montgomery, on a scramble, let fly to tight end Pat Morrison. Cannon again broke it up.

The next time Arkansas got the ball, on its 23,

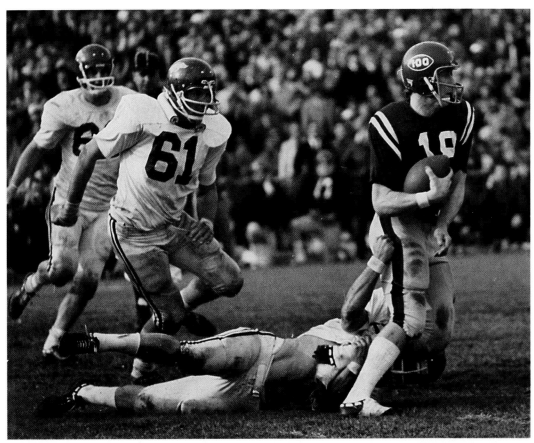

Manning
leads Rebel charge.

there were two minutes and 32 seconds left in the game. Montgomery, on fourth-and-four, ran out of the pocket for 13 yards and a first down at the 42. Two plays later he did the same for 18 yards and reached the Rebel 40. Montgomery went back to Dicus, who made a catch at the 25 but fumbled when he was hit by Cannon, who recovered on the 29. There was 1:08 left when the fumble occurred and Ole Miss was home free.

"I just hit Dicus," said Cannon, "and when I saw the ball jump loose, I hopped on it . . . I knew it was over then." "As I recall," said Dicus, "I was really tired because we had a lot of success throwing on them. But Cannon reacted very well. I don't remember whether I actually had the ball or not, but I turned when it got to me and he hit me immediately. I was so tired, I didn't even remember losing the ball."

Ole Miss, in what had to be in some ways its most frustrating season, had upset its fourth Top 10 team. The Rebels and Arkansas each broke three Sugar Bowl records in amassing a whopping total of 954 yards. If not the most important game played that day, it was the most entertaining.

Unfortunately, only a few more than the stadium crowd of 82,500 would know just what a spectacle the 1970 Sugar Bowl really was. The game drew a television rating of 8.3. Since records have been kept, going back to 1964, it was the worst rating for any major bowl. The prime-time production would give the Orange Bowl a $451,000 payday per team in 1971, and the Texas-Notre Dame game kept Dallas close to Miami. The Sugar, paying $100,000 less, was a weak third in a three-horse race.

Years later Manning, who became the quarterback of the New Orleans Saints National Football League team, was given a videotape of the game by a member of the Sugar Bowl. Watching it with his family, Manning was startled when his young son Cooper exuded, "Wow, dad! You sure were fast . . . then."

Tennessee-Air Force

FRIDAY, JANUARY 1, 1971

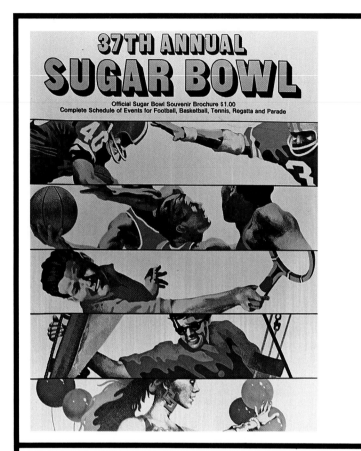

Captain Joe Katz, first director of the Sugar Bowl since 1958.

"I've already been bombed."

For 12 years, since the death of Fred Digby, the Mid-Winter Sports Association had basically been run by committee. Edna Engert, the secretary hired by the organization in 1936, carried out the day-by-day duties of the office, and the various committees of the membership made the hard-and-fast decisions. The Sugar Bowl had realized for some time that it needed an executive director.

Navy Captain Joseph T. Katz, a native New Orleanian, was retiring. His last tour of duty in a 28-year military career was as head of public relations and special projects for Vice Admiral Tom Connolly. On July 27, 1970, Joe Katz was appointed executive director.

The pickings for bowl eligibles outside the South were slim in 1970. Nebraska, Notre Dame, and Air Force, in that order, were the obvious choices to fill the 1971 berths. At an early date it appeared that Notre Dame and Nebraska would meet in the Orange Bowl, though the Irish had a late-season game with formidable LSU. The Sugar Bowl wanted either of those teams or, in lieu of the Southeastern Conference champion, the higher-ranked SEC runner-up Tennessee Volunteers.

Voting for the Associated Press national champion would again be done after the bowls, and this situation added some spice to postseason games. When the champion was picked before the bowls, the higher-ranked teams seemed to look more for the easy mark and a good time.

The No. 3-ranked Cornhuskers wanted the No. 6-ranked Irish because Notre Dame was viewed as Nebraska's stepping-stone to the national championship. It was reported that some Orange Bowl officials wanted Notre Dame win, lose, or draw against No. 7-ranked LSU; others wanted the Irish-Tiger victor.

Texas, with a No. 1 ranking, was a huge attraction for the Cotton Bowl, and it was also keenly interested in the LSU-Notre Dame winner.

As it turned out, Notre Dame won a somewhat controversial 3-0 victory over the Tigers and accepted a Cotton Bowl invitation. The snubbed Orange Bowl was then left with a choice of LSU or Arkansas. Any chance the Sugar had with LSU may have been dashed the year before when the Mid-Winter Sports Association opted for Ole Miss.

LSU accepted a provisional invitation from Miami that stipulated the Tigers had to defeat its final two opponents, Tulane and Ole Miss. At the same time, the Sugar invited No. 8-ranked Tennessee, which in most years would have been a prime bowl target, and No. 10-ranked Air Force, an exciting offensive team, though both had difficult games remaining.

The Vols handled their assignments well, defeating Vanderbilt 24-6 and UCLA 28-17 and rose to 4th in the polls. Air Force did not do as well, beating Rose Bowl-bound Stanford 31-14 but getting drubbed 49-19 by Colorado in its final game.

Charles Zatarain represented the Sugar Bowl at the Air Force-Colorado game, trying to keep a smile on through the darkest moments of the ordeal. An officer came to Zatarain's seat and informed him there had been a crank call about a bomb planted in the press box. "Don't worry about me, Colonel," smiled Zatarain, casting an eye toward the scoreboard. "I've already been bombed."

So, while the Cotton Bowl and Orange Bowl had the earmarks of No. 1 shoot-outs, the Sugar and Rose Bowls had only outside shots at one of their teams becoming the national champion.

Still, New Orleans would be getting an interesting contrast. Air Force averaged 423.6 yards in offense, third best in the nation. The Vols were second nationally in defense, surrendering a miserly 88.4 yards a game.

The pragmatic Sugar Bowlers made a concession to realism for this game. New Orleans and Dallas, the only bowls that competed in the same approximate time slot, had been inflicting damage on each other's television ratings. The Cotton Bowl had come out the better in recent years. With No. 1 Texas and an attention-grabber like Notre Dame, the Sugar realized there was no way anybody was going to top the Cotton Bowl's viewer interest. The Mid-Winter Sports Association moved its kickoff to noon, which gave it an hour jump on Dallas. It was also realized that the move would hold the Sugar viewers until just about the half.

Tennessee, under 29-year-old Coach Bill Battle, opened a 10-point favorite. Battle, who felt that a bowl trip was a reward, worked his team hard in practice but allowed the squad freedom to enjoy the city. On the other hand, Air Force Coach Ben Martin appeared grim and determined to make up for the Colorado defeat. Writers, noticing this and Tennessee's mediocre 6-10 bowl history, began picking the Falcons.

Tennessee 34-
Air Force 13

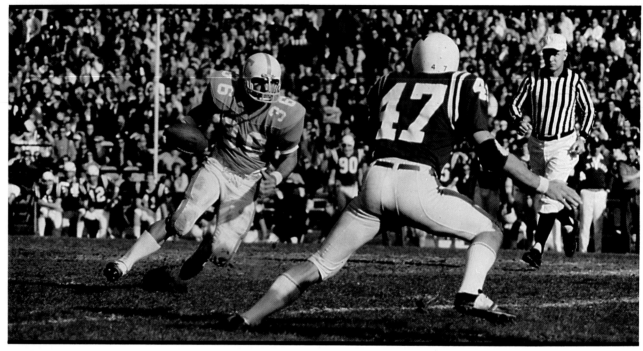

Don McLeary (36) of Tennessee turns on the afterburners while Air Force's Cyd Maattala (47) moves in.

"We had the momentum going."

It was over quickly, if not painlessly. Tennessee made the shortest work of any Sugar Bowl offering, virtually putting an end to Air Force's expectations nine minutes after the opening kickoff.

Kevin Milam returned the kickoff from his 8 to the Vol 41. Air Force threw up an eight-man line to try to slow down the potent Tennessee running game. Quarterback Bobby Scott neutralized that and outguessed a constant blitz threat, and the Vols drove 59 yards in seven plays for the first touchdown. Two minutes and 45 seconds were gone in the first quarter when Don McLeary took a pitchout from Scott, cut behind a block by Curt Watson, and scored from the 5. "We had the momentum going," said Scott of the opening march.

Bob Parker nudged the Falcons to a first down at the Air Force 34, but Brian Bream fumbled and the Vols recovered. George Hunt, with 8:44 left in the quarter, kicked a 30-yard field goal for a 10-0 Tennessee lead.

The strapped flyboys couldn't move, punted to the Vol 42, and shortly found themselves out of the running. Scott, rolling right, zipped a pass to Lester McLain at the 20. McLeary found a hole at left tackle, broke a tackle, and cut to his left. Another defender slipped off, and McLeary scored his second

TD of the afternoon. There was 6:07 remaining in the opening quarter, and Tennessee was up, 17-0.

There was more to come. Parker inched his unit out to its 32, then hit Bream in the left flat. Bream fumbled when smacked by David Allen and linebacker Jamie Rotella recovered on the 26. Four plays later, Scott passed to Gary Theiler at the five and the receiver completed the 10-yard play by stepping into the end zone. In four possessions, Tennessee had scored four times and led 24-0 with 3:12 remaining in the first period.

Air Force finally saw the other side of the 50 in the quarter's waning moments with a pass interference call at the Vol 45. That was followed by the day's most exciting moment, though it had nothing to do with football. A dog raced on the field and held up the game for more than three minutes. "I tried to chase him off the field," said Vol split end Joe Thompson, "and he almost bit me." So much for exciting moments—the time the dog was on the field represented the longest first-half span that Tennessee did not score.

Scott Hamm punted out on the Volunteer 8, which turned out to be one of Air Force's most effective plays. Scott fumbled the next snap, and ran back to pick up the ball at the 1. There he was knocked into the end zone and fumbled again. Darryl Hass recovered to slice the first quarter to 24-7.

"I tried to pick it up," said Scott, "and knock it out of the end zone. But a Falcon grabbed my arm and Air Force fell on it for a touchdown."

Bobby Majors put the next points on the board with a swirling 57-yard punt return the first time Tennessee touched the ball in the third quarter. Majors fielded the ball, stepped to his left, picked up a convoy, and headed toward the faraway goal line. Hamm, the kicker, had the last chance of stopping Majors at the Falcon 30, but Majors whizzed past. "After I caught the punt," said Majors, "I looked downfield and right away (Jackie) Walker got the first man, and I saw a lane there. The punter had a shot, but I sidestepped him and turned it on."

Each team scored again in the 34-13 Tennessee victory, but the final score, convincing as it was, didn't reflect the Vol mistakes. Tennessee, which cut down the Air Force running game to minus 12 yards, came up empty on six other legitimate scoring opportunities: 1) a fumble on the Falcon 17; 2) a missed 32-yard field goal; 3) a missed 30-yard field goal; 4) a fumble on the Falcon 15; 5) a missed 42-yard field goal; and 6) an interception in the end zone from the Air Force 21.

The Vol defense was more than impressive in the mismatch. Rotella had eight tackles and an assist, recovered two fumbles, and broke up a pass. Fellow linebacker Ray Nettles had nine tackles, three assists, and one sack. Coach Bill Battle said in the locker room, "I'd like to thank all the writers who picked Air Force."

Nettles added, though, "I didn't like them (Air Force). They said things on the sidelines and seemed awful cocky."

Bobby Scott (10) passes to Steve Wold (32) for gain against Air Force.

McLeary cuts behind a block to score Tennessee's first touchdown against Air Force.

Oklahoma-Auburn

38th Annual Sugar Bowl

Official Sugar Bowl Souvenir Brochure $1.00
Complete Schedule of Events for Football, Basketball, Tennis, and Regatta

"Now we had invited another one."

The switch in the Sugar Bowl kickoff time to noon had exactly the anticipated effect: The ratings were fine—for a half. As soon as Texas-Notre Dame got under way the viewers changed channels. Tennessee-Air Force went into four million homes with a 8.3 rating, the same as 1970. Texas-Notre Dame was beamed into 20 million homes. The wipeout caused ABC to start thinking of a radical change in time—a New Year's Eve game.

It was strange, this merry-go-round the Sugar Bowl had boarded. Because of something out of its control—the segregation legislation of the 1950s—the Sugar Bowl entered an era of essentially regional games. Because of it, and some extraordinary bad fortune when race was no longer an issue, its television ratings were weak. The Orange and Cotton Bowls had, conversely, gotten stronger with television. It added up to this: The Dallas and Miami games received more television money because of ratings. New Orleans didn't do as well but could hardly do better since its network, ABC, was reluctant to provide more money, money that could be used to attract better teams for the higher ratings.

What ABC wanted, beginning with the 1972 game, was a Monday night, prime-time attraction. In this case, ABC was talking about January 3. The Mid-Winter Sports Association was opposed, though it realized its $500,000 contract was up for renewal and that outcome could depend upon the ratings of the next Sugar Bowl.

The parties compromised. The Sugar Bowl stayed on New Year's Day, but agreed to move its kickoff back to 11 A.M. where most of the attraction would be unopposed.

The Big Eight Conference, where Nebraska, Oklahoma, and Colorado held sway, lorded over the 1971 polls. Alabama and cross-state rival Auburn were the standard-bearers in the South. Penn State was the best in the East, and Notre Dame held its usual magic in the rankings. It was the Big Eight and SEC teams that were most coveted. The only question was the match-up. Nebraska, ranked No. 1 all season and leaning to New Orleans, and No. 2 Oklahoma would play in the regular season finale for the Big Eight championship. Also undefeated, No. 4 Alabama was to play No. 5-ranked Auburn for the SEC title in their last game.

Of course, the selections would have to be made before those outcomes. The Orange Bowl wanted the schools to put off committing to the bowls until the championships were resolved; then the Nebraska-Oklahoma and Alabama-Auburn winners would be welcomed to Miami, and the losers to New Orleans. The Sugar wouldn't agree to this and neither would the schools. Miami had to take its chances, too.

ABC wanted to pair Alabama and Penn State. For sheer glamour and business, Alabama-Oklahoma was the people's choice.

New Orleans' prospects were excellent. On a motion by the Executive Committee, Aruns Callery was sent to Tuscaloosa the weekend of the bowl selections. He was to invite Alabama and consult with Bear Bryant on an opponent. After Alabama's Saturday afternoon game, Bryant asked Callery to meet him at his office at 6 A.M. Sunday.

Bryant told Callery that he had made a decision and wanted to go to the Sugar Bowl. Assured the bowl most certainly wanted him, Bryant said, "I think I'll call Chuck (Fairbanks, the Oklahoma coach) and see if we can't have a national championship game for New Orleans," said Bear to a startled Callery. And Fairbanks agreed. The only thing Bryant asked of Callery was to wait until noon Monday to announce it.

On the phone with the Sugar Bowl at noon, Callery told the committee members things were looking good, but Bryant didn't want to say anything until noon the following day. He couldn't be more explicit than that. The rest of the afternoon Callery was out of phone reach, driving to Birmingham and then flying to New Orleans. And while Callery was traveling, Auburn Coach Ralph "Shug" Jordon was putting the squeeze on the Executive Committee. Jordan wanted his team invited to the Sugar Bowl and if he didn't get an immediate invitation, he would not wait until Monday. He wouldn't play in New Orleans—win, lose, or draw.

Auburn was undefeated, untied, 5th-ranked, and readying for an SEC championship game. It had a Heisman Trophy-winning quarterback in Pat Sullivan and was an excellent, exciting offensive football team.

In an emergency meeting Sunday afternoon the Executive Committee of the Sugar Bowl agreed to accept Auburn.

"When I got home," Callery remembered, "I had a message to call Bernie Grenrood immediately. Bernie asked me to meet him at his house. 'I have terrible news,' he told me when I arrived. 'The committee called an emergency meeting at 4 o'clock this afternoon and picked Auburn.'

"I was just frozen when I heard," said Callery. "We had, in essense, already invited two teams that morning—Alabama and Oklahoma. Now we had invited another one. I had to pour myself a couple of drinks before I called Coach Bryant. It must have looked like I was a fraud. You can't print what Bryant said when I told him. He did tell me to tell the Sugar Bowl that he was going to beat the hell out of Auburn."

And he did. Alabama walloped Auburn, 31-7, and Nebraska edged Oklahoma 35-31 in a game matching two of college football's all-time teams. Those results set up a national championship game for Miami and a runner-up game in the Sugar. It was just what Miami was angling for, but this time New Orleans kayoed itself.

Auburn-Oklahoma wasn't a bad match, pairing an awesome Sooner ground game against a devastating Auburn aerial display. The Sugar could have been in far worse shape. But it was still a runner-up game.

Oklahoma 40-Auburn 22

"I knew they were going to score a lot."

Oklahoma quarterback Jack Mildren (11) pops through Auburn line.

The 1972 Sugar Bowl ought to have been a spectacular game offensively. Oklahoma, averaging 566 yards a game in a 10-1 season, was the most efficient offense in NCAA history. The Sooners were so potent they punted only 26 times in those 11 games. Auburn was no slouch either, averaging 393 yards a game. Whereas Oklahoma inflicted most of its damage on the ground, Auburn was air-minded. Quarterback Pat Sullivan passed for 2,012 yards and 20 touchdowns that season. Terry Beasley, a superb wide receiver, caught 12 of those touchdown passes.

If the luster of a 9-1 record was smudged by the 31-7 loss to Alabama, Tiger Coach Ralph "Shug" Jordan expected that to be a weapon in his favor in the Sugar Bowl. "We have a chance to redeem ourselves," said Jordan, whose team was a 10½-point underdog.

But there was no redemption for Auburn, and only Oklahoma was spectacular. Like the 1971

Tennessee-Air Force game, the suspense in the 1972 Sugar Bowl ended shortly after the coin toss.

Greg Pruitt, a 5-foot-9 junior, returned the opening kickoff 24 yards to the Oklahoma 23. Quarterback Jack Mildren gained 17 yards on a keeper on the first play from scrimmage and the Sooners, as they say, never looked back. Pruitt and Leon Crosswhite alternated carrying and the Oklahoma line took immediate control. Twelve plays into the game Mildren fumbled on the Auburn 4, but Crosswhite recovered.

The following play, 6 minutes after the 77-yard drive began, Crosswhite scored. John Carroll missed the conversion.

Sullivan misplaced a handoff onto Tommy Lowry's hip after a punt exchange, and Ray Hamilton recovered on the Auburn 41 for Oklahoma. Mildren had the wishbone humming perfectly and in eight plays the Sooners scored again. The quarterback faked to Crosswhite, who took the Tiger defense with him,

176

TOUCHDOWN!

G

Mildren

LINE OF SCRIMMAGE

5

Mildren of Oklahoma dashes in with the first of his record three touchdowns against Auburn.

and Mildren went in untouched from the 5. He also scored on a sweep in a 2-point conversion attempt, but Oklahoma was penalized for illegal motion. Carroll kicked the PAT to make the score 13-0.

Joe Wylie was the next Sooner to touch the game ball. Auburn lost 9 yards in three plays on its possession and David Beverly punted to Wylie at the Oklahoma 29. Joe gathered in the punt, slipped through two onrushing Tigers, and headed down the right sideline. Mark Driscoll chopped down the last man with a chance of catching Wylie, and Joe completed the 71-yard journey.

"It was as if we had put it on the drawing board," laughed Wylie. "It was perfect . . . Steve O'Shaughnessy and Geoffrey Nordgren blocked the first two men down, and I ducked behind the wall. I thought I could go all the way when the wall formed."

Mildren again went for a two-point conversion, but Mike Neel broke up a pass to Albert Chandler.

With 1:55 remaining in the first quarter, Oklahoma held a 19-0 lead. After that, the outcome of the game was never in doubt, but the score would change considerably.

Nordgren intercepted Sullivan on the Auburn 35 and in short order Mildren scored on a 4-yard keeper. Pruitt attempted to sweep left for the two-point conversion but was stopped short by David Langner and John Hayworth.

Driscoll intercepted Beasley on a gimmick pass and returned it 19 yards to the Auburn 41. With 47 seconds remaining to halftime, Mildren set a Sugar Bowl record with his third touchdown, a 7-yard sprint that, after still another two-point conversion was missed, made the halftime score a record 31-0.

Carroll kicked a record 53-yard field goal in the third quarter to put Oklahoma ahead, 34-0.

Harry Unger finally put some points up for the Plainsmen on a 1-yard run after Sullivan drove Auburn 80 yards in five plays. A 35-yard pass to Beas-

Joe Wylie (22) leaves War Eagles in his wake in 71-yard punt return.

Sooner Coach Chuck Fairbanks, left, greets Ralph 'Shug' Jordan after 40-22 Oklahoma victory.

ley got the Auburn offense hinged again. Gardner Jett kicked the PAT.

Pruitt swept left from the 2 early in the fourth period after Oklahoma stopped Auburn at the Sooner 31, then drove 69 yards for the touchdown. Carroll missed the extra point.

Sullivan passed 11 yards to Sandy Cannon for the Tigers' second touchdown after a heads-up effort by defensive tackle Tommy Yearout, who grabbed a Wylie fumble out of midair and returned it 49 yards to the Oklahoma 32. Jett made the conversion.

Another Oklahoma fumble, this time at the Sooner 19, gave Auburn a last opportunity at points. Unger went in at left guard from the one with 2:45 left in the game. Dave Beck, the holder on the apparent placement, ran the ball around end to slice the final difference to 40-22.

There was little excitement or spice to the match. "I just started out playing bad," offered Sullivan. "As big and strong as they were, I knew they were going to score a lot, and we were just going to have to out-score them. We just weren't able to." There were many reasons why things got out of hand for Auburn. Sullivan found the best one when he sighed, "If there is a team in the country better than Oklahoma, I'm sure glad we don't have to play them."

The only balm for Auburn was the Orange Bowl. Alabama played a better team than Oklahoma and Nebraska ground up the Crimson Tide in another game that was over fairly quickly.

Oklahoma-Penn State

SUNDAY, DECEMBER 31, 1972

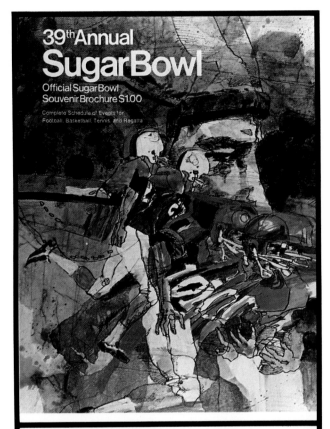

"They got that idea from 'Monday Night Football.' "

The noon kickoff, a time change that for all practical purposes excluded West Coast television viewing, was a disaster. The ratings for the Sugar Bowl were only slightly higher than those for regular season NCAA telecasts (14.6 to 14.0), and it had the smallest audience of the major bowls. ABC, whose sports operation was headed by Roone Arledge, decided drastic measures had to be taken and began pressing for a New Year's Eve game over the objections of most of the Mid-Winter Sports Association membership.

"They (ABC) got that idea from 'Monday Night Football,' " said Sugar Bowl member Charles Zatarain. "On a night when people are planning to go out to celebrate, it didn't seem logical that a football game would keep them home that extra couple of hours. And in New Orleans it sure wouldn't work. This is a party town, so we were going to lose people in the stadium because of New Year's celebrations. The thing was a network decision. They wanted it, and, of course, they were buying it and we went along with it."

For going along with it, ABC increased its yearly payment to the Sugar Bowl from $510,000 to $575,000 and spent an additional $100,000 improving the Tulane Stadium lighting. For a New Year's Day game, ABC would have paid $300,000.

The NCAA granted the Sugar Bowl permission to move the date of the game. A Sugar Bowl was scheduled for New Year's Eve, 1972, for 8 P.M. in-

Joe Katz sets a facsimile of a bond on fire while banking officer Morgan Shaw, center, and Sugar Bowler John W. Boebinger watch. The 1972 ceremony was symbolic of the Sugar Bowl retiring the last portion of a $500,000 bond issue floated in 1947 to expand and improve Tulane Stadium.

stead of the more logical 7 P.M. because the network didn't want to preempt its popular series, "The FBI." They pointed out that the Orange Bowl had been hurt during the opening 30 minutes the year before while "All in the Family" was being telecast in opposition to the Nebraska-Alabama national championship match.

New Year's Eve, 1972, would also break another tradition. The game would be played on a Sunday. All the major bowls historically sidestepped Sunday games and played on January 2 in those years when New Year's fell on the Sabbath. "We kind of expected protests from the churches and religious groups," said Joe Katz, of the Sugar Bowl committee, "but nobody made anything over it at all."

Of the events important to the Sugar Bowl in 1972, none may have been bigger than the retirement of the last bonds indebted by the Mid-Winter Sports Association. Now it was free and clear of debt.

Bear Bryant held the keys to the makeup of the bowl games that season. Practically everyone agreed that for pure talent Nebraska had the best team in the country. But the Cornhuskers, playing their last season under Bob Devaney, had a loss and a tie on their record. Undefeated Southern Cal was ranked No. 1, making also unbeaten and 2nd-ranked Alabama the team every bowl wanted and the team any national championship contender would have to play in order to have a chance at the title.

Devaney had a no-strings-attached invitation to New Orleans that he seemed to relish, but he wanted to play Alabama. Bryant hinted early that he would play in either the Sugar or the Cotton Bowl, but let it be known if he played in New Orleans he wanted to play Penn State. Notre Dame was interested in the Sugar if it did not have to play Nebraska. The team preferred to play Alabama, Penn State, or Louisiana State. LSU was the second SEC choice (Alabama, the first) for the Sugar's host spot, and the Tigers wanted Penn State.

Bryant accepted a bid to the Cotton Bowl. With its only chance for a national championship gone, Nebraska went to the Big Eight's port of call. LSU, thinking Penn State was out of the Sugar Bowl picture, accepted a Bluebonnet Bowl berth. But the Sugar took 6th-ranked Penn State and, with its two SEC favorites no longer on the scene, went for 4th-ranked Oklahoma. Notre Dame ended up as Nebraska's Orange Bowl partner.

Oklahoma still had a game to play—with Bob Devaney's dreadnought—but the Sooners had an outside chance at No. 1, with a potential 11-1-0 season.

Upset coaches began sniping at Bryant. Devaney complained, "He got three shots at me when I was

unbeaten, and he won two of them. Now he won't play me." Notre Dame's Ara Parseghian criticized Alabama for taking on Southwest Conference champion Texas instead of Nebraska, or presumably Notre Dame. "From everything I've read, and by their own admission, Alabama took the easy way out," said Parseghian. "They were in the driver's seat, being undefeated, and their decision dictated the structure of the other bowls."

Bryant responded, "I just can't see playing a team in a bowl that has lost two games. We would be honored and privileged to play Notre Dame at any time except at this time."

Oklahoma made Nebraska's chance at No. 1 academic when, on Thanksgiving Day, the Sooners, a 2-touchdown underdog, scored 17 points in the final 17 minutes to beat the Cornhuskers 17-14.

Charles "Tinker" Owens, a Sooner freshman receiver, added excitement to the first Sugar Bowl in 23 years without an SEC team. He was the brother of former Oklahoma Heisman Trophy winner Steve Owens.

The coach of the 10-1 Nittany Lions Joe Paterno—a man whose .838 winning percentage (64-12-1) was the best in the country and who had never lost (3-0-1) in a bowl—was in a reflective mood when he met the press in New Orleans.

Paterno spoke about his team, a talented offensive unit featuring quarterback John Hufnagel, the school's total offensive leader, and John Cappelletti, who gained 1,117 yards at running back. The potent Lions averaged 32 points a game. Paterno also spoke of Oklahoma, which averaged 478 yards and 37 points a game—the nation's best. Befitting a 6-point underdog, Paterno said, "There are only two great teams in college football today—Oklahoma and Southern California. Sure, there are several good teams . . . Texas, Ohio State, Tennessee, Alabama, but only two great ones.

"When you talk about what makes a great team, you must consider its size, speed, balance on offense and defense. That's Oklahoma!"

Taking his mind off the awesome Sooner wishbone, though, Paterno spoke of his first Sugar Bowl on January 1, 1952. He was then a 26-year-old assistant who wanted to see the Tennessee-Maryland game and bought a scalper's ticket to do so.

"I can still see Ed Modzelewski ripping into Tennessee's wide-tackle-six," he reminisced. "I drove down from Penn State with two friends, drove all night to see that game, my first trip to New Orleans. I paid twenty bucks for my ticket. My friends sneaked in with the Boy Scouts. "It was one of those trips I'll never forget. We left New Orleans early the next morning—after doing the town—and we turned the car over on the way home."

Oklahoma 14-
Penn State 0

Freshman Tinker Owens (11) makes touchdown grab on '346-S-Post.'

"It didn't bounce at all."

A virus hit Penn State and bad news hit Oklahoma. Joe Paterno learned the day of the game he would be without his ground game—John Cappelletti, who had a 102-degree fever. The Penn State coach had a virus himself, but refused to have his temperature taken so that no one could command him from the sideline.

Chuck Fairbanks, coach of the Sooners, decided the day of the game that starting split end John Carroll's injured knee still hadn't recovered sufficiently. It was a major decision because a lot of Paterno's concern centered on Carroll. And just before the game, freshman Tinker Owens was told he would start.

Early in the second quarter, Oklahoma quarterback Dave Robertson began flaring his backs for consistent gains into the defensive front. "We couldn't go outside early because they were overplaying us outside," said Robertson, "and then we began to hammer away inside and that's where most of our success came from."

Ten consecutive running plays used five minutes of the clock and placed Oklahoma at the 27. "Then we called what we referred to as '346-S-Post,' " said

Owens. "It was a fake dive and I would go downfield. Penn State was playing me man-to-man and really watching for Joe Washington to get the ball." Owens made an over-the-shoulder catch at the 7 between two defenders, worked loose from a tackle, and scored. "It was funny," said Tinker. "I didn't even think I would catch it. The ball was right there but it was over my shoulder and I had to look up and back. After I caught it, I just kept running and the guy on me slid off." Rick Fulcher added the PAT.

The half ended with the same 7-0 score, and it was obvious that without Cappelletti, Penn State was playing with only one arm against the mobile Oklahoma defense. At halftime, Walt Addie was the leading Lion rusher with 18 yards on 7 carries. Quarterback John Hufnagel was 5 of 15 in passing attempts as several were dropped, and the Sooners concentrated on a suddenly one-dimensional offense.

Two minutes into the fourth period, Gary Hayman dropped an Oklahoma punt, and Ken Jones recovered on the Lion 33 for the Sooners. Greg Pruitt weaved through the Lion line on consecutive carries to the 18. Joe Wylie was the trigger in a

Penn State Coach Joe Paterno.

halfback pass in the spectacular (and disputed) highlight of the night. "I ran a post pattern again," said Owens, "and the ball was a little underthrown. I dove for it and caught it between my elbows. It didn't bounce at all."

Penn State fans and some reporters felt the catch at the Lion 1 was trapped. The film was unclear. Owens maintained it was a legal catch. "I caught it," he said. "I knew it had it then, I know I had it now."

Leon Crosswhite scored two plays later and, after Fulcher's kick, Oklahoma led 14-0 with 9:46 remaining.

Owens, in his third starting assignment, had 5 catches for 132 yards, which resulted in 1 touchdown and set up another. He was the MVP.

Three months later there was some question of having to change the score. A joint investigation by the University of Oklahoma and the Big Eight revealed that the high school transcripts of freshman quarterback Kerry Jackson and center linebacker Mike Phillips had been tampered with.

As a result, Oklahoma voluntarily forfeited every game in which the pair participated, including the Sugar Bowl. Penn State Coach Joe Paterno refused to change the outcome. "It's a shame that a great effort by an Oklahoma football team has to be marred by an inexcusable recruiting violation such as this incident," said Paterno in a prepared statement. "However, irrespective of what action Oklahoma or the Sugar Bowl would take in regards to the forfeit, our players and the Oklahoma players know who won the game."

The Sugar Bowlers' objections to the 8 P.M. kickoff proved to be well-founded. "This game's running so late," cracked a sportswriter eyeing an Eastern time deadline, "it might be the first bowl game to be played in two years—1972 and 1973."

Penn State-Oklahoma was a game for trivia buffs. It was the only Sugar Bowl ever played on a Sunday, and it was the first time two Sugar Bowls (January 1, 1972, and December 31, 1972) were played in the same calendar year. Oklahoma won two Sugar Bowls in the same year, and a freshman won the Miller-Digby trophy (MVP).

Penn State defense rises to stop Oklahoma.

Oklahoma quarterback Dave Robertson (15) flashes past Nittany Lions.

Notre Dame-Alabama

MONDAY, DECEMBER 31, 1973

Fighting Irish of Notre Dame vs. Crimson Tide of Alabama

Bear Bryant and Ara Parseghian chat before New Year's Eve, 1973, classic of classics.

"I just have players."

A series of events, some reaching back to the opening days of the decade, had a deep effect upon the Sugar Bowl in 1973. The Mid-Winter Sports Association had opened its membership and taken in a select group of capable, civic- and sports-minded individuals in 1966, but immediately thereafter slipped back into comfortable insulation. Though the intention in 1966 was to consider and sponsor new members periodically, new people were not admitted for six years.

A coalition of primarily younger members, realizing the organization had to expand itself in order to regain its former stature, began pressing for new admittances at the start of the 1970s. Moon Landrieu, newly elected mayor and the most progressive New Orleans government head in a decade, urged that the Sugar Bowl admit blacks to its membership.

"Because it had come to mean so much to the city and region," reflected Landrieu, "because its membership included names of individuals that meant something in business, government . . . meant something to New Orleans, the Sugar Bowl had become almost a 'quasi-public' organization. It was an organization that served exceedingly well, but also one that did business each year with schools that had more and more black representation while the Sugar Bowl had none."

For three years of Landrieu's first term nothing was done by the Sugar Bowl. In August of 1973 several black groups represented by an Ad Hoc Committee put together by Carl Galmon, (a New Orleans member of the Southern Christian Leadership Conference) charged the Mid-Winter Sports Association with racial discrimination. The Ad Hoc Committee, identifying itself as composed of members of the National Association for the Advancement of Colored People, the Urban League, the Southern Media Coalition, the Modern Organization for Dynamic and Effective Leadership, and the Community Organization for Urban Politics, requested that NCAA President Allen J. Chapman conduct an investigation into Sugar Bowl operations. They asked that the NCAA approval of the Sugar Bowl be lifted if discrimination was found in its operations, but this question was out of NCAA's jurisdiction.

Unquestionably, there was a lingering hold from the past on some Sugar Bowl members, as there seemed to be on a large segment of American society. The feeling remained that the Sugar Bowl was, after all, a private organization and as such was entitled to choose its makeup. A significant portion of the Sugar Bowl membership, particularly the younger people, disagreed. Finally, a group of 11 men were invited to join the Sugar Bowl. Six of them were among the most influential people in the black community. They were: Xavier University President Dr. Norman C. Francis; Dr. Leonard Burns; educator Elliot Willard; banker Sidney Cates; newspaperman Jim Hall; and Juvenile Court Judge Ernest N. Morial.

The 11 new members were asked to serve on a 23-man advisory committee called "Ambassadors" for one year before being considered for full membership. The usual probation period was two years. All the blacks declined, feeling the offer was made to placate them rather than to provide meaningful participation. After the Sugar Bowl talked with all parties concerned again, the six blacks were elected to associate membership on December 10. Five others, Louisiana Lt. Gov. James E. Fitzmorris, Jr., Richard Gaiennie, Lloyd F. Gaubert, Ronnie J. Kole, and 24th Judicial District Court Judge Thomas C. Wicker, were also elected to membership.

On November 8, Alabama's Coach Bryant announced in what was described as a sugarcoated challenge that his team wanted to play Notre Dame in New Orleans. The key words were "in New Orleans" because Alabama-Notre Dame was a match anyone would have loved.

The 5th-ranked Irish, with a week to think about the prospects, had to consider the $100,000 or so more the Orange Bowl would pay, no small sum to an independent that doesn't have to share with conference members. Coach Ara Parseghian, speculating on what would happen, said, "We will select the competition first and the site second . . . it doesn't take too much intelligence on the part of anybody to figure what will happen."

Bryant had hinted this could be his best team. Parseghian had done the same. The thought of Alabama and Notre Dame, titans of the college football world, meeting was exhilarating. "Look at the possibilities," wrote Dave Lagarde in the *Times-Picayune*, "Alabama undefeated and untied; Notre Dame undefeated and untied; North against South; Catholic against Protestant; Parseghian against Bryant; the Bear against the Pope."

There was another dimension to add to the excitement. Alabama had risen to No. 1 and Notre Dame to No. 3. Oklahoma was the No. 2-ranked team, but it was on NCAA probation and ineligible for bowls. This meant the Alabama-Notre Dame game would probably be played for the national championship. "This will be one of the biggest moments in

Alabama's history," said Bryant in anticipation. "We've talked about this game for years," Ed "Moose" Krauss, the Irish athletic director said. "There's no question that this could be the most important game ever, certainly since Ara Parseghian has been here. We have a chance to go undefeated and win the national championship and become one of the greatest teams in the history of this school . . . and there have been some great ones."

While the football world awaited the game, political currents continued to swirl around the Sugar Bowl. After the appointments of the six blacks to the Mid-Winter Sports Association membership, the Ad Hoc Committee asked that four more blacks be appointed. They wanted at least 33⅓ percent blacks involved in meaningful participation by 1975 and an agreement in writing for an affirmative action program before the Alabama-Notre Dame game on December 31.

Asked if he had discussed the situation with his black players, Bryant shot back, "I don't have any black players and I don't have any white players. I just have players."

The winner, both coaches agreed, would be the defense that could control the other's offense. It would be 'Bama odd-man front defense against the Irish wing T with motion and misdirection. And the Irish even-odd defense would face the Tide wishbone. Notre Dame gave up only 201.2 yards a game during the season—the second best in the nation. Alabama, on the other hand, averaged 366 yards offensively—the country's second best. The Irish averaged 350 yards offensively while the Tide defense gave up 244.8 yards.

ABC, in a gesture of sportsmanship to the New Orleans fans, lifted the local blackout. Alabama entered the game a 6-point favorite, but the words of Southern California Coach John McKay should've kept Crimson Tide feet on the ground. "Now listen, Paul," McKay advised Bryant, "you're going to look at films and you're going to write them (Notre Dame) off. Don't, because they're faster than they look and are even bigger than the program says they are."

Notre Dame 24- Alabama 23

"Oh (bleep), this is one I better not miss."

It wasn't the afternoon showers that caused the lightning to zigzag over Tulane Stadium in the evening. It was simply an indication of how much electricity was in the air. The most celebrated miracle workers of the religion of football, Ara and Bear, were preparing to match miracles, and the prospect was thrilling.

Awaiting was a duel involving seemingly hexed extra points, almost magical fumbles being taken from the air, a quarterback catching a touchdown pass, and a freshman shattering a record twice as old as he.

Notre Dame and Alabama sparred early on the slick turf with the Irish gaining the upper hand. On Notre Dame's third possession, quarterback Tom Clements began challenging the Tide secondary and covered 59 yards to the 3 on three passes to split end Pete Demmerle. Fullback Wayne Bullock, on third down, flung his 230 pounds into the end zone. A weak snap cost Irish kicker Bob Thomas any chance at the conversion, but the underdog Irish led, 6-0.

Notre Dame gained another shot at quick points before the quarter ended when Greg Gantt shanked a punt of only 23 yards out at the 'Bama 49, but Notre Dame couldn't take advantage. Seconds later when the period ended, southern fans may have begun to suspect voodoo in the Notre Dame kettle. There was a mind-boggling no first downs and zero offensive yards in the Tide column after 15 minutes of football. It wasn't just that Notre Dame had five first downs, 144 yards, and six points. The Irish offense had controlled the ball for more than 10 minutes. This was unsettling.

Alabama quarterback Gary Rutledge began solving the changing Notre Dame defense by the second quarter. He drove the Tide to the Irish 17 when the quarterback was smacked by Jim Stock on a pitchout that went bouncing 19 yards back. Stock recovered at the 36. Bullock fumbled shortly, and Alabama got the ball at its 48.

Avoiding middle linebacker Gary Potempa, who was feasting on the Tide front whenever possible, Rutledge guided Alabama smoothly, covering the 52

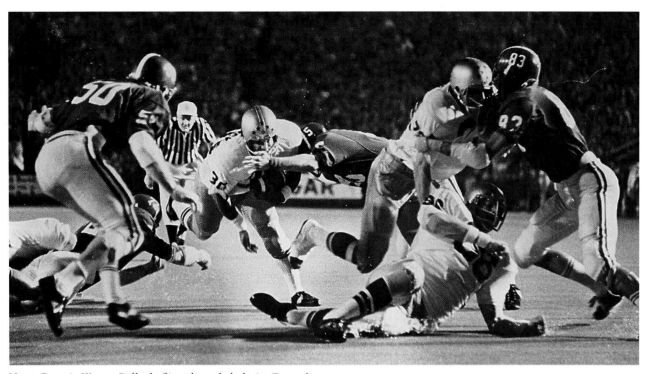

Notre Dame's Wayne Bullock flies through hole in 'Bama line.

Bullock holds ball high for touchdown emphasis in Tide-Irish classic.

Al Hunter (25) of Notre Dame takes off on record-breaking 93-yard kickoff return.

A throw for the national championship: Tom Clements of Notre Dame passes from the end zone to tight end Robin Weber to maintain control of the ball . . . and of the game.

yards in seven plays. Randy Billingsley scored on a 6-yard run. Bill Davis (younger brother of Tim, who kicked four field goals in the 1964 Sugar Bowl, and Steve, who kicked in the 1967 Sugar Bowl) booted the extra point to put 'Bama ahead, 7-6. It also gave Notre Dame a chance to use a play put in especially for Alabama.

Ara Parseghian installed a new kickoff return system in which five linemen would be responsible for taking out the first wave of defenders. Two ends and two fullbacks would form a semicircle around the receiving back who would yell "Go" as he received the ball, the signal to the second cluster.

Freshman Al Hunter took the kick at the 7 on the extreme left side of the field, and ran toward the middle behind his shield of blockers. Alabama bodies were flying as the escort picked off the defenders and Hunter veered diagonally at the 35. In seconds Notre Dame was back in front. The 93-yard return broke the record set by Claude "Monk" Simons in the inaugural Sugar Bowl almost 40 years before. Simons, who carried the ball 85 of the 90 yards against Temple, was sitting in the press box as a Sugar Bowl officer and smiled at the end of Hunter's run. "I'm just glad I'm here to see it," he joked. A 2-point conversion—Clements to Demmerle—made it a 14-7 game.

Late in the period, sub quarterback Richard Todd led 'Bama on a drive from its 18. Keeping the Irish off-balance with passes, rollouts, and play-action

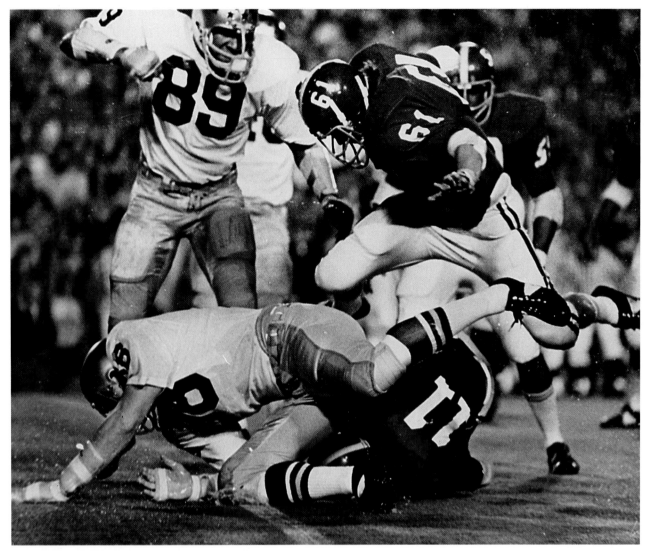

Bodies fly in 1973 classic as Alabama's John Rogers (61) hurdles downed Tide quarterback Gary Rutledge (11) and Notre Dame's Mike Fanning (88) as Ross Browner (89) moves in.

calls, Todd left only 39 seconds of the 3:19 he started with when Davis kicked a 39-yard field goal to make the score 14-10. Clements nearly got the three points back after an interference call gave Notre Dame the ball at the Tide 31. But Thomas was very short on a 48-yard field goal attempt on the last play of the half.

With one miracle play (Hunter's run) already in the books, Parseghian exhorted his troops with the reminder, "We're one-half away from the national championship!" The Irish coaching staff also decided to use more of the "mirror" defense they had used so successfully against Texas' wishbone three years before in the Cotton Bowl.

A clipping penalty on the second-half kickoff return placed the Alabama offense on its 7. The Tide was hot at that point and decimated the Irish front line, covering 93 yards in 12 plays. A 15-yard personal foul penalty and a 21-yard pass from Rutledge to Wilbur Jackson that put the ball at the Irish 18 set up Jackson's eventual 5-yard scoring run. Alabama went back ahead, 17-14.

Two long field goal attempts, 45 yards by Alabama and 54 yards by Notre Dame, failed later in the third period. Linebacker Greg Collins added a bit more sorcery by separating the Tide's Willie Shelby from the ball at the Alabama 20, and fellow linebacker Drew Mahalic caught it in midair and ran 8 yards.

One play and 12 yards away, Eric Penick circled into the end zone behind two blocks by tight end Dave Casper. Notre Dame went into the fourth quarter with a 21-17 lead.

The Irish fumbled another opportunity at the Tide 25; then Rutledge threw an interception at the Notre Dame 32. But Bullock fumbled and safety David McMakin recovered at the Irish 39. Bryant, five plays later at the 25, yanked Rutledge and sent Todd in at quarterback. He was setting up his opponent for a sucker play. Todd handed off to Mike Stock on an apparent sweep. As the play developed, Todd rolled to the short sideline. Stock stopped, whirled, and threw back to the quarterback who made the catch and flew untouched to the goal line. Davis missed the all-important PAT, leaving Alabama in the lead by a precarious two points, 23-21 with 9:33 left to play.

Davis' Notre Dame counterpart, Thomas, said of

the botched conversion, "I didn't want to say I believe in fate, but when their guy missed that extra point, I KNEW something was up."

The Irish offense uncoiled for ground gains of 15, 4, 8, 0, and 9 yards, bringing up a third-and-one at the Alabama 45. Clements faked a run and passed to Casper. "When it left my hand," Clements said, "I thought it was going to be picked off. I didn't get enough into it." Casper, tightly covered by McMakin and Ricky Davis, recalled, "It was a 'quacker' all right. But the two defensive guys were playing me, not the ball. So I was able to come back for it." The tight end made the catch and went down on the Alabama 15.

Hunter gained 3 yards wide, and Clements rolled right for 8 more. Thomas, the kicker, came in on fourth-and-goal from the 2.

Thomas said, "Normally I don't chip the ball, but I decided to this time, and I decided not to follow through as much to make sure I got it over their rush. I knew it would probably go a little to the right or left, but at 19 yards I knew it couldn't drift far enough to miss. I knew I could put points on the board." And he did—by a couple of feet—making the score 24-23 Notre Dame with 4:12 to go. "That was a little close, don't you think?" asked Parseghian as Thomas went to the bench. "I was thinking on the way out," the kicker responded seriously, "that if I stuck it right down the pipe nobody would ever remember it. This way they'll be talking about it for years."

Robin Carey returned the kickoff from the 22 to the Tide 40, putting Alabama in position for a late victory. Rutledge lost yardage on two plays and threw incomplete on the other. Gantt punted a 69-yard missile on 4th-and-18 that was downed on the Irish 1. All 'Bama had to do was hold Notre Dame, force a punt against the steady wind, and regain possession. It would be well within Davis' field goal range.

Notre Dame inched itself out to the 5 when, on third down with 2:12 remaining, Parseghian told Clements to go with a long count in hope of pulling Alabama offsides. Instead, Dave Casper jumped offsides and the Irish were penalized to the 2 with one play to get themselves out of immediate danger.

Parseghian, during a conference with his quarterback, called "Power-I-Right, tackle-trap-left," the second of two plays buzzing through his brain. "I was either going to have Tom Clements bootleg the ball around left end," said the intense Armenian, "or we were going to the pass."

With his team hemmed in on the south end of Tulane Stadium, Parseghian remembered, "I didn't want to kick because we were so deep, and it would have been against the wind. Alabama almost surely would have gotten the ball in position to beat us with a field goal. Secondly, they figured we were going to run, and we sent in another tight end (Robin Weber) to be sure they knew we were going to run."

Weber, who had not practiced in two days and needed a cortisone shot for a knee injury before the game, was a forgotten man entering the Sugar Bowl. "Heck," he asked rightfully and rhetorically later, "why should they worry about me?" He had caught only one pass (in the opener) all season.

Casper was the intended receiver, but an Alabama defensive back, expecting the run, froze. Suddenly Casper was double-teamed, and Weber was alone. "Dave was held up," said Clements, "and I saw the safetyman come up to protect on the run. Robin ran by him and all I had to do was hit him." Weber, cutting diagonally, thought, "Oh (bleep), this is one I better not miss."

He made the catch—a national championship catch—after juggling it, and Notre Dame had possession on the 38. It would be six more plays before the horn went off, but the game ended there.

Bryant said he missed the play because he was getting the punt return team ready for the anticipated fourth-down kick. "We were going to rush and try to block it," the coach said. "Two points would have won the game, at least on a field goal. When we had them backed up like that, if I had been a betting man I would have bet you anything we were going to win . . . I think Notre Dame is a great team. But I wouldn't mind playing them again tomorrow. In fact, I'd like it."

It was a game for the ages, a classic. The Irish dressing room, filled with young athletes, echoed the sounds of exuberance and achievement. "Roll, Tide, roll," the Irish mocked with glee. "Everywhere we went," explained Casper, "all we heard was 'Roll, Tide.'" The final score, 24-23, would later make Notre Dame No. 1.

The Alabama locker room was quiet and disconsolate. "It's worse than that loss to Nebraska (in the Orange Bowl)," said linebacker Wayne Hall. "It's even worse than losing to Auburn."

Of course, it was really a game that no one lost. No one had to be ashamed of less than a sterling effort. "We beat a great football team," said Parseghian, putting the game in perspective, "and they lost to a great football team."

But perhaps the woman outside the Alabama dressing room, drained by the night's miracles and heroics, put the 40th Sugar Bowl in the best perspective when she admitted, "Maybe I've been praying to the wrong coach."

Aruns Callery joined Bear Bryant at his hotel after the game. Friends came in and out of the suite for drinks and condolences as 1973 turned to 1974, but the atmosphere was subdued. The coach would read, put aside, and then read some more of the mountain of telegrams he had received. After reading each, he'd crumble it and throw it into the wastepaper basket. It was Bryant's only Sugar Bowl defeat, and with one of his finest teams. He was disappointed.

Nebraska-Florida

"The Sugar Bowl means everything to me."

Notre Dame-Alabama was a spectacular success and immediately ranked among the finest collegiate games ever played.

A very respectable 25.3 television rating, the highest the Sugar had received since records began being kept in 1964, was gratifying. It was also third behind comparatively weak attractions in the Rose and Cotton Bowls. The inescapable conclusion was if a game like this didn't rank higher than third on New Year's Eve, no game ever would. Returning the Sugar Bowl to its natural spot—New Year's Day—seemed inevitable after Notre Dame-Alabama.

Everyone, of course, wanted a duplicate of the Irish-Tide match the following season, setting off an early scramble for those teams. New NCAA rules allowed the bowls to set up matches as early as possible, though there was a gentleman's agreement among the various committees not to firm up anything until November 16. Word seeped out of Miami two weeks before that Alabama, then ranked 3rd, and the Irish, ranked 8th, would have a rematch in the Orange Bowl.

Coach Paul "Bear" Bryant's Crimson Tide had played in Dallas and New Orleans the previous two years. As the story went, Bryant allowed Notre Dame Coach Ara Parseghian to select the site of their showdown since Bear chose the Sugar Bowl the previous year. The Orange Bowl was paying approximately $100,000 more than the Sugar.

Oklahoma, the No. 1 team, was again ineligible for postseason football because of NCAA probation, but the Sugar had several options. ABC-TV wanted to put on a Penn State-Nebraska telecast because of the eastern audience the Nittany Lions would draw. Also, the Cornhuskers (ranked No. 6) appeared to have a legitimate chance of beating Oklahoma.

Florida (7-1), Auburn (7-1), Texas A&M (7-1), and Texas (6-2) were also in the picture with the Cornhuskers (6-2) and Penn State (7-1). Nebraska-Auburn figured to be the best draw in terms of bringing fans to the game. When the Cornhuskers played Alabama in the 1967 Sugar Bowl, 16,000 fans followed Nebraska. When Auburn played Oklahoma, 18,000 fans followed the War Eagles. When Penn State played Oklahoma, it brought only 8,500 fans.

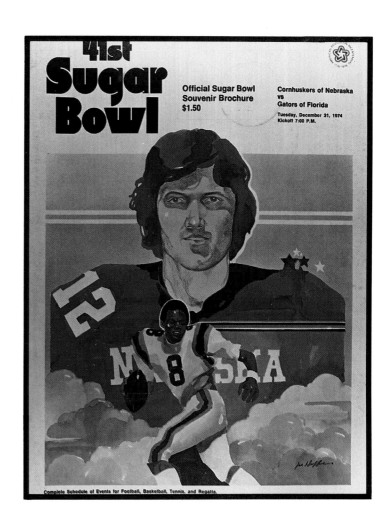

Nebraska Coach Tom Osborne.

And just 6,000 Gator fans followed Florida to New Orleans in 1966.

In terms of rankings, the best bet the Sugar seemed to have was Penn State-Florida, and both teams seemed capable of winning the remainder of their games. Penn State, although the Sugar didn't know it at the time, was already spoken for—by the Cotton Bowl. The Sugar took the best it could from this assorted grab bag: Florida and Nebraska.

Later, Florida missed on a two-point conversion in the final 12 seconds and lost to Georgia, 17-16. A week later the Gators lost to Kentucky, 41-24. By the end of the season Florida was barely in the Top Twenty. Both the Gators and the Cornhuskers, 8th-ranked after a 28-14 defeat to Oklahoma, were 8-3 entering the Sugar Bowl.

As a footnote, the Alabama-Notre Dame rematch soured somewhat, too, though those teams were 2nd and 9th entering the Orange Bowl. Southern California waxed the Irish 55-24, removing the luster.

An offensive game was anticipated in the Sugar Bowl. Nebraska averaged 32 points and 412 yards a game. Florida averaged 22 points and 371 yards. A closer glance at the opponents, though, was intriguing. In one corner was bowl-tested and tradition-steeped Nebraska. Alabama defeated the 'Huskers in the 1967 Sugar, but that was the last time Nebraska had lost a bowl game. A victory in the Sugar Bowl would be Nebraska's sixth straight and would tie it with Georgia Tech for the national record.

The Cornhuskers hadn't lost often in recent history. In the decade from 1965 to 1974, Nebraska finished in the Top Ten seven times. On the other hand, Florida, though it had a program on the up-swing, astoundingly had never finished in the Top Ten. The 18th-ranked Gators felt they had an out-side chance at breaking that barrier with a victory over Nebraska.

Florida brought some tradition in the form of Ray Graves, a distinguished Sugar Bowl alumnus. Graves was the starting center on the Tennessee team that was upset by Boston College in 1941. He later returned as a Georgia Tech assistant in 1953, 1954, and 1956, then as the head coach of the Gators in 1966. His return as athletic director made Graves the first person to compete on all levels in the Sugar Bowl. Unfortunately, his school had little of that kind of background.

The odds-makers felt strongly that this Gator team would not be the one to crack the Top Ten. Nebraska was a 12½-point favorite, a line that obviously reflected a lack of respect for the angered Gators. "You hear so much about Nebraska and how we're a 12-point underdog," fumed linebacker Glenn Cameron, "but I don't think Nebraska is a super team. I ask this question: Who has Nebraska played this year? They played Oklahoma, one of the greatest teams this year, and lost. But, who else have they played this year? When people start talking about Nebraska they are talking about the Nebraska team of three years ago that won the national championship."

Lee McGriff wasn't as belligerent. He wore his heart on his sleeve as he summed up the game. "Being a senior," said the wingback, "the Sugar Bowl means everything to me. It's my last game in a Gator uniform. We have a chance to finish in the Top Ten, and a chance for the seniors to go out with the feeling we gave something to this university. It's everything we ever dreamed of boiled down to one night."

Nebraska 13-Florida 10

Crisp play between Nebraska and Florida on New Year's Eve, 1974.

"It had that famous Coyle hook on it."

Florida linebacker Ralph Ortega summed up the main concern of the Gator defense when he analyzed, "I don't want to take anything away from the Nebraska running game, but it's their passing game that can hurt you the most and that's because of quarterback David Humm."

Humm, a 6-foot-2, 186-pound son of a Las Vegas casino dealer, was the trigger in the Nebraska offense. He held several Big Eight passing records, including 42 career touchdown passes.

Early in the game, however, it became apparent that Humm was not going to be the Cornhusker fuse. It was also apparent that Nebraska had as much as it could handle with the aggressive, swarming Gators. Humm fumbled and recovered on the third down of Nebraska's first possession, forcing a punt. A 25-yard run by James Richards, behind a devastating block by Mike Williams, put Florida on the Nebraska 45. Three plays netted 9 yards and 35 inches. Quarterback Don Gaffney tried to sneak for the drive-sustaining inch, but the 'Husker middle stopped him short.

The two possessions established the tempo for most of the night—a floundering 'Husker offense and a threatening Gator attack.

Humm went to the air and Randy Talbot intercepted at the Florida 49 and headed down the sideline. He reached the Cornhusker 21. On the following play, Tony Green, darting in and out of the line, cut behind a block by Richards and covered the 21 yards to the end zone. David Posey's conversion put the underdog Floridians ahead, 7-0.

Gaffney, taking all the thunder away from Humm, had the Gators back in position again with an excellent pass to Wes Chandler. He caught a 22-yard pass downfield between defenders George Kyros and Jim Burrow (a former walk-on at Ole Miss, where he had been told he was too small). The play gave Florida a first down on the Nebraska 29. Eventually Posey attempted a 38-yard field goal. It was low and short.

With two minutes until the half, Florida went for the jugular. Gaffney, with a first at the Gator 30, threw to wide-open Lee McGriff, who made the reception and rolled out-of-bounds at the 'Husker 31.

Jimmy DuBose hit the middle for 17 yards, but Tom Pate snuffed touchdown hopes by sacking Gaffney at the 29. Posey kicked a 40-yard field goal, and the 12-point underdogs had a 10-0 halftime lead.

When the teams started the second half, Florida had a chance to put the game away. Alvin Cowans intercepted Humm at the Gator 38 and returned it to the Nebraska 34. Gaffney inched Florida to the 18 where, on third-and-four, he pitched to Green who bolted for the end zone. Knocked off-balance, Green went the final 5 yards sideways while trying

Don Gaffney (8) has 'Husker defense running in circles.

Mike Fultz (72) has Gator quarterback Gaffney hanging by a thread.

to stay inbounds. He got into the end zone, but the officials ruled he stepped out at the 5. Films later showed Green had not stepped out.

There was a 2-yard loss before Green drove for 6 yards. DuBose gained nothing at the 1. Coach Doug Dickey passed up the field goal and Gaffney pitched to Richards who slipped, then was dropped at the 1 by defensive back Burrow.

Dickey didn't really feel the situation was a gamble. "I thought maybe if we left the ball there (at the 1)," said Dickey, "we're going to get it back and kick the field goal anyway."

When Richards went down short, 'Husker Coach Tom Osborne made a change in strategy. He benched Humm and sent in reserve Terry Luck with orders to junk the passing game and go to the running offense.

Nebraska began worming its way out of the shadows. Don Westbrook, Monte Anthony, and Tony Davis put some consistency into the offense. By the end of the third period, the Huskers were planted on the Gator 12. Anthony bounced into the end zone 2 minutes later to cut the lead to 10-7. The 18-play, 99-yard drive consumed 8 minutes and 50 seconds of playing time.

Seldom has a game turned so completely on one play as Florida's failure to score from the 1.

Nebraska forced a punt and took over on the Gator 41. In three downs, Luck's unit had moved to

the 49, bringing up a fourth-and-two. Tom Osborne signalled "Go-for-it," and Anthony gained 3. The drive eventually fizzled, and Mike Coyle's line-drive field goal of 37 yards tied the score with 7:12 remaining.

Again Florida couldn't move, and the 'Huskers got the ball with four minutes to play at their 25. Davis put Nebraska into position for victory when he broke off tackle 40 yards to the Gator 31. The last minutes wouldn't have been an issue except that Cowans brought Davis down when no one else could.

With 2:22 left, Coyle came back in for Nebraska, facing a fourth-and-one at the Florida 22. Coyle's 39-yard kick was good. "I didn't think that last one was good," the kicker said, "but it had that famous Coyle hook on it."

Nebraska had somehow pulled itself not only from defeat but also from humiliation.

The Florida dressing room was steamy and somber after the 13-10 defeat. Dickey spent a lot of time talking individually with his warriors. Preston Kendrick, who was absolutely superb on the field with two interceptions, eight tackles, and four assists, couldn't look up.

In another corner, defensive back Talbot stopped taking his jersey off, looked around, and expressed everyone else's thought aloud: "I'll tell you what, I'd like to play them again."

Alabama-Penn State

"I think we ought to consider it."

It had been demonstrated that ABC's New Year's Eve experiment was failing. The Nebraska-Florida game, at least as attractive as the Penn State-Baylor Cotton Bowl, was overwhelmed (25.3 to 16.0) by 3rd-place Dallas in the ratings. The Notre Dame-Alabama Orange Bowl, a rematch without nearly as much sizzle as the previous year's Sugar Bowl, pulled a much higher audience. There was simply no question that New Year's Day was a stronger date than New Year's Eve for bowls.

Other factors that could change the entire bowl structure were coming into play. The Big Ten and Pacific Eight were about to break their traditional Rose Bowl-only affiliation. Champions from those conferences, of course, would continue to play in Pasadena, but runners-up and others would be free to participate in other postseason games. Also, the Orange Bowl, which had expressed interest in the Southeastern Conference but was turned down, was close to resuming its tie-up with the Big Eight after a hiatus of several years.

Those changes would have an effect on the SEC. The SEC, which on occasion had sent as many as seven of its teams to bowls in one year, would have stiff competition for minor bowl berths as the number of available quality teams increased. And with the Miami tie-up, a New Year's Day berth would be gone. Theoretically, the SEC champion, under the right set of circumstances, could be shut out of a New Year's Day game.

For years, as the Sugar Bowl's fortunes nosed downward, the Mid-Winter Sports Association concluded that a tie-up could rejuvenate an ailing bowl. The arguments of past decades against such an arrangement were no longer valid.

It seemed to become an annual ritual: The Sugar Bowl would inquire about the feasibility of a tie-up with the SEC, and the SEC would politely decline. New Orleans began pressing harder in 1973.

By 1975 things were different. Realizing that shortly the Sugar Bowl again would be the only New Year's Day game without a tie-up, and that the SEC champion could be shut out of a New Year's Day game, some members began to perceive the situation differently. For New Orleans to host a

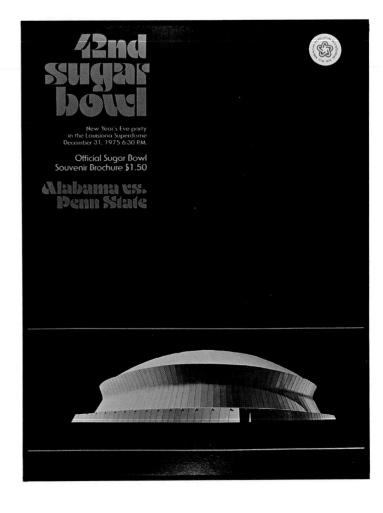

No. 1 game without the SEC champion would require a highly ranked independent or a rare national contender that was not a champion of the Southwest, Big Eight, Big Ten, or Pacific Coast Conferences. For the first time, there seemed to be a mutual need by both parties.

Sugar Bowl President Cliff Kern, Sam Corenswet, Jr., and Charles V. Cusimano drove to Baton Rouge in the spring to talk with Louisiana State University Athletic Director Carl Maddox. Maddox would chair the athletic directors' meeting at the SEC convention in December, and the delegation wanted the chance to make a definite proposal. Maddox promised to get them on the docket.

Conference Commissioner Boyd McWhorter was contacted for advice. "I gave them the proper procedure," said McWhorter. "They would have to get the athletic directors to approve of it, and to make that recommendation to the conference presidents. Personally, I did not think at the time it would pass because the conference simply had not shown any tendency toward tying up with any bowl."

McWhorter advised the Sugar Bowl that the possibility of a tie-up would be greatly enhanced if there was a financial guarantee.

The Mid-Winter Sports Association went to work. "We put together a group that had very close relationships with the athletic directors around the conference," said Kern. "A.B. Nicholas was very close with Johnny Vaught at Ole Miss and Bob Woodruff at Tennessee. So he contacted those gentlemen. I was about the only one in the group that knew Clay Stapleton at Vanderbilt very well, so I got in touch with him. John Boebinger was good friends with Joel Eaves at Georgia. Charles Cusimano was on the Board of Supervisors at LSU. And Aruns Callery contacted Bear Bryant."

Bryant was the fly in the ointment. He had only one vote, but his stature was such that no one would seriously try to tell him where his team was to play over the holidays. Bryant had made Alabama into the most glamorous bowl team in the region, if not the country, and in the process had become something of a kingmaker. Alabama was so coveted as a bowl commodity that frequently it was only when Bryant decided where and who he was to play that the year's bowl pairings fell into place.

Bear told Callery he would not consider a tie-up, that he could go where he wanted and felt it was in the best interest of the University of Alabama. This put a practical end to the matter.

Months later, Bryant called Callery and thoughtfully said, "I have to think about the rest of the conference, too." Callery knew the Sugar Bowl was about to change.

Sports in New Orleans was approaching a new age with the completion of one of the world's unique buildings, the Louisiana Superdome. It is the most multifaceted building ever designed. The Battle of Gettysburg conceivably could have been fought within its walls. A 25-story structure could fit under its roof, which spans 9½ acres. It took two years and nine months to complete, with 800 construction workers swarming over the 13-acre site on any given day. The scope of the Superdome was so vast that its architect, Buster Curtis, concedes that no single man could have put it together on paper— computers did it. It is a ludicrous statistic, but the Superdome has 125 million cubic feet of space and was built at a cost of $163 million.

Bryant wanted to coach in the first Superdome Sugar Bowl and asked to be considered. Who could have turned him down? After a season-opening loss to Missouri, the Crimson Tide tore through its schedule and was on the verge of another Southeastern Conference championship. Bryant also winked at the Cotton Bowl where he might have the opportunity to play a higher-ranked team.

There was no question he could play a higher-ranked team in the Orange Bowl. Either 2nd-ranked Nebraska or 6th-ranked Oklahoma would be waiting there. But not only was Alabama refusing to play either of those schools in Miami, but the Tide wouldn't play them in New Orleans either. The Sugar Bowl was informed that should Bryant play in the Sugar Bowl, he would like to play Penn State. Eleventh-ranked Penn State was a fine ball club, but was not of the same caliber as Oklahoma or Nebraska. "This is a helluva note," stormed Oklahoma's Barry Switzer. "It would have made no difference if we were 10-0 like Nebraska. The Sugar Bowl still wouldn't have taken the loser of our game, even though that would have guaranteed them at least one 10-1 team." "Tell that son of a buck not to duck us," an angry Nebraska Coach Tom Osborne told Sugar Bowl official John Barr.

"I want to make it clear that we want to play in the best bowl against the best team," Osborne went on. "Any team that doesn't feel that way doesn't belong in competitive athletics. I know that's a pretty strong statement, but it's time this thing is brought out in the open."

"We have no apologies to make to anyone," retorted Bryant in Birmingham. "If the Big Eight wanted to play Alabama, why did they sign with the Orange Bowl?" It was a weak response, and the whole situation was ironic since a strong argument against a tie-up in the early days was the possibility a team might want to call the shots on its opposition.

There were two reasons why Bryant would have been interested in Penn State. The first was obvious. Alabama, for all its success, had not won a bowl game since the 1967 Sugar against Nebraska. There were some who were saying Bear had quit eating soup because he couldn't handle the bowl. While this Penn State team was capable and deserving, it did not have the weapons of the Big Eight contenders. Second, Penn State seldom used its entire allotment of tickets. Alabama fans could never get enough. A Penn State-'Bama bowl gave Bryant an excellent chance at victory and more tickets for his legion of supporters.

An indication of the ticket pressure at Alabama was illustrated one Sunday morning at Birmingham's St. Paul's Cathedral. Aruns Callery, who had been following the Tide, attended early Mass attired in his Sugar Bowl blazer. As he went for a seat, an usher with whom he'd become friendly handed Callery a folded church pledge card. Callery put it in his pocket. After church Callery found a $20 bill attached to the card with a note requesting two Sugar Bowl tickets.

After Bryant's turnabout concerning the tie-up, he joined with Ole Miss' Johnny Vaught in buttonholing their fellow athletic directors in the cause. The proposal probably would have failed without them. Bryant felt he could deliver three votes, which left seven for Vaught. "I guess part of the reason we

Pete Fountain and his famed clarinet charm an audience of attentive football players.

Joe Paterno, left, and Bear Bryant toast each other with café brulot at Antoine's.

were able to do it," said Vaught, "is because Bear and I went to so many bowls. We were kind of the dominant teams as far as the bowls were concerned, and I think the other athletic directors recognized that if we stood behind it, it had some merit."

Vaught, who lobbied vigorously and successfully, said he had never been for tie-ups per se, and that if he could he would abolish them all. "I have a lot of friends with the Sugar Bowl," he said, "but I pushed for it because it seemed like the thing to do. If we hadn't tied with the Sugar Bowl we eventually would have had to tie up with another bowl. If we were going to go that way, I think we were better off with the Sugar Bowl."

In the meantime, Sam Corenswet, Jr., and other members of the Sugar Bowl were negotiating with ABC. This would be the final game of the television pact and since the Sugar Bowl wanted to guarantee the SEC a payment, those talks were as important as the conference vote in Birmingham.

Cliff Kern, Executive Committee Chairman Marshall Davis, A.B. Nicholas, Aruns Callery, and Charles Cusimano went to Birmingham for the November 30 SEC meeting and were prepared to offer a $750,000 guarantee. The reception was warm. "I think we ought to consider it," Tennessee's Bob Woodruff. "It would be a fine thing for our conference." Apparently the groundwork laid by the Sugar Bowlers, Bryant, and Vaught was solid. The SEC athletic directors voted unanimously to recommend to the university presidents a tie-up with New Orleans.

"I stood aghast when the vote came in," recalled SEC Commissioner Boyd McWhorter. "I wasn't disappointed, just surprised at the unanimous vote."

There was no way of knowing it at the time, but the Orange Bowl's matchup of Oklahoma and Michigan influenced the Sugar Bowl's proposal. McWhorter and others throughout the SEC were concerned that a tie-up would have the effect of limiting it to one team in a major bowl. "But right after that," recalled the commissioner, "the Orange Bowl invited the runner-up from another conference (Michigan). So I thought if a runner-up from that conference can get it, all of us can get it."

The SEC presidents would have to make the final decision, but after 42 years and many attempts, the SEC and the Sugar Bowl were engaged.

On the football front, things were not moving smoothly for Bryant. Quarterback Richard Todd, a two-time All-SEC athlete from Mobile, sliced the middle finger of his right (throwing) hand Christmas Day and required two stitches.

"If it had to happen I'm glad it happened yesterday and not the day before the game," Todd said. "If we had to play tomorrow night, I don't think I could take a snap. But I'm gonna play in the game unless I break my leg."

Some thought was given as to whether Todd would play. Twenty-three Alabama players, including Todd, were anywhere from 15 to 90 minutes late returning to their hotel after a Saturday night on the town. This happened to the coach that once suspended Joe Namath before a Sugar Bowl game. But Bryant tried to be understanding, calling the incident "no big thing." Then more players were late coming in Monday night, and Bryant stripped two of their starting assignments.

Todd, meanwhile, was gaining a healthy respect for the Nittany Lions. He and Penn State linebacker Greg Buttle sized each other up in a press conference. Todd listened attentively as the 6-foot-2, 228-pound linebacker joined a New Orleans barbershop quartet for a song. When asked what he thought of Buttle, Todd laughed, "Well, the way he sings you can smell his breath from here. I hope he doesn't get that close during the game."

Alabama 13-Penn State 6

"Lordy, it sure didn't come easy."

Bear Bryant was typically downplaying his chances, even against a preferred opponent, one that figured to be 13½ points behind Alabama at game's end. "I think we'll win," Bryant said, then hastily added, "if I don't overcoach 'em."

It was the classic Bryant style—laid-back, understated, and homespun. But Bryant wanted to break his bowl jinx badly. He walked out for the kickoff without his trademark houndstooth hat. Bryant would later say he was taught never to wear a hat indoors. But he hoped that by adding a different touch, he might render his team a victory. That was the reason Mary Harmon Bryant asked if she could ride in the team bus to the Superdome.

John Andress quarterbacked Penn State to two consecutive first downs on the opening possession of the game. The Lion's misdirection plays kept Alabama a bit off-balance until they reached midfield. Chris Bahr tried a 62-yard field goal that was short and to the right.

Todd came out with his finger bandaged, and Penn State dared him to pass. Overloading the line and hoping to force 'Bama into mistakes on the Tide side of the field, the Lion defense was singed. Joe Dale Harris, a starter because of the curfew violations, ran a simple turn-in pattern that Todd got off just before being engulfed by the defense. There weren't enough Lions in the secondary to take all the receivers and Harris was free, turning the short yardage pass into a 54-yard gain.

That play eventually was converted into a 25-yard field goal by Danny Ridgeway and a 3-0 Alabama lead that held up to the half.

Andress moved the Lions in position to score early in the second half when he scrambled from his 35 to a first down at the Penn State 49. The drive went to the 25 where Bahr kicked a 42-yard field goal.

Todd brought the Tide roaring back, though admittedly the quarterback was never sure of what he was doing against the changing Penn State defense. At his 35, Todd called a time-out. "There were times that I didn't know who to read or who to give the ball to. I called the time-out because they shifted to our tight end side, right where we wanted to run a play," said Todd. "I went over to the sidelines and Coach Bryant sort of winked at me. He called the pass. We felt they'd be single-covering Ozzie (Newsome)."

Freshman Bill Crummy was inserted in the Penn State secondary in the first period when Tommy Odell suffered a rib injury. Crummy had played well, but on this play he took Todd's pump fake and Newsome broke back to the sideline and caught the pass 30 yards upstream. He was brought down at the 10.

Todd lost 4 yards recovering a fumble, but Mike Stock swept into the end zone behind a ferocious block by Newsome.

Bahr cut the margin to 10-6 with a 37-yard field goal in the fourth quarter, but Ridgeway answered with a 28-yarder. With 3:19 left, Penn State got one last chance, hinging the outcome on a fourth-and-one at its 39. Alabama held with 1:15 to play and Bryant's bowl jinx was broken. "Lordy, it sure didn't come easy," grumbled Bryant, noting that Penn State had dropped his offense for losses nine times. "We beat a helluva football team tonight. Anybody who doesn't think that is an idiot."

Richard Todd's bandaged throwing hand may have been the single reason why others didn't believe Penn State was an elite team. Todd completed 10 of 12 passes for 210 yards and in the process probably prevented a Nittany Lion victory. "Believe it or not," said standout linebacker Kurt Allerman of 'Bama's lean but effective air game, "we wanted them to pass. But they mixed up their passes well and they executed them exceptionally well. They executed the big play and had no turnovers—what more can you say?"

Todd was unsure before the first snap. "I don't throw a spiral when I have a good hand," he cracked. "It didn't hurt any."

It only hurt Penn State and Coach Joe Paterno, who weaved his way into Alabama's dressing room, where Todd was surrounded by newsmen. "I want to congratulate you on a great game," said the Nittany Lion coach. When he learned Todd was planning on going to the Senior Bowl, Paterno quipped, "I'd like to recommend you for that one. It's the least I can do since Bear recommended me for this one."

Pittsburgh-Georgia

SATURDAY, JANUARY 1, 1977

"We think it will be a very popular move."

Bear Bryant, as unselfish as he was in helping weld the support necessary for the SEC-Sugar Bowl tie-up, made a last plea after the Penn State game to open all the bowls, to let them all compete for the best match. His argument was parallel to the one the Mid-Winter Sports Association had made for years. But no one really listened. "What I'm for is all bowls to open up for everybody, nobody have a tie-up," said Bryant, who was also opposed to the voting of national champions after bowls. "If we are going to stay with the polls," he stated, "take it out of the bowls. It puts too much pressure when bowls are used for it. It takes all the fun out of the bowls."

Voters would continue to decide the national champion after postseason games because the general public enjoys seeing grand matches with something riding on the outcome. Instead of decreasing the number of bowl tie-ups, there would be an increase. The SEC presidents, after studying the Sugar Bowl's proposal, approved it.

On March 3, 1976, after 42 years of infatuation, spats, and courtship, the SEC and Sugar Bowl were finally hitched. "We think it will be a very popular move," said Harry M. England, who had succeeded Cliff Kern as Sugar Bowl president. "We recognize that the SEC has been a very contributing factor in the Sugar Bowl for many years. Unofficially it has been almost a partner."

With what England called the Sugar Bowl's "new arsenal of weapons"—the tie-up and the Superdome —the Mid-Winter Sports Association also believed it was time to call an end to the experiment with a New Year's Eve playing date. The December 31 date was a failure because the traditional celebrations interfered and further, there was a drop-off in eastern press coverage because of early deadlines on newspaper holiday runs. ABC agreed, and the Sugar Bowl petitioned the NCAA for a return to its New Year's playing date. "We hope it will be a mere formality," said England. "We tried New Year's Eve for four years and found it was not the best time to hold a football game."

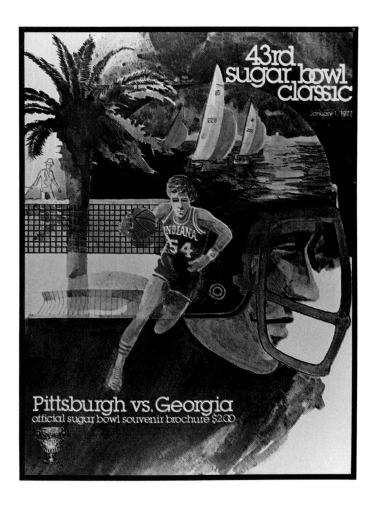

43rd sugar bowl classic

January 1, 1977

Pittsburgh vs. Georgia
official sugar bowl souvenir brochure $2.00

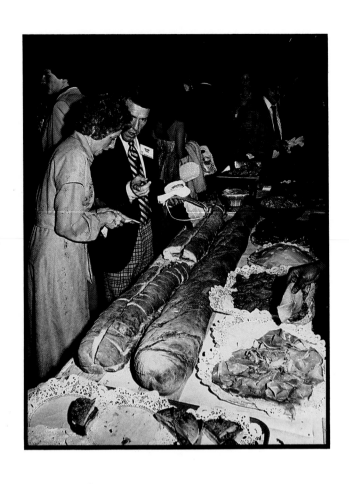

The NCAA approved the request, not only putting the Sugar Bowl back on New Year's Day, but also creating two questions for sports trivia buffs: What year was there not a Sugar Bowl? The answer is 1976, since the December 31, 1975, game would be followed by a January 1, 1977, game. The companion question is, of course: In what year were there two Sugar Bowls? The switch to New Year's Eve had made possible a game on January 1, 1972, and another on December 31, 1972.

These significant changes were taking place without Joe Katz, who resigned as executive director of the Mid-Winter Sports Association shortly after the Alabama-Penn State game. Katz wanted to pursue other business ventures. A search committee was formed to find his successor, the third director of the Sugar Bowl.

The 1976 SEC season was wild and woolly, and there was a certain irony in that the first year of the tie-up, after an unyielding five-year hold on the throne by Alabama, the conference had a horse race. This was also evident elsewhere; as late as November 1 it appeared that of the nonaligned bowl berths, only 2nd-ranked Pittsburgh in the Orange Bowl looked definite.

Pittsburgh, on the other hand, was also the team New Orleans wanted and, for the first time in a long while, all the Sugar Bowl's resources were going to be used to get a favored team. Coach Johnny Major's Panthers were more than just very good. Pittsburgh featured an extraordinary runner, Heisman Trophy winner Tony Dorsett. He was college football's all-time ground gainer with 6,082 yards. The Panthers also had an underrated but suffocating defense. Uppermost in Majors' mind was playing the best opponent he could find, an opponent whose defeat would push the Panthers to No. 1, or solidify that position if it were achieved beforehand.

ABC helped overcome the difference in money between the Orange and Sugar Bowls by putting the Panther-West Virginia game on regional television, which was perfectly legal and ethical, though some other bowl officials squirmed. It wasn't as if Pitt didn't belong on TV. "The opponent is more important than the money," said sources at Pitt. "The main goal is the best way of getting No. 1."

Pittsburgh rose to No. 1 after Purdue defeated Michigan early in November. A week later, Iowa State assured the Orange Bowl of a host with at least two losses when it whipped Nebraska and put the Big Eight in a five-way first-place tie. At the same time, 4th-ranked Georgia emerged as the Southeastern Conference champion and the highest ranking available opponent for the Panthers. The Panthers voted to play in New Orleans against the 10-1 Bulldogs.

Georgia won the SEC championship on the merits of a ball-control offense and an effective defensive unit called the "Junkyard Dogs." The dedication of the defense was reflected in a supreme sacrifice of the 1970s—shaved heads—a symbol that so inspired Georgians that Coach Vince Dooley shaved his head, too. Ironically, Majors built Pitt from a 6-5-1 team to 11-0 in four years, and the first game his seniors had played was a 7-7 tie with Georgia.

"The winner of the Rose Bowl (between USC and Michigan) is the national champion," said Trojan Coach John Robinson of his 2nd-ranked team, "and the hell with the rest of them. If we win, we're going into the dressing room and declare ourselves unanimous national champions." His Rose Bowl rival, Bo Schembechler of the No. 3 Wolverines, chimed in, "I can hardly believe that Pitt could beat Southern Cal, and if we beat them we're going to claim the national championship."

Majors was incredulous, pointing out that USC's 21-point loss to Missouri was a pretty wide margin for a national contender. "That's the most ridiculous farce ever perpetrated," said Majors. "If Georgia beats us, they'd have more of a claim than Michigan or Southern Cal."

Pitt raised two questions in the public's mind, neither of which had anything to do with its ability. The first was how the loss of Coach Majors would affect the Panthers' bowl effort. Bill Battle resigned from the University of Tennessee, and Majors leaped at the opportunity to return to his alma mater after this last game. The second question was how Majors' treat-'em-like-men attitude would hold up.

Majors gave his team of mostly seniors run of the town until just a couple of days before the game. He wouldn't have done it, he said, with a less-mature team. This team could handle it. The gesture was in keeping with the coach's personality.

Twenty years before, when Majors' fumble was instrumental in Baylor's 13-7 upset of Tennessee, Johnny recalled, "I went out and partied. I wasn't feeling too good, but I knew back then you'd always have to take the bad with the good. I remember I stayed up all night, drove to Mobile, and was at practice for the Senior Bowl the next afternoon."

While the press wondered about the Panthers prowling the French Quarter, Dooley fretted about them prowling the Superdome. A lot of attention was given Dorsett, who gained a single-season record 1,948 yards as a senior; but the Georgia coach knew that in order to stop Dorsett he had to contain multitalented quarterback Matt Cavanaugh. If the Georgia defense was on the field too long, Dooley knew he was in trouble.

Greater love hath no man . . . Georgia Coach Vince Dooley wears the trademark of his defensive unit.

Dooley watches practice intently.

Dooley covers skinhead after Pitt skinned Georgia.

Pittsburgh 27-Georgia 3

"Well, I guess they're drinking Bloody Marys."

Tony Dorsett juggles a pitchout in Pitt's steamrolling of Georgia.

It was over almost before it began. Matt Cavanaugh would face a 6-2 stunting Georgia defense by the run-conscious Bulldogs. This defense would give the Panther receivers one-on-one coverage, and Cavanaugh put points on the board minutes after the kickoff.

Pitt, a 2½-point favorite, zipped 80 yards on a 12-play drive on its second possession. Split end Gordon Jones caught a 13-yard pass to midfield, then fullback Elliot Walker beat linebacker Jim Griffith and took a pass over the middle that turned into a 36-yard gain. "On that first long pass," moaned linebacker Ben Zambiasi later, "the ball actually hit my finger. It was just broken coverage by one of our linebackers."

The play went to the Georgia 10 and two plays later Cavanaugh scored on a keeper from the 6. If Georgia could take any solace, it was that Dorsett gained only 10 of the 80 yards.

Georgia held on from there until seven minutes were gone in the second period when Cavanaugh, running along the line on an option, pulled up and threw to a slanting Jones who split two defenders and loped 59 yards to the end zone.

"They've got eight people up there to stop Tony," explained Cavanaugh, "and that means single coverage on our receivers. All you have to do is get them the ball."

Dorsett finally got loose and was 11 yards from the goal just before the half. He scored with defenders sprawled in his wake and made the score 21-0 to seal Pitt's national championship. "When did I think we had it won?" asked tight end Jim Corbett. "That's easy. At halftime. There's no way any team is going to score 21 points on our defense in one half if the points meant anything."

While statisticians were breaking down the half's figures, a reporter broke up the press box by glancing solemnly toward the Pitt locker room and musing, "Well, I guess they're drinking Bloody Marys."

Some of the halftime stats read like a Georgia obit. The "Junkyard Dogs" had done a reasonable job on Dorsett, holding him to 65 yards on 17 carries. Cavanaugh, however, was 7 of 11 passing for 185 yards. Georgia fell victim to solid Pitt defensive strategy. On running plays (almost all Bulldog plays were) the Panthers went to a six-man front to which Georgia didn't seem able to adjust. Georgia was unable to put together back-to-back first downs and could gain only slightly more than a yard (a total of 17) on its first-down opportunities.

In the second half things changed a bit, though the outcome was never in doubt. Cracks in the line seemed to widen and Dorsett began swinging right and left, anywhere there was daylight. He gained 137 yards on 15 carries in the 30 minutes for a Sugar Bowl record 202 yards rushing. Cavanaugh, who got Pitt over the hump, was the Most Valuable Player, though.

Allan Leavitt kicked a 25-yard field goal for Georgia, but Panther kicker Carson Long countered with 42- and 31-yard field goals to end the point tallying.

The Pitt defense was extraordinary, perhaps the finest aspect of this excellent collection of athletes. The three points Georgia scored was not only 26 below its season average, it was Georgia's lowest

score in 52 games. The Bulldogs averaged 279.5 yards rushing during the regular season, but got only 135 against the Panthers. It wasn't until 22½ minutes had elapsed that Georgia crossed midfield. The Pitt defense caught more (5) of Georgia's passes than Georgia (3) did. And three of Pitt's five scoring drives came after the defense forced a turnover.

"I think some people thought we might miss the 11:30 kickoff because we'd be hung over," cracked middle guard Al Romano, obviously relishing the complete dressing down of his rival and the early practical end to the national championship question. "What they should do now is call off the Rose Bowl," Romano added.

"All year long," said Johnny Majors, "I haven't waved my finger in the air, and I haven't worn a No. 1 button." Waving a finger in the air and sporting a No. 1 button, he added, "But after the game I told the team it was No. 1 and they all agree that we are."

Georgia quarterback Ray Goff (10) shot down by Pittsburgh defender.

Tony Dorsett (33) on record-breaking day.

Pitt's Matt Cavanaugh (12), Pitt's decisive 1977 Sugar Bowl weapon, rears up and fires at Georgia.

Alabama-Ohio State

MONDAY, JANUARY 2, 1978

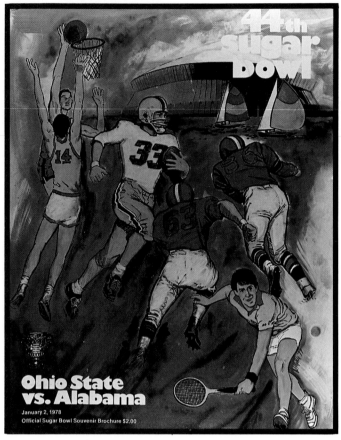

"You'd better get the grandfathers involved."

The look of the Sugar Bowl was changing in many ways. The football game was back on New Year's Day, with the Southeastern Conference champion automatically in one corner. Edna Engert, after 41 years of running the business office, decided to call it a career.

She had once said, "I was very involved with the piano as a young girl. My mother said I must make up my mind to either attend college and study music or take a job. I took a job and I've never regretted it. It led me to the Sugar Bowl." The feeling was obviously mutual. This woman, who started with 37 bosses, was entrusted with command of the Sugar Bowl's nerve center for most of her tenure with the Mid-Winter Sports Association. She served well. If Fred Digby was "Mr. Sugar Bowl," Edna Engert was the "Mrs."

At a testimonial given by her "bosses," Edna was presented with a gold charm and desk set. Until then, it was a gift reserved only for Sugar Bowl presidents.

Carl James, the 48-year-old athletic director of

Duke University, was named executive director in July; but the position was again open the following year when James resigned to become Athletic Director at the University of Maryland.

Alabama and Notre Dame again seemed to be the champagne pairing for the holidays. After an early season loss to Nebraska, the Crimson Tide had developed into a potent football team. The Irish were in and out, and indeed a loss to a very weak Ole Miss seemed to knock the Notre Dame aspirations for No. 1 askew. But it was the only Irish loss.

What the pairing appeared to be riding on was a Texas defeat before November 19, the day the invitations would be issued. A loss by the No. 1 Longhorns should lift the Tide to No. 1, and Dan Devine's Fighting Irish would go wherever No. 1 went for the chance to swipe the crown.

A more likely occurrence would be Texas steaming into the Cotton Bowl with the Irish tagging behind, and Michigan edging Ohio State in the Big Ten's annual showdown. That would send Michigan to Pasadena and the co-champion Buckeyes looking

Edna Engert on January 20, 1977, the night she retired after 40 years at the Sugar Bowl. She is surrounded, from left to right, by bowl pioneers Paul DeBlanc, Ralph Barry, Dough Watters, Charles Zatarain, Bernie Grenrood, Albert Wachenheim, Jr., and Alan Smuck.

for other vacancies on New Year's. Since the Big Ten and Pac-Eight had broken their Rose-only binds, their representatives had played in other bowls, though not in New Orleans.

Notre Dame was more desirable, but the novelty of a Big Ten team in the Sugar Bowl was intriguing—particularly if it were a game between Coach Bear Bryant, with 270 victories, and Coach Woody Hayes, with 231 victories, the biggest winners on football's active roster. It was interesting also to ponder the insurance the Sugar had with the SEC tie-up. Without it, Bryant surely would have been angling for a No. 1 showdown.

In spite of being generally outplayed, Michigan somehow beat Ohio State. The fiery Hayes, gentleman and history scholar off the field and occasional firebrand on the field, slugged an ABC cameraman in the game's final moments. Hayes' temper had become part of football lore and New Orleans braced for it.

Alabama and Ohio State were 3rd and 8th in the polls at the time of the selections. The Tide's wish-

bone gained 416.7 yards a game, the 11th-best offense nationally. Ohio State was 14th with 413.8 yards a game and 2nd in rushing with 321.2 yards. On the opposite side of the ledger, the Buckeyes gave up only 230.8 yards a game (7th nationally) while 'Bama surrendered 252 yards. Sprinkled on the Buckeye roster were names like Pete Johnson (fullback), Chris Ward (tackle), Ron Springs (tailback), and Tom Cousineau (linebacker). Alabama had names like Ozzie Newsome (receiver), Jeff Rutledge (quarterback), and Tony Nathan (running back).

The only names the press seemed interested in were Bryant and Hayes. The growl vs. the scowl was the way the New Orleans press painted the game.

"I don't know why you people keep making such a big deal over Woody Hayes and Paul Bryant," rasped the Bear. "I can assure you that I'm not going to play . . . and I hope Woody does." Hayes made a case for the vintage years. "When (Egyptian President Anwar) Sadat and (Israeli Prime Minister Menachem) Begin got together," said Hayes, "it's

Woody Hayes and Bear Bryant prepare café brulot at Antoine's.

Ohio State Coach Woody Hayes.

the same as when Bear and I get together. If you want a good contest or a good agreement, you'd better get the grandfathers involved."

Even the players got into the act. Springs said, "This is a game between Bear Bryant and Woody Hayes. They are the two best coaches of all time. We (Ohio State) wouldn't want to say we play for the second-best coach."

Gil LeBreton, who covered Ohio State for the *Times-Picayune*, however, believed the Buckeyes were priming themselves for a tumble. "They found a ready-made excuse and used it," said LeBreton, referring to an Ohio State feeling that the Buckeyes rightfully belonged in Pasadena as the undisputed Big Ten champion.

A victory and a Texas loss could put 'Bama on the top of the polls. Ohio State was trying to redeem itself for two losses and a conference co-championship instead of a national championship.

"Coach Hayes has been saying all along that there's one more great game left in this team," said Aaron Brown. "This has got to be the one." Springs added, "We really felt this was the best Ohio State team we've had here in a while. Those Oklahoma and Michigan losses were just so disappointing. They kinda all stay on your mind. "In a way I'm glad we're playing Alabama. It's like a second chance for us."

Alabama 35-Ohio State 6

John Crow (40) of Alabama fires out of 'Bama backfield and past Ohio State's Michael Guess (12).

"We thought we had 'em then."

Alabama's lines were completely in charge from the kickoff. Quarterback Jeff Rutledge directed a lethal dose of ball-control offense at the school most associated with it. Guard Lou Green felt he had as much to do with keeping the Ohio State defense off-balance as anyone. He had cut out pictures of Aaron Brown, Tom Cousineau, Byron Cato, and Dave Adkins and put them in his sock.

"I wanted to paste Brown's picture in my helmet," he deadpanned, "but some of the guys talked me out of it. I just kept them down there where they couldn't raise any hell."

"The plan," said center Dwight Stephenson, "was to take it right to them." Sixteen of Alabama's first 17 plays were straight into the eyes of the Buckeye defense. The Crimson Tide held the ball for 8 minutes and 60 yards while Ohio State appeared to be just hanging on. David Sadler, Green, Bob Cryder, and Jim Bunch, the 'Bama offensive line, thrashed their opposition as Tide backs consistently gained yardage off tackle. The drive ended short of points when Rutledge was stopped on a 2-yard pickup on fourth-and-goal from the 5.

"We had a little further to go than I thought," commented Alabama Coach Paul Bryant. "We should have kicked the field goal. It was a stupid call and I made it."

The ease in which 'Bama handled Ohio State, points or not, on that first drive brought a message home early. "We thought we had 'em then," admitted Rutledge.

With embarrassing efficiency, Rutledge moved the Tide 76 yards on its second possession. A 29-yard pass to Ozzie Newsome, with a 15-yard roughing-the-passer penalty added on, again had Ohio State backed up to the player end zone. Tony Nathan bounded into the end zone from the 1 after Bruce Bolton put the ball there on a 6-yard run that wasn't supposed to be. "Ozzie came off when Bolton went in and he (Newsome) was supposed to carry on the play," Bryant moaned with a smile later. "The Good Lord called that one for us."

Bolton also figured in the next 'Bama touchdown, which came on a play Bryant hadn't used all season. Rutledge and the Tide line had Ohio State backpedaling on its next possession, an 11-play, 76-yard

Tony Nathan (22) holds ball high after Alabama touchdown as Ohio State linebacker Tom Cousineau (36) checks scoreboard.

touchdown drive. The points came when fullback Johnny Davis swung right on a fake at the Buckeye 27 while split end Bolton, who had lined up as a right halfback, rolled out of the backfield, and fired down the sideline.

Anticipating the run, the Buckeye cornerback stepped forward, and Bolton was almost instantly clear. Rutledge dropped back and eased the ball into Bolton's hands barely inbounds. The extra point was missed; but with 4:32 remaining until the half, Alabama led, 13-0. They had scored on two of only three first-half possessions.

Buckeye quarterback Rod Gerald completed a 22-yard pass to tight end Jimmy Moore, and on the next play, tailback Ron Springs took a pitchout, shot off tackle, and ran 42 yards to the 'Bama 11. The Buckeyes seemed to be back in business. Three plays gained 6 yards. Gerald pitched to flanker Jim Harrell, sweeping right on fourth-and-four. For a second there was a hole in the line, but Harrell continued wide where Don McNeal, after shedding a blocker, brought the runner down at the 3.

Alabama's defense stiffened. And Woody Hayes passed up a field goal on fourth down. "I thought about it being bad football," he said. "When you're down 13 points, field goals don't look so big . . . If we had gotten the touchdown, we may have played better ball."

Rutledge fumbled early in the third quarter, but the Buckeye offense couldn't get a first down or inch any closer than the Tide 29. On Ohio State's next possession, they were unable to dent the Tide 28. Rutledge went from that spot 67 yards to a 3-yard TD reception by Rick Neal. Another pass to Nathan on the two-point conversion made the score an out-of-reach 21-0. "There in the third quarter, when we had the ball on the short side of the 50 twice and didn't move, their defense rose to the occasion and our offense didn't," smoldered Hayes. "That definitely sealed the ball game right there."

Gerald spurred his team to an 85-yard, seven-play, somewhat face-saving scoring surge. Harrell turned a 20-yard, first-down play into a 38-yard touchdown, but Ohio State missed a two-point conversion and that was their last gasp.

For the following seven playing minutes, Alabama controlled the ball, driving 84 yards and ending with freshman running back Major Ogilvie scoring from the 1. When Ohio State got the ball again, Gerald threw an interception on the Buck 24, and Davis spurted in from the five to make the final margin 35-6.

An unhappy Hayes said, "They beat us with about one-half as much material as we have, and we played them with about one-fourth as much coaching as they got—because we sure got outcoached here today. They just outplayed us in every department they could have."

In the locker room, the Bucks continued to talk about their exhaustive defeat in the Michigan game, and why they should've been in Pasadena as Big Ten champions. While embarrassed Sugar Bowlers cleared their throats and avoided eye contact after one of their worst matches, reporters wondered how one team could fumble 10 times and still win by 29 points.

Answers came from the Alabama locker room. Tackle David Sadler felt it was because there was no better team. "Anyone who doesn't vote for us," he said with an eye toward the final poll balloting, "isn't voting with a clear conscience."

The game of coaching legends, the growl vs. the scowl, never came into play according to Bryant, who repeated in different words what he had said earlier. "Winning or losing has nothing to do with how bad or good a coach we (Hayes and Bryant) are," said Bear. "Woody is a great coach. And I ain't bad."

'Bama fans tear down goalposts under the delusion that their Tide is No. 1.

Alabama-Penn State

"It's not life or death."

"**E**verything coach told us turned out to be right—except the vote," said Alabama linebacker Barry Krauss of the 1978 bowl sequence. "He said we had to beat Ohio State convincingly. He said Oklahoma would lose, Michigan would lose, and Notre Dame would beat Texas. We just looked at him, feeling it couldn't all happen like he said. Damn if it didn't. "Man, I was driving home, sure we'd be national champions. Then we go and get ripped off."

The victory Bear Bryant forecast for the 5th-ranked Irish over No. 1 Texas catapulted Notre Dame into the top spot in both polls while Alabama inched to No. 2, forcing a lot of fans to wonder if the pollsters voted for the name rather than the game. It was fair to speculate that had the positions been reversed—Notre Dame No. 3 and Alabama No. 5 before the bowls—and if the Tide beat No. 1 Texas 38-10, it would not have leapfrogged Alabama to the top.

It must have frustrated the man many considered the best collegiate coach of all time. Bryant had won three Associated Press national championships, four in United Press International. But Notre Dame was directly responsible for Bear not having an incredible seven AP No. 1s.

In 1966, Notre Dame had been voted No. 1 despite a 10-10 tie with Michigan State and despite Alabama's 11-0 record. Now the Irish had leapfrogged over Alabama to No. 1 despite the Tide's slaughter of Ohio State. The Irish beat him, 24-23, in the 1973 Sugar Bowl, and then upset him, 13-11, in the 1975 Orange Bowl.

There was a change in the masthead of the Mid-Winter Sports Association. The name was formally changed. No one bothered to call it anything but the Sugar Bowl, so after 44 years the membership gave up the ghost. The Sugar Bowl was now the Sugar Bowl.

An odd thing occurred in 1978 as the season opened and the time came to choose the participants for the Sugar Bowl: The weaknesses in the

Carl James succeeded Joe Katz.

215

SEC-Sugar Bowl contract caught up with Alabama's Bear Bryant. After beating Nebraska and Missouri, the Crimson Tide lost 24-14 to Southern California in a game Bryant would say was "worse than the score." The loss was damaging to the Sugar because 'Bama was the SEC's best chance for a No. 1 team and, thus, the attraction for the highest-ranked opponent on January 1.

Georgia, which lost one early season nonconference game, was knocking on the Sugar's door most of the season. The Bulldogs were not a bad team but had little chance at No. 1. But they held the inside track for the Sugar Bowl. Bryant, it seemed, had written himself out of the Sugar Bowl. His Crimson Tide improved and continued to improve after the USC loss, rising to No. 3 in the polls. In some way, Bryant had to be able to play No. 1 Penn State in order to have a shot at a national championship. With the Big Eight tie-up in the Orange Bowl and the SWC tie-up with the Cotton Bowl, the Sugar was the only major bowl in which such a pairing could occur.

When the original contract between the SEC and Sugar Bowl was drawn up, Bryant influenced the formula for selecting the conference representative. As the perennial champion, and because he wanted the freedom to go elsewhere on occasion, it was agreed in the event there was a tie for the conference title, the "most recent appearance rule" would prevail. That is, the team last appearing in the Sugar Bowl was free to go to another bowl. Alabama's better overall record would not come into play as the Sugar had less say in the representative than either the Orange or Cotton Bowls.

All Georgia had to do was beat Auburn to tie 'Bama for the conference championship, and the Bulldogs would host the Sugar Bowl, probably against Oklahoma. There was some talk of matching Penn State and Alabama in the Gator Bowl, but nothing came of it. Nothing had to.

Penn State Head Coach Joe Paterno had never won a national championship, nor had Penn State in 92 years of playing the game. He let the Sugar in on a secret. Penn State seemed ready to play in Miami, but Paterno allowed that should Missouri upset Nebraska and should Auburn beat Georgia, which would put Alabama in the Sugar, he wanted to play the Crimson Tide.

Sure enough, Missouri beat Nebraska, and Auburn and Georgia tied. After the Lions beat Pittsburgh and the Tide defeated Auburn, Alabama moved up a notch in the polls. The Sugar Bowl found itself with the No. 1 and No. 2 teams, only the fifth time this had happened in postseason football.

Why would Paterno look for the toughest foe? The answer was he had a team that could look anyone in the eye and not blink. The Penn State defense gave up an average of 54.5 yards rushing while quarterback Chuck Fusina, second in the Heisman Trophy balloting, directed an offense that averaged almost 31 points a game.

Paterno, unlike Bryant, did not believe winning a national championship was as important as the challenge of playing for a national championship. "This is my third 11-0 team," Paterno said in indirect reference to what seemed to be a prejudice by voters against Eastern football.

Paterno reiterated his fundamental belief in the chase for the title. "I think the important thing is that we have an opportunity to go for it," said Paterno. "Certainly it is important to have goals to attain." The talented quarterback Fusina echoed his coach. "We want to be No. 1," he offered, "and we're going to work as hard as possible. But it's not everything . . . If we don't win a national championship, I won't feel the four years are a waste. There are a lot of things other than a national championship. It's not life or death."

Alabama's aspirations were clearly more singleminded. "Sure, I'd like to win another national championship," growled Bryant. "Every year I want that to be our goal and the objective of our team. Every day when they come in that's what we talk about. We write it down and we talk about how we're going to get there." "It is," said Barry Krauss, "the reason a lot of us came here."

Bryant and Paterno were, of course, more concerned with each other's teams. Bryant characterized his Alabama squad as "a bunch of average players who don't know they're not supposed to be able to play as well as they do." The figures backed Bear up. Uncharacteristically, this Crimson Tide team was not a reckoning force, particularly on defense where it surrendered 309.2 yards of total offense a game. "We used to not give up that much yardage in a season," moaned Bryant.

The thought came up that perhaps a replay of the 1978 bowl season could occur. If Alabama beat Penn State and 3rd-ranked USC (early season conquerors of Alabama) beat Michigan badly in the Rose Bowl, then the Trojans could rise to No. 1.

Tide defensive tackle Marty Lyons seemed self-assured. "If we beat the No. 1 team in the nation," he said, ". . . they're 11-0 and no one else could beat them. That has to say something for us . . . We weren't brought here to play football for the fun of it. We were brought here for achievement."

Alabama 14-Penn State 7

"You better pass."

Jeff Rutledge (quarterback) and the Alabama coaching staff played a constant guessing game with Penn State. "We used a lot of misdirection because of those two tackles (Matt Millen and Bruce Clark). Those two guys just come right across and you can't play straight up football against them and succeed."

Meanwhile, Joe Paterno was hanging his hopes on quarterback Chuck Fusina, "the best passer I've ever coached." Alabama was vulnerable to his passes. "Rushing the passer is the worst thing we do," said Bryant. Everywhere 'Bama looked there were leaks to be plugged.

Tide Coach Ken Donahue put in a pinching, looping, stunting defense that would have to serve as the linchpin to victory—if it worked. Wayne Hamilton and E.J. Junior at the ends, Marty Lyons and Byron Braggs at tackle, nose guard Curtis McGriff, and linebackers Barry Krauss and Rickey Gilliland were woven into a defensive pattern designed to slow an offense that hadn't been tamed in 19 consecutive games.

The noise and tension were gripping in the Superdome as the curtain went up on the 45th Sugar Bowl. And this atmosphere would remain for 60 playing minutes.

Rutledge broke the wishbone, used misdirection plays, then reconstructed his basic formation in a "show-'em-this-and-run-that" offense. In the first half, the Tide wiggled down to the Penn State 33, 38, 38, 33, and 18. Each time, Penn State would stop the threat. At the same time, the Tide defense more than held the Lion offense in check. Fusina was harried and pressured so that his rhythm seemed considerably slower. The Lion backs appeared to step into a storm with each carry, and by the half Penn State was neatly under control with Donahue's defense. They had minus rushing yardage, only two first downs, and a quarterback whose timing had been disturbed by a savage defense.

Just before the half, Alabama squeezed in a touchdown in a development as surprising to the Tide as to the Lions.

An 80-yard drive in the last two minutes ignited when Tony Nathan went off tackle and fireballed into the secondary for 30 yards. Rutledge pushed the Tide to the Penn State 37 with 15 seconds remaining in the half. "We weren't really trying to score," said Rutledge of the drive, "but I saw them in a certain defense and checked off to a play. It was wide open and then we had a chance."

Rutledge dropped back, felt Millen pulling at his

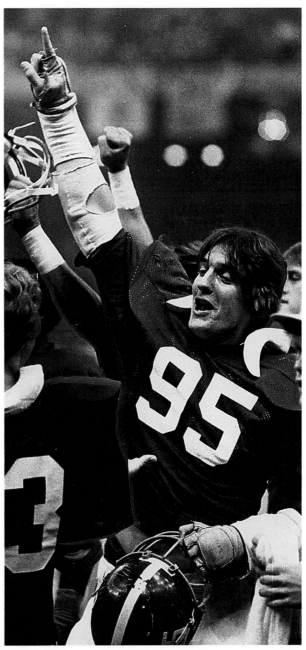

Danny Collins (95) proclaims the message 'We're No. 1,' but it was premature.

jersey, and noticed receiver Bruce Bolton toward the goal line. The quarterback threw short and behind the receiver, but Bolton reached back, made the grab, and curled around the ball on the end zone turf.

"Bruce was supposed to take somebody deep," said Rutledge, "to clear out the area. He wasn't the primary receiver, but he was open. It wasn't a good pass, but it was an exceptional catch."

The drive took one minute and three seconds and left eight seconds in the half.

Matters didn't change much during most of the third quarter until Pete Harris made Rutledge pay for testing the Penn State secondary with a diving interception at the Tide 48. Two plays later, Fusina perked the dead Penn State offense with a 25-yard completion to tailback Mike Guman to the 19. A running play gained 2 yards, then Fusina tied up the game with a 17-yard touchdown pass to Scott Fitzkee at the flag over defensive back Don McNeal. "It was a two tight end set," explained 'Bama safety Murray Legg. "The two tight ends ran a crossing pattern. One of our safeties overplayed the receiver and he got open."

Matt Bahr tied the score with a PAT. The next time Penn State had the ball, Legg fired in to sack Fusina for the sixth time—an 11-yard loss. Fitzkee toed a 50-yard punt over the thundering Lion coverage to Lou Ikner at the Alabama 27. Ikner, an inexperienced kick returner with only one return all season, was subbing for Major Ogilvie. The veteran performer had been dazed on the previous series. "I

probably would have fair-caught it," said Ogilvie with a smile.

Ikner caught the punt, found an alley on the left side, and cruised 62 yards to the Penn State 11. Two plays netted 3 yards. On third down, Rutledge moved left, sidestepped a stunting Millen in time to see Harris zeroing in.

"I was out of position," Harris later admitted. "I figured the defensive end would see me going for him (Rutledge) and drop off to cover the pitch man, but he didn't." Just as Harris got to the quarterback, the ball was pitched to Ogilvie who had no trouble beating two defenders to the end zone. There were 21 seconds remaining in the third period when Alan McElroy kicked the extra point that put Alabama ahead, 14-7.

Penn State fans added to the crescendo of sound with a Lion drive beginning on the Lion 31 and reaching the 'Bama 33—only the fourth penetration of Tide turf that afternoon. McNeal choked off the threat with an end zone interception when Fusina was forced to throw into double coverage. Then suddenly, Millen, who seemed to spend as much time in the Alabama backfield as Rutledge, forced the quarterback to pitch badly to Nathan. Joe Lally recovered at the 19 with 7:57 left.

Fullback Matt Suhey, in one lightning stab, flashed through the Tide defense to the 8. It was abundantly clear that the fight for No. 1 very likely rested on this drive.

Guman gained 2 yards. Alabama then proceeded to make three consecutive touchdown-saving plays.

The Stand: Matt Suhey is stopped by Rich Wingo on third and goal from less than a foot away.

Mike Guman of Penn State is stopped on fourth and goal from inside the 1 as Alabama takes national championship from Nittany Lions.

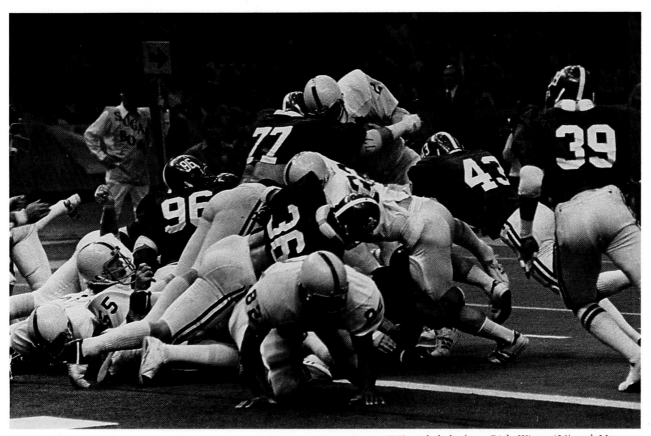

On fourth down, Mike Guman picks up not a centimeter as Barry Krauss (77) with help from Rich Wingo (36) and Murray Legg (19) preserve Alabama's lead and ultimate national championship. The stand is perhaps the most memorable feat in Sugar Bowl history.

Fusina sent Bob Bassett deep into the end zone corner, taking McNeal with him. Then Fusina threw to the delaying Fitzkee near the flag. As the ball left Fusina's hand, defender Legg fell, his hands reaching desperately to the receiver who gathered in the ball. McNeal meanwhile had somehow recovered and reacted, flying into the split receiver before he was able to turn his body toward the end zone. The tackle was made two feet short of the goal.

"When I started to fall, about all I wanted to do was cry," said Legg. "I thought I was gonna score," Fitzkee commented, "and I went to dive in to make sure. Then someone hit me—I don't know where he came from—and his momentum carried me out-of-bounds."

Suhey was met helmet-to-helmet on a third-down dive by linebacker Rich Wingo and Legg. The play gained inches.

"Fusina came out to look at the ball," Alabama tackle Lyons recalled, "and I was standing in the way, in between him and the ball. He started smiling. 'How much is it?' he asked. I told him 'Bout that much.' 'Ten inches?' 'Yeah,' I said. 'You better pass.' "

"Man," said linebacker Krauss, "it was gut-check time. We looked at one another. We knew this could be it. When they broke the huddle, everything got silent. Boy, talk about gut-checks."

Legg reminded his teammates emotionally, "We're Alabama and they can't score."

After conferring with Joe Paterno, Fusina brought his team to the line and, ignoring Lyons' advice, sent Guman diving into practically the same spot as Suhey had flown. This was a power play into the galelike force of the defense. Almost in symphony, the opposing lines crested. Lyons and tackle Braggs submerged and Krauss went over the top like a heat-seeking linebacker and met the ballcarrier face-to-face. Legg finished the tackle, and Penn State remained the same 10 inches from the goal.

"When I heard the yell, I thought it was Penn State," said David Hannah with a wide smile. "When you're pinned to the ground and you look over and see the blue and white shakers everywhere, you think, 'My gosh. They've done it!' I thought we could hold them. Then I felt this guy jumping behind me and I knew we'd stopped them."

The Alabama defense left the field following Legg who was jumping and yelling with tears flowing under his helmet. Krauss, unnoticed, remained prone on the field. The dazed linebacker picked himself up, and wobbly made his way to the sideline where Bryant embraced him. "A knock like that," said the Bear, "is the nicest kind of feeling you can get."

Penn State had one more realistic chance. Tide punter Woody Umphrey sliced a punt off his foot and the Lions would have had possession on the Alabama 20 with six minutes left. But the Nittany Lions had 12 men on the field, and 'Bama retained the ball on the penalty. It was ironic, because Penn State won the 1969 Orange Bowl against Kansas on a 12-man penalty.

Coach Ken Donahue's defense had more than done its job. Penn State gained only 19 yards rushing, and Fusina had four interceptions. There was no question that No. 1 rightfully belonged to the Crimson Tide, though it was felt that Alabama had bested a superior team. "When you're No. 2 and you beat No. 1," analyzed Lyons, "there is only one place to go."

Some felt the No. 1 moment of the 1979 football season occurred in the Penn State locker room when the superb tackle Millen watched bitterly disappointed Chuck Fusina walk, helmet half on, half off, with a constant and glazed stare at the Superdome concrete floor. Fusina tried to shake his teammate when he reached for him. Millen caught the quarterback again and clamped his shoulders.

"Listen to me. Listen to me!" the tackle ordered, pushing his friend to the wall. "I just want to tell you that I love you."

Paterno, after saying he had been outcoached, commented on the finish to Penn State's closest brush in its star-crossed quest for No. 1. "I told my players not to go into hibernation because they finished 11-1," he said. "That record gave them something (a chance at a national championship) few ever get. What they get now is a chance to love each other a little more. I know that sounds cornball, but . . ."

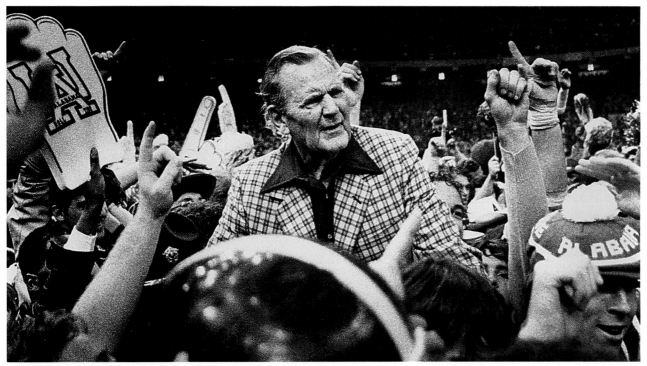

Bear Bryant, on the crest of No. 1.

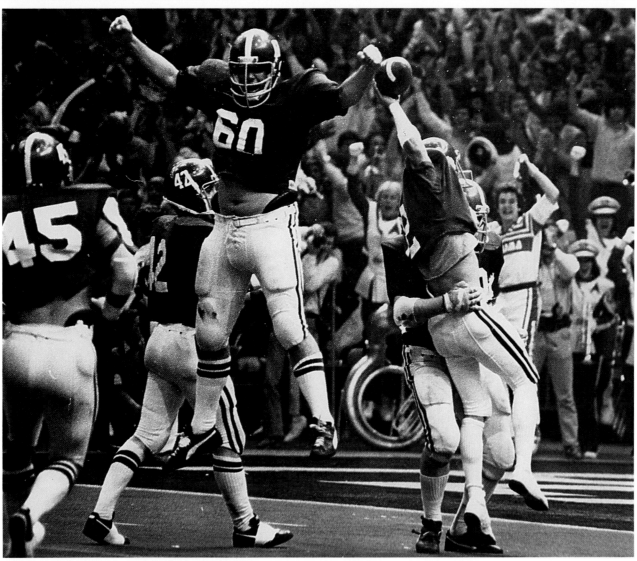

'Bama's Vince Boothe (60) displays the emotion of victory.

Alabama-Arkansas

TUESDAY, JANUARY 1, 1980

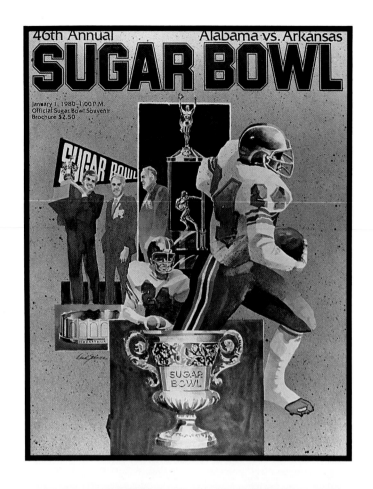

"What can you do here?"

A chance encounter with Charlie Glueck of the Sugar Bowl and Missouri Valley Commissioner Alan "Mickey" Holmes in the Dallas airport resulted in the filling of the organization's most pressing need: an executive director. The bowl had formed a committee a year before to search for a successor to Carl James, and Glueck felt the savvy, stogie-smoking, red-haired Holmes might be just the person they needed. Holmes had been mildly interested in the Sugar Bowl nine years before, when Joe Katz was selected executive director. "I met with Dr. Fred Wolfe and Sam Corenswet, Jr., at a Nebraska football game in 1969," recalled Holmes. "I was interested, although I was a little concerned about the makeup of the bowl at the time. I felt it was a little too inbred. Also, some people were talking to me about the possibility of an assistant athletic directorship at the University of Missouri."

The then 28-year-old Big Eight official received advice from Wayne Duke, the conference commissioner and a close friend. "A lot of good opportunities are going to come your way," counseled Duke. "Be patient. Be patient."

The timing was perfect when Glueck and Holmes bumped into each other in Texas. "I was making my swing around the (MVC) conference to talk rules changes and so on with coaches and ADs," recalled Holmes. "I was on my way from New Mexico State to Creighton, and I ran into Charlie in Dallas. He mentioned that the Sugar Bowl was looking for someone. Well, we didn't sit together on the plane, but after we landed I said, 'Hey, let's go to the game tonight.' Creighton was playing Indiana State, with Larry Bird.

"I pumped him a little, thinking this sounded like a fine opportunity. I knew the Sugar Bowl was coming on—it had the contracts with the SEC and ABC, it was a relatively broad program for a bowl. From the outside looking in, it really interested me."

A note was mailed to Robert J. Fabacher, president of the association, and he passed it to Jerry Romig, who was on the selection committee. Romig got in touch with Holmes at the NCAA basketball tournament at Salt Lake City and agreed on a date for an interview. Of the multitude of applicants, Holmes was the consensus choice to become the Sugar Bowl's fourth executive director. He had prepared himself well for the task.

"I started out to be the world's greatest architectural engineer," said Holmes, who began college at the University of Iowa, transferred to Upper Iowa University, then switched back to Iowa in pursuit of newspaper and sports information internships. This was during a golden age of Hawkeye football and, aside from his other duties, the enterprising Holmes started his own newspaper stringing service.

Executive Director Mickey Holmes.

His high school in Iowa offered no foreign language, and realizing he would need one to graduate from college, Holmes, with world crises in Crete and Suez fresh on his mind, along with the draft, decided to tackle the language he felt would do him the most good in the future: Russian. That, he felt, would keep him out of any foxholes.

He ended up with one of the strangest mixtures of disciplines from any university. "I reached a point when I thought it was time to get out of school and go to work. But I had so many hours in so many different fields," Holmes laughed, "it was difficult to pick my major." He could have ended his five-year collegiate career by graduating with degrees in Russian, journalism, or physical education. He chose Russian with minors in the other two disciplines.

Grinnell (Iowa) College, where he conducted the school's news service and was sports information director, was Holmes' first stop. Soon he was also employed as publicity director of the Midwest Conference, retaining his duties at Grinnell. As an outgrowth of this job, Mickey became executive secretary for the league.

In 1963 Wayne Duke left the NCAA office to head the Big Eight Conference. Holmes applied for Duke's position, but Charlie Thornton was hired. Holmes then went after a spot on Duke's staff with the Big Eight, where he stayed for eight years.

Duke left the Big Eight in 1971 to take the job opened by the death of Big Ten Commissioner Bill Reed, and Holmes, then 30, went after his friend's spot. "I told them (the selection committee) there were three things I couldn't do anything about: my red hair, unless I dyed it and I didn't want to do that; my freckles; my age. But I could be a heck of a lot older and not have this experience."

However, Chuck Neinas was selected. Holmes resigned in order to give Neinas, an old friend, a free hand. The new commissioner talked Holmes into staying. "The chemistry was right," smiled Mickey. "We didn't always see eye-to-eye philosophically, but that doesn't hurt. It probably expands things because it makes people look a little closer at what they are doing."

But a year later, Holmes was a conference commissioner. The Missouri Valley took advantage of the vast experience Holmes had accumulated for the previous eight years. Holmes was happy and satisfied with himself until he ran into Charlie Glueck in Dallas.

The most important tie Holmes had with New Orleans was his third child, Sara. Sara, in a way, represents the intertwining of Mickey's career and family. "When I was with the Big Eight in 1971, my wife was pregnant with Sara," explained Holmes. "I was in downtown Kansas City for our holiday conference basketball tournament. From there I was to fly to New Orleans for the Auburn-Oklahoma Sugar Bowl," said Holmes, sheepishly. "Before halftime of the first game of the last afternoon I got word that Judy was about ready to deliver and had taken herself to the hospital. I left immediately, got to the hospital, went up to see Judy for a minute. After that I went downstairs to get her admitted. This was the 30th of December. When I went back up she seemed fine and I asked her if she would mind if I still went to New Orleans.

" 'What can you do here?' Judy responded. So a policeman took me back to the tournament. I got there at halftime of the second game. The next morning I flew to New Orleans. I saw the Sugar Bowl, flew to Miami for the Orange Bowl, flew back to New Orleans, and then had to stay in town a couple of days for meetings.

"That done, I flew back to Kansas City, picked up my wife and Sara from the hospital and went on our way."

"I'll let y'all take care of the polls."

Mickey Holmes' initial brush at a bowl pairing nearly caused him to do what nine years before he had told the Big Eight he didn't want to do: dye his hair. The University of Georgia was turning the hair of all the Sugar Bowlers white.

Vince Dooley's Bulldogs were unable to win outside the Southeastern Conference but were perfect within and knocking on New Orleans' door. It was possible, with Auburn wins over Georgia and Alabama coupled with a Bulldog loss to independent Georgia Tech, that a losing Georgia (5-6) team would hold down the host spot in the Sugar Bowl.

At the same time, Alabama, the nation's No. 4 offensive team, No. 1 defensive team, and No. 1-ranked team, was cruising effortlessly to at least a share of the SEC championship with the Bulldogs. Alabama and Georgia didn't play, and the Bulldogs would earn the invitation in a tie because of the "most recent appearance rule." New Orleans could lose a possible national champion and gain a team with a losing season record. "We'd welcome them with open arms and go on with our bowl," Holmes said diplomatically of Georgia's chances.

Auburn, 15th-ranked but ineligible for bowls because of NCAA probation, put the Sugar on hold by unleashing James Brooks and Joe Cribbs on Georgia. Brooks gained 200 yards and Cribbs 166 in a 33-13 War Eagle whoop. But the Sugar Bowl could rejoice only momentarily. Alabama's last game was with these same War Eagles, a very good team. If Auburn beat the Crimson Tide, Georgia and Alabama would be tied in the final SEC standings and the Bulldogs would spend the holidays in New Orleans.

Coach Bear Bryant said of his state rivals and the bowl situation, "It's not up to me, but if we can't beat Auburn, I'd just as soon stay home and plow." The Auburn faction went up in arms over the comment, which added more fuel to a rivalry that needed none.

Georgia officials removed the fear of having a losing team in the Sugar by requesting that the "most recent appearance" rule be waived should the Bulldogs lose to Georgia Tech. The request applied only in that instance, though. If Georgia won, and Auburn broke Alabama's longest-in-the-nation victory string at 19, the 'Dogs wanted their rightful berth.

The SEC Sugar Bowl opponent would be either Arkansas or Texas (tied with the University of

Houston for the Southwest Conference lead). Texas appeared to be the odds-on choice; but the Longhorns were upset 13-7 by Texas A&M, and the Sugar had Arkansas, a 10-1 conference co-champion.

Bear Bryant, now hard on the heels of Amos Alonzo Stagg's all-time coaching record of 314 victories, showed up on the field more than an hour before the Auburn-'Bama kickoff. As he and Assistant Athletic Director Charlie Thornton strolled around Legion Field, Auburn students began chanting, "Plow, Bear, plow." Bryant had Thornton put his hands behind his back, whereupon the coach grabbed them, turning the bent-over assistant athletic director into a plow. The students roared approval.

With Vince Dooley in the press box along with some very nervous Sugar Bowlers, Bryant's team played an uncharacteristic Alabama game. The Tide had third-quarter fumbles on its 21, 23, 37, and on the Auburn 12-yard line. Alabama was letting a national championship slip away.

Auburn took an 18-17 lead with less than 12 minutes remaining; then the Tide composed itself and drove 88 yards for a touchdown and a 25-18 win. The Sugar Bowl had dodged a silver bullet.

Lou Holtz, the Arkansas coach who was knocked out of the Cotton and into the Sugar with Baylor's upset of Texas (because of the SWC's most recent appearance rule) said, "There were just four minutes left in the Alabama-Auburn game when we found out we'd be playing the Bear." He spoke of his first game against Bryant when he was an assistant on the South Carolina staff. "I was coaching the defensive secondary and, boy, it was going to be a great thrill. But it wasn't so because we got beat something like 42-0, or some ridiculous score like that.

Heck, lots of teams get excited about playing Alabama before the game . . . They're so good I don't vote for second and third place behind them. Nobody's is close to them."

Others thought differently. After the close call with Auburn, the Associated Press poll dropped Alabama to No. 2 behind Ohio State by a point and a half, upsetting Tide fans who jammed the telephone circuits to AP headquarters in New York. The coaches who vote in the United Press International poll kept the Tide on top; but if 'Bama was to regain its AP ranking, it was going to have to be impressive in the Sugar Bowl and Ohio State would have to stumble in the Rose.

Holtz had done a masterful job with Arkansas. With five freshmen in his starting lineups and a defense ranked no higher than 6th in the SWC, he put together a team that played excellent field position football. "We use a rope-a-dope defense," said Holtz. "Everyone always seems to have us on the ropes." The "Cinderella Pigs" were 6th-ranked after giving up an astounding 320 yards but only 9.8 points a game. And if the bowls fell just right, Arkansas had as much claim to No. 1 as anyone.

"Polls, polls, polls," groused Bryant, "that's all I've heard about. I just want to beat Arkansas . . . by one point or a half point, I don't care. Then I'll let y'all (the press) take care of the polls."

Which is what Crimson Tide defensive back Don McNeal, who unlike his coach had polls very much on his mind, was counting on. "This is it," said McNeal. "Everybody comes here (Alabama) to win the national championship. That was my goal when I came here. I've accomplished it once. I'm hoping for two."

Alabama fans celebrate 1980 victory over Arkansas.

Alabama 24-Arkansas 9

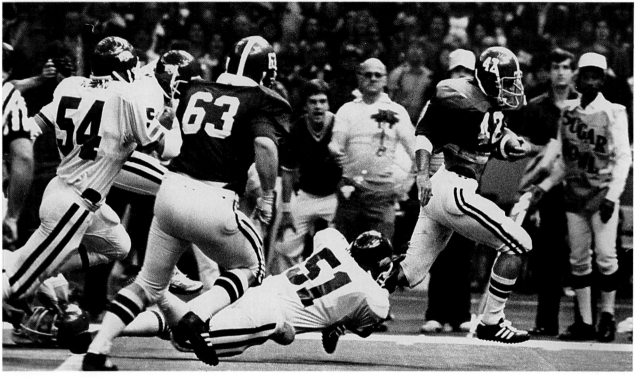

Major Ogilvie (42) was a major problem for the Hog defense.

"Steve just went psssst!"

Bear Bryant may not have wanted to talk about national championships with the press, but he certainly had no intention of letting one out of his grasp. "Bear told us if we're going to do anything about the polls," said quarterback Steadman Shealy, "we had to do it on the field. He said, 'The apple's there. Grab it.' "

For the first time since a 10-7 loss to Ole Miss in 1976, Bryant installed a double wing set off the wishbone formation with motion. Alabama could run its basic plays off the set, yet it added another twist for Arkansas to think about.

Ten seconds into the game, it was the Razorbacks who had the Crimson Tide slightly stirred. With a crashing smack on the kickoff, Rusty Hill sent Don McNeal spinning in one direction, the ball in the other. George Hill recovered for Arkansas on the Alabama 43. The Tide held, but Ish Ordonez kicked a 34-yard field goal.

Shealy got the Tide moving on its second possession, using a fullback in motion while countering to the weak side to Billy Jackson, slowing the Hog thrust. Major Ogilvie, who was also put in motion, finished off a seven-play, 82-yard drive by rocketing

22 yards after Shealy pitched out at precisely the last instant. It was the third straight year Ogilvie had scored a Sugar Bowl touchdown. "We weren't expecting as much double wing," admitted Arkansas Coach Lou Holtz. "We weren't expecting an unbalanced line. We knew they'd run at least two wide-outs and two tight ends . . . but with five freshmen (in his defensive alignment) we made some mistakes. We got in wrong calls, shifted the wrong way, and did a lot of wrong things."

Right after Ogilvie's touchdown, Arkansas made another mistake. Four plays after receiving the kickoff, quarterback Kevin Scanlon and center Mike Burlingame mishandled a snap, and linebacker Thomas Boyd recovered for 'Bama on the Hog 22. Ogilvie scored his second touchdown from the one to put Alabama ahead 14-3 with 3:46 left in the first period, forcing Arkansas into a Scanlon passing exhibition.

Scanlon, a very capable quarterback who was being wracked on virtually every play by the relentless Tide defense, pushed the Razorbacks into threatening position twice in the second quarter. A sack (one of five Scanlon endured during the game)

Steadman Shealy (10) pitches to Billy Jackson as Tide wishbone performs almost flawlessly.

by defensive end Wayne Hamilton at the Alabama 36 put a practical end to one drive. Later linebacker Randy Scott made a fourth-and-two tackle at the Alabama 23. "We probably should have gone for the field goal," said Holtz of the second situation later, "but it was quite obvious by that time that field goals weren't meant in the football game."

Alabama wasn't adverse to field goals. Ogilvie returned a Bruce Lahay punt 50 yards, and Alan McElroy kicked a 25-yarder just before the half.

With a 17-3 score at the half, Alabama seemed content. Scanlon took every advantage. He connected on four of six passes and turned a busted play into a 20-yard gain, sweeping the Razorbacks 80 yards after the second-half kickoff. The payoff came on a 3-yard pass to Robert Farrell, who made an over-the-shoulder catch. Arkansas opted for a two-point conversion, but Hamilton and Boyd stopped Scanlon well short of the goal. The score was now 17-9, and the game was taking on the look of a dogfight.

Scanlon kept coming. By the fourth quarter he had the nine-point underdog Hogs threatening once more, but the Tide stopped Arkansas at the Alabama 33. The Tide couldn't quite put the Razorbacks away—until Mike Burchfield downed a Lahay punt on the Alabama 2.

Fullback Steve Whitman barrelled out 6 yards, and Ogilvie gained 7 more. Shealy again timed an absolutely perfect pitch to Jackson who raced 35 yards. Jackson got 14 more running wide and, after Ogilvie gained 3, Shealy gained 22 on an option. The Tide nudged down to the Arkansas 7 where the Razorbacks stopped a third-down play. Illegal motion was ruled before the play, however, and the down was rerun from the 12.

On third-and-11, offensive coordinator Mal Moore suggested a play—"43-Read"—to Shealy. "I would not have called it," said Shealy. The quarterback glided down the line, "read" the right defensive end, and then stuck the ball into 230-pound frame of Whitman, who shot up the middle for the touch-

Ogilvie rockets out of the arms of linebacker Ozzie Riley (51).

down. He muscled right over defensive back Kevin Evans at the goal. "I read the end on the play and Steve just went psssst!" explained Shealy.

The 98-yard drive, Alabama's longest that season, broke Arkansas' back. Holtz offered no excuses, though he did remember that Alabama scored the last touchdown on a second chance. "They (the officials) said somebody moved. They called the play dead. I wish they'd called the next one dead."

Alabama and Arkansas gained 696 yards between them. The double wing took the Hogs out of their planned defensive schemes. Holtz put matters more succinctly, "Alabama's offense is fourth best in the nation, and it's the team's major weakness. How could we know the nation's best team would play a perfect game?"

Amidst all the clamor and reasons why Alabama should be ranked No. 1, Bear Bryant was saying that injuries may have kept his team from being one of the greatest of all time. "We hit some peaks," said Bryant, "against Baylor, and later against Tennessee

when we came back from being down 17-0. No team has ever done that against Tennessee. It was a team that did what it had to do. When Auburn went ahead of us, we marched 82 (actually 88) yards. When the Sugar Bowl was hanging in the balance, we went 98 yards. Things like that say something about a football team."

That football team said something about Bear, too. The victory was not only his 296th, within 20 of Amos Alonzo Stagg's 314, but this team was the 17th of Bryant's 22 at Alabama to finish in the Top Ten, an unmatched feat for a coach since the Associated Press voting began in 1936. Also, South Cal defeated Ohio State (17-16) that day in the Rose Bowl, rectifying the AP voting and moving Bryant past Frank Leahy, who had won four AP national championships at Notre Dame in 1943-'46-'47-'49.

Georgia-
Notre Dame

THURSDAY, JANUARY 1, 1981

GEORGIA vs. NOTRE DAME

"The road to the Sugar Bowl goes through I-85."

Auburn, in a very real sense, had been the key to the Sugar Bowl's national championship role. In consecutive years, the War Eagles had prevented Georgia, an SEC-challenging team with only average credentials, from playing in New Orleans. The complexion of the 47th Sugar Bowl would also be influenced by the Auburn-Georgia feud, but this time New Orleans had a strong hankering for the Bulldogs.

Vince Dooley had fashioned a textbook team in Athens, one that used limited resources to maximum efficiency. Georgia had a capable, big play defense (ranked only 4th in the SEC), excellent special teams and kicking units, and a battering ram offense based on the extraordinary talents of an 18-year-old freshman. Herschel Walker, a 220-pound tailback with sprinter's speed, became the ingredient that made Dooley's team the nation's best. Walker accounted for 40 percent of Georgia's 1980 offense.

Out first-downed, with less total plays and less possession time, Georgia outscored its opponents with a combination of Walker's running (which totalled 1,616 yards—30 yards better than Tony Dorsett's freshman record); Rex Robinson's placekicking; and an opportunistic defense. It forced the opposition into a nation-leading difference in average turn-

overs (2.09 per game) and made the Bulldogs a fearful foe. Georgia also had a best-in-the-nation 16.6-yard average in punt returns while allowing only a half-yard. Georgia's 9-0 reeord and No. 2 ranking before the Auburn game made the Bulldogs the South's favorite.

The prospect that had the Sugar Bowl excited was a match between No. 1-ranked Notre Dame and the Bulldogs, though each had tough games at the end of the season.

After Georgia defeated Florida on a 93-yard pass play in the final minutes, a myriad of possibilities still existed for the Sugar Bowl's host berth. Alabama, LSU, and Mississippi State, right behind the 'Dogs in the conference standings, were waiting for Georgia to stumble. The complex SEC tie breaker had them all in the running should Georgia lose just once. If the Bulldogs could put Auburn away though, something they hadn't done since 1976, the shouting would be over.

Georgia vs. Notre Dame or Georgia vs. Alabama (SEC rivals that didn't play during the regular season) were the matches that intrigued the Sugar Bowl. The feeling in New Orleans was that either the Irish or 'Bama, who had lost to Mississippi State, would be far more attractive against Georgia

Georgia fans make a point for No. 1.

than either Florida State or the winner of the Penn State-Pittsburgh game. Since Notre Dame and Alabama played late in the season, the Sugar wanted to tie up the victor. There were questions, however.

Rather than play Georgia, Notre Dame might well opt for the Cotton Bowl and its additional riches. An influential Irish alum told columnist Peter Finney, "Notre Dame would go anywhere if it meant $800,000." Finney disagreed, pointing to Baylor (with one loss) and Texas (with two) as the main contenders in the Cotton Bowl sweepstakes. "Could Notre Dame afford to pass up the challenge of playing No. 2 Georgia?" asked Finney. "I don't think so."

Another thought was whether Bear Bryant would enjoy the idea of an all-SEC bowl. For that to happen, Alabama would have to beat Notre Dame. Then Georgia, with a win over Auburn, could move to No. 1. Given those circumstances, Bryant's only chance at a third consecutive national championship would be to play Georgia. Bryant wouldn't commit himself for the record, but Crimson Tide running back Major Ogilvie summed up matters when he said, "If we beat Notre Dame and Georgia is the No. 1 team, I don't think there's any question we'd like to play Georgia. Our main objective all season

has been the national championship. We'll do whatever it takes."

Would Vince Dooley like the idea of playing a fraternity brother? Probably not, but he didn't have to make the decision.

As it turned out, lowly Georgia Tech knocked the Irish out of No. 1 the week before the Alabama game with a 3-3 tie. That lifted Georgia to the top rung for the first time in 38 years and meant that the Irish would probably have to play the 'Dogs to have any opportunity to reclaim No. 1. Auburn couldn't wait for a chance to knock its conference next-door neighbor down a couple of pegs on the national ladder. The battle cry in the sleepy little Alabama hamlet that is home to the War Eagles was "The road to the Sugar Bowl goes through I-85 (the highway that passes Jordan-Hare Stadium)."

Defensive back Greg Bell followed Georgia's season-long script by blocking a second-quarter punt that was picked up and returned for a touchdown. That put the Bulldogs ahead for the first time at 10-7 and was the catalyst in a 31-21 defeat of the gritty War Eagles. "We're shooting for No. 1," Buck Belue added as Vince Dooley accepted the Sugar Bowl invitation.

Two hours later, Notre Dame (which dropped to

6th after the Tech tie) awaited Coach Dan Devine in Legion Field's dressing room chanting, "Sugar Bowl, Sugar Bowl, Sugar Bowl!" Irish arms were held aloft as the bodies continually swayed, elated above a 7-0 victory over Alabama.

A 20-3 defeat by Southern California in the season finale put a practical end to Notre Dame's national championship aspirations, and the Irish opened a one-point favorite over the team no one could quite believe. Georgia was finally going to get its chance to play Notre Dame 34 years after Wally Butts had tried. The Bulldogs were an undefeated, No. 1-ranked underdog.

Scott Zettek felt it should have been more. "I hear we're favored," the Irish defensive end said. "My own personal (line), I give them 10 points. It's a chance to maybe be No. 1, and a chance to regain some of the respect we lost. We can prove ourselves again with a win. This game will get a lot of attention, not only because Georgia's No. 1 but because people want to see what Notre Dame does against them." Devine, who would be coaching his last game for the Irish, also figured in Zettek's handicapping. "We've been an emotional team all year, as all Notre Dame teams are, but the fact that it's Coach Devine's last game will be an additional factor."

The mammoth Notre Dame defense, outweighing Georgia's offense 15 pounds a man, had limited opponents to 109 yards a game rushing, a per-play average of 2.8 (in contrast to Georgia's offensive average of 4.5). The mobile Irish offensive line averaged 6-foot-6, 255 pounds against Georgia's front which checked in at 6-foot-2, 236 pounds.

Notre Dame diehards spoke in smirks of Georgia's relatively easy schedule, and how South Bend troops were battle-hardened, conveniently forgetting some of the past paper-thin schedules the Irish had ridden to glory. Never, however, would Notre Dame have as much fraternity support as it would have against Georgia. There had not been a season quite like this, where so many schools remained alive for the national championship as New Year's Day approached. A Notre Dame victory and the right set of circumstanaces could vault Pittsburgh, Oklahoma, Florida State, Michigan, or even Baylor to No. 1. But any change hinged completely on one factor: Notre Dame had to defeat Georgia.

Former Bulldog idol Charley Trippi said it best, though, when he assessed, "Georgia can beat anyone because it's a very opportunistic team. And football often comes down to opportunism."

It was left to Rex Robinson, the second most prolific field goal kicker (59) in NCAA history, to capture just what this Georgia team was and what could be expected in its 12th game. "I know we've been a fortunate team in many respects," Robinson said New Year's Eve. "What we've been, more than anything else, is a team of survivors. Somewhere, someone has been there to pick us up. The reason we're here is that we've survived."

Georgia 17-
Notre Dame 10

"They were dying but they didn't crumble."

Buck Belue, who quarterbacked this strange Georgia team through its season, had to unlock the Notre Dame defense to unleash Herschel Walker on the opposing white jerseys and gold helmets. Although Belue didn't pass much on this infantry-oriented team, he was the most accurate passer in the SEC. He would have to pass and pass well. So that the Irish Goliaths couldn't aim all their defensive guns at Walker, Belue would have to keep them off with sprint-outs and play-action.

At first it seemed that the Georgia game plan would not be put into effect until the second half. Notre Dame took the opening kickoff and agonizingly wormed its way from the 20 to the Bulldog 32. From there, Harry Oliver kicked a 50-yard field goal. The nine-play drive used four minutes and 19 seconds, though it seemed longer to the crowd of 77,895 which included President Jimmy Carter.

George shoved its offense in reverse on its first possession, starting at its 22 but having to punt from the 6 after Belue was sacked. The possession was significant for two reasons, however. On the second play Walker found daylight at right end and picked up 9 yards before being knocked out-of-bounds at the Bulldog 31 by safety Dave Duerson. The play was called back because of holding and Walker separated his shoulder, though he didn't realize it. Second, Notre Dame got the ball again at the Bulldog 41, only 9 yards from where Oliver had just kick his field goal.

Freshman quarterback Blair Kiel used Phil Carter in four of the ensuing six plays that put the ball at the 31 on fourth-and-11. Oliver came back in for a second kick. From the 48, it appeared to be a routine three points for the Irish kicker. But then Terry Hoage came in, a reserve defensive back who had five minutes of game time during Georgia's season and who had made only two road trips. During Sugar Bowl practices the coaches had the backups attempt to block kicks, simulating game conditions. Hoage had a knack for it and was placed on the Sugar Bowl squad.

As the ball was snapped, the freshman sliced through the Notre Dame middle, leaped, and caught Oliver's kick on his chest. "I saw kind of a little

Georgia honeys check scoreboard with smiles and some concern to reassure themselves that one of the most opportunistic football teams in history, Herschel Walker & Co., can continue its season-long sorcery.

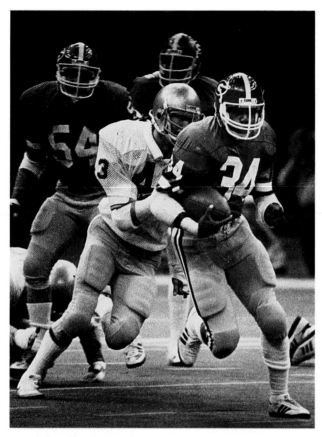

Herschel Walker begins his one-man destruction of the Notre Dame defense.

Walker goes up and over for Georgia's first touchdown against the Irish.

hole and just sailed through," Hoage explained. Belue put Walker to work at the Irish 49. On four of the next five plays Walker carried for gains of 7, 7, 8, and 7 yards. Only a Belue incompletion interrupted the thundering cadence of No. 34. He carried twice more for 2 yards before Belue was sacked for a loss of 11 yards at the 29. Rex Robinson kicked a 46-yard field goal to tie the score.

Robinson kicked off to Notre Dame's deep backs, Jim Stone and Ty Barber, each of whom drifted away from the ball before it hit near the goal and began bouncing laterally. "I called for Ty to take the ball," Stone said, "but he didn't hear me. It was hard to hear with all that noise." Barber shrugged, "I guess he thought I had it and I thought he had it. I think we both were too anxious to block." A Georgia brother act, Steve and Bob Kelly, closed on the live ball. Steve dived at the offering, hit it, and, he said, "the ball popped into my brother's hand. At the one. The play has come to be remembered in Athens as 'the world's longest on-sides kick.'"

Walker launched himself over the Notre Dame line two plays later to put Georgia in front, 10-3.

Early in the second quarter John Sweeney, the Irish fullback, dropped the ball as he veered into the middle. Rover Chris Welton recovered for the Bulldogs at the Notre Dame 22. Walker slammed off right tackle for 12 yards, and Belue gained 7 by sweeping left. Walker then beat two defensive backs to the outside. With two turnovers, Georgia was ahead, 17-3.

The senior member of Notre Dame's quarterback tandem, Mike Courey, moved his unit right back downfield on another nine-play drive that reached the Bulldog 13. But when Courey tried to lob a pass to Pete Holohan in the end zone, Scott Woerner intercepted.

Notre Dame was ahead in virtually every statistic by the half, with the exception of three significant figures: Georgia had claimed three Irish turnovers, and Walker already had 95 yards against a defense that hadn't surrendered 100 yards to any runner all season. And Walker got his yards without the benefit of Belue's passing. Buck had no completions in six attempts, and on five other plays he was unable to get a pass off.

Dan Devine decided to overlook the threat of Belue's arm, and moved his linebackers up for a second half salvo at Herschel. Field position and size became Notre Dame's offensive components. On its first possession in the second half Notre Dame moved from its 34 to the Georgia 46; on the second possession Kiel jockeyed the Irish from the Irish 40 to the Bulldog 13, where Tony Hunter caught a pass outside the end zone. Then Scott Woerner batted down a pass to Holohan, and Oliver kicked a 30-yard field goal wide to the right.

Georgia couldn't move and punted, and the Irish took over again on their 43. Kiel—who would quarterback the entire second half after Courey broke a

Walker goes up and over again

. . . and again.

hand just before halftime—drove Notre Dame 57 yards in 10 methodical plays. Carter scored at right tackle from the 1 with 57 seconds remaining in the third quarter.

On its next possession, Notre Dame drove from its 46 to the Georgia 27. The Bulldogs were clearly in a clench now. On third-and-three at the 20, Georgia again came up with a big play. Woerner fired through the line and dropped Carter for a yard loss. Oliver then missed a 38-yard field goal attempt. "We were wearing down," Bulldog defensive coordinator Erik Russell said of the mounting Irish momentum. "We had guys out there dying . . . but that's typical of the kind of guys we've got out there. They were dying but they didn't crumble."

Mike Fisher gave Georgia one more chance to put the game away by intercepting a deep sideline pass to Hunter at the Irish 37. Robinson ended up missing a 48-yard field goal with nine minutes to play, and Notre Dame was very much alive.

Starting at its 43 with 5:10 remaining, Notre Dame gained 9 yards in three plays. Kiel, on fourth-and-one at the Georgia 48, decided to go for the whole ball game. He dropped back for a pass to Dean Masztak, but the Georgia defense wasn't fooled. Kiel was pressured by two linemen and had to hurry the play. Woerner intercepted at the Georgia 34.

Belue still had not completed a pass. This severely slowed Walker's ground game after the half. Offensive guard Tim Morrison saw that Belue was beginning to get discouraged and perhaps a bit intimidated. He spoke to the quarterback just before Woerner's interception, "I told him he's got to get his act together. He had to remember we're in this as a team, and as a team we're still ahead. That we were in this together and we were still counting on him."

Belue picked up one first down with a 6-yard rol-

lout on third-and-three. On the next third down, with seven yards to go at the 50 and 2:05 left, Belue completed his first pass—7 yards to Amp Arnold. "That was the only one we needed," smiled Dooley. From there Belue was able to run the clock out.

"It was frustrating," Belue admitted of his one-for-12 day. He was even more concerned with the pre-game disbelievers. "I got the impression they didn't expect much of a game," he said of the Irish. "It was to our advantage that they felt that way. I read where (ND defensive end Scott) Zettek said Notre Dame should have been a 10-point favorite. Well, I want to know where those 10 points are. He's got a big mouth!"

Notre Dame outrushed (190-120), outpassed (138 yards to 7), and out first-downed (17-10) Georgia. Walker finished with 150 yards, 55 in the second half. His individual total may have been the most impressive rushing performance in Sugar Bowl history, considering his separated shoulder and the fact his total was 30 yards more than his team's. Take away Walker's 36 carries and Georgia had a minus 30 yards, partly due to four sacks of Belue. Georgia did win two stats it had won all season: turnovers, 4-0 (not including Notre Dame's goal line fumble), and the scoreboard, 17-10.

"I don't know how good we are," said Vince Dooley, "but I do know we're 12-0 and nobody else is."

Woerner stood in the middle of the locker room, a football tucked under one arm and his other holding a towel around his bare midriff. "You see this," he asked, holding the ball which had "Notre Dame" stenciled on it. "I sneaked it off the field and gave it to a manager on the sidelines. Maybe this will wake everyone up and they'll discover that Georgia has a pretty good football team."

Georgia was an undefeated, untied, and slightly unbelievable national champion.

Georgia players give Vince Dooley a ride following their Sugar Bowl triumph.

Pittsburgh-Georgia

FRIDAY, JANUARY 1, 1982

"Pitt was No. 1 at the time."

The Georgia-Notre Dame game was a hit in every way. The pairing gave the Sugar Bowl one of its highest television ratings (23.3). But due to the nature of the Orange Bowl's prime-time telecast, and because the Sugar obviously lost a share of the afternoon audience to Dallas, Miami (24.1) was the ratings king. ABC, which had pressed the Sugar and the Southeastern Conference to switch to prime time, was pleased with the result, yet unhappy with the thought of what might have been.

ABC had a sweetheart deal with the Sugar Bowl because the Bowl gave the network all the high cards when the last contract had been signed in 1976. The Sugar, because of its contract with the network, could now pay competing football teams $1 million apiece. Meanwhile, CBS was paying the Cotton Bowl enough to allow its teams to get approximately $1.8 million. NBC's Orange Bowl contract was helping the Miami teams to pick up an estimated $1.3 million.

In four of the previous five years, the Sugar Bowl had showcased a No. 1 team in what was in effect, a national championship game. ABC, the college football network, had the best of all worlds—the finest attractions for the lowest pay. And there were three more years remaining on the agreement.

In March at the conference basketball tournament in Birmingham, the SEC's Bowl Committee informed the Sugar that its tie-up would end after the January 1, 1982, game if more money was not forthcoming for the competing teams. The Committee pointed out that under the existing contract, its champions had nothing to lose by being free to play in Dallas and Miami as well as New Orleans.

"We agreed to get back to the SEC people," said Mickey Holmes. "All we did here was to give our side and listen to their side. It's been a great relationship for both parties. As for raising the payoffs, the only way to do it is through TV money. You can't make any substantial increase in payoffs by increasing ticket prices."

The first thing the SEC-ABC-Sugar troika did was petition the NCAA Extra Events' Committee for the 7 P.M. kickoff that the network wanted. Mickey

Holmes had to convince the Committee as well as suppress intense Orange Bowl lobbying. Miami, understandably, wanted to keep New Year's night to itself. For a prime-time kickoff, and a change in the SEC's most recent appearance rule in favor of letting the Sugar choose a representative in case of a championship tie, ABC was willing to come up with a $20 million, escalating, six-year contract. Both were approved.

The Fiesta Bowl, a relative newcomer based in Phoenix, announced a move to New Year's Day opposite the Cotton Bowl. Nineteen eighty-two would be the first New Year's since 1961 that more than the traditional four bowl games would be played on January 1.

Finding quality teams to fill the bowl vacancies wasn't difficult. A record seven teams (Michigan, Notre Dame, Southern Cal, Texas, Penn State, Pitt, and Clemson) were ranked at the top of the polls at one time or another during the 1981 season. From the start, Pittsburgh and Penn State caught the Sugar's fancy. It was the SEC spot that caused the most headaches. Georgia lost its No. 1 ranking in the third week of the season when it lost nine turnovers and a game to Clemson, 13-3. Vince Dooley used the defeat as a springboard; his team constantly improved and headed toward the end of the season as a probable 10-1 entry. Alabama, which lost to Georgia Tech and was tied by Southern Mississippi, kept even with Georgia in the SEC standings.

Georgia recovered sufficiently from the Clemson defeat to climb back to No. 3 in the national polls. And, of course, Georgia had Herschel Walker as a calling card. Alabama, in the season that Bear Bryant eclipsed Amos Alonzo Stagg as college football's winningest coach, was ranked No. 6 when the Tide thrashed No. 5 Penn State 32-16. Alabama, seldom impressive during the 1981 season, was awesome. Penn State, a solid football team that probably played the most difficult schedule in the country, went down for its second loss.

Pittsburgh, ranked No. 1, was the obvious choice for the Sugar Bowl. But a local debate raged over the merits of the SEC co-champions. The argument for 'Bama, No. 4 after the Penn State game, was Bryant's record and the unpublicized fact that Bear was eager for a shot at Pitt and his protégé Jackie Sherrill. It was his most direct route for a chance at No. 1. There were those on the Sugar Bowl's Executive Committee acutely aware of what the organization owed Bryant.

The Sugar Bowl also had an obligation to itself, the SEC, and ABC to select what it felt was the best attraction. Georgia not only had the better record and the higher ranking, but the Bulldogs' only defeat was to Clemson, who would finish the season unbeaten. 'Bama's only loss was to Georgia Tech (1-9), a matter of striking significance. Also, the Sugar Bowl would choose between Bulldog running back Herschel Walker and Crimson Tide Coach Bear Bryant. The nod had to go to the combatant.

"We were in a 'can't win' situation with the SEC," said Holmes. "We had to choose between two excellent football teams. We made our choice. Now I feel we're in a 'can't miss' situation with No. 1 and No. 3."

Penn State made it a 'could miss' situation with a 48-14 comeback win over the Panthers, dropping Pitt to No. 8. Clemson, scheduled to play No. 4 Nebraska in the Orange Bowl, rose to the top spot in the polls. That, of course, put Miami in the position New Orleans had held before the kickoff: the game with the glitter.

No team may ever have lost as much talent at one time as did Jackie Sherrill when 20 members of his 11-1, 1980 Pitt Panthers decided to play professional football—12 by way of the draft, 9 as free agents. In what could only be expected to be a rebuilding year, Sherrill molded an extremely potent offense revolving around 6-foot-4 junior quarterback Dan Marino. With 2,615 yards and 34 touchdowns, Marino could already be throwing against pro defenses observers believed. The Pitt defense also glittered, leading the nation by allowing only 224.8 total yards a game. Seven turnovers and 13 penalties defused any chance Pitt may have had against Penn State, an extremely good team in its own right.

After the slow start, Vince Dooley was convinced his Bulldogs had evolved into a team better than the one that won the national championship the year before. Herschel Walker gained 1,891 yards, yet his longest run was 32 yards. As a sophomore he was more consistent, although less spectacular. Buck Belue, who lead Georgia to 27 victories in his 29 starting assignments, completed 60 percent of his 188 passing attempts, taking pressure off Walker.

Both teams were downright miserly on defense. Pitt gave up 62.4 rushing yards a game, Georgia 72.5 yards. Both appeared vulnerable in the secondary. Pitt surrendered 162.5 passing yards, Georgia 164.5. That was only because opponents couldn't run on either.

In 563 passing attempts over two seasons Marino had been sacked only 16 times, so Dooley suspected the course for his team was patience.

As much as Dooley respected Pittsburgh's capabilities, there was an intangible that kept gnawing at him. "Pitt being undefeated, and then jumping up with two relatively easy touchdowns (against Penn State) may have been the worst thing for Pitt, the best thing for Penn State. Pitt had not been in stress situations before and did not respond. Penn State (which had played a much more difficult schedule) had, and did. That loss was the worst possible thing for us. I would rather have had Pitt undefeated. Now they've been embarrassed and have an opportunity to make amends for that."

Sherrill studied the match-ups, went through the game plan at a chalk session two days before the Sugar, stopped and looked at the board again. With sudden insight he said, "They've got problems."

Pittsburgh 24-Georgia 20

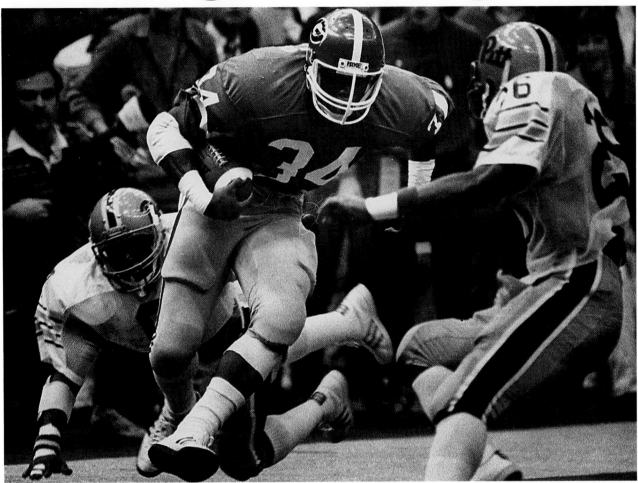

Herschel Walker breaks through the iron Pittsburgh defense.

"He'll burn you."

"There's one sure way to get in trouble against Pitt," explained Vince Dooley, "and that's to try to blitz Dan Marino. He'll burn you." Jackie Sherrill agreed with the Georgia coach's summation, saying, "Danny knows where the dots are going."

In the end, both appeared prophetic. Marino knew exactly where the dots were going, and burned Georgia with the same effectiveness as William Tecumseh Sherman, a field general of an earlier era.

Early though, Dooley's possession game appeared sound. Georgia took the opening kickoff and moved to the Pittsburgh 42 in eight plays. It wasn't necessarily a perfect drive but it was effective. On the ninth play, a third-and-five, Buck Belue rolled right looking for flanker Lindsay Scott. Belue threw the pass a half-second later than he should have, allowing Tom Flynn to cut in front of the receiver and make an interception, which he returned 9 yards to the Panther 39.

Pitt didn't go anywhere then, but its next posses-

sion summed up the tenor of the game. The Georgia secondary double-teamed Panther wide threats Julius Dawkins and Dwight Collins, and Marino drove using a short passing game and an effective running offense from the Pitt 26 to the Bulldog 8 in 15 plays. On fourth-and-one from there, Marino threw into the end zone for Collins, but Dale Williams worked an arm in front of the receiver and slapped the ball down. The drive had taken the game into the second period, where, with the presence of Herschel Walker and Marino on opposing sides, the 0-0 score was surprising.

Jim Broadway punted after three downs to Flynn at the 'Dog 42, but the safety fumbled when hit and Clarence Kay recovered for Georgia. Belue put some steam into things when he dropped back on second-and-17 at the Georgia 42 after a penalty, scrambled out of a collapsed pocket, and picked up 12 yards. On the next play Belue hit Walker over the middle. Herschel shucked off three defenders as he twisted and bounced 31 yards to the 15.

Dan Marino unleashes last minute pass.

John Brown scores the winning touchdown after the catch.

Three plays later, Walker swept right, hesitated to let one Panther overrun the play, and flew into the end zone. Kevin Butler kicked the conversion to put Georgia ahead, 7-0.

Undaunted and utilizing the short pass and run again, Marino came right back and drove to the Georgia 25. Marino was 11 of 13 at one point during the drive, and the Panthers were in control of the line. Possession time was beginning to favor Pitt. Georgia, showing the incredible resiliency that was its trademark the past two seasons, forced a field goal situation. Snuffy Everett kicked one 41 yards to slice the score to 7-3 with 1:59 left in the half.

Two stats stood out. Marino finished the first 30 minutes with 14 completions in 19 attempts for 100 yards. But Pitt only had three points. Walker, who was being fenced into the middle by the Panther defense, had only 28 yards. Bryan Thomas, who Sherrill had dreamed would outrush Walker, had 40 rushing yards.

Two new wrinkles—two tight ends at times and three wide receivers at other times—were installed by Sherrill for this game. The first helped Thomas' running, but so far all Pitt had was a stat sheet.

Pitt came out prepared to change matters. Eight plays after the second half began, with Pitt at the Georgia 30 with a first-and-10, Marino anticipated Dawkins would draw single coverage on a formation in which the Panthers had three receivers on the right side. Dawkins sped out on a post route, turned, and Marino put the ball on the numbers for a 10-7 Panther lead.

Later in the period, after an exchange of fumbles, Georgia found itself camped on the Pitt 10 after Eddie Weaver recovered a Thomas bobble. Walker made it a four-second drive by breaking out of Pitt's "fence," buzzing wide, shedding two tacklers, and scoring. Butler's PAT was wide.

Pitt suffered its ninth procedure penalty and fifth turnover early in the fourth quarter during another long drive. Ronnie Harris intercepted a second Marino pass at the goal line after the quarterback went to Collins from the 22. "I can't believe it," bellowed Panther assistant Joe Moore in the coaching booth. "We're killing them but we're losing!"

Moore's frustration subsided shortly as linebacker Rick Kraynak hit Walker who fumbled. Michael Woods recovered for Pitt at the 23. Bryan Thomas got the Panthers to the 6 on consecutive runs of 8, 7, and 2 yards. Marino felt by running his backs to the right, he could roll left and have a choice of two targets, a tight end going deep and a back angling out in the flat. When safety Steve Kelly came up to take the short man, Marino lobbed a 6-yard pass to tight end John Brown, who was all alone deep in the end zone.

Belue responded with Georgia's most impressive

march of the night. When the Bulldogs didn't gain on the ground, Belue went to Walker by air, moving to the Georgia 46. There Belue scrambled for 23 yards. Walker slammed into the right side, found a crack of daylight, and ran over linebacker Sal Sunseri before Flynn saved a touchdown at the 10. After two plays netted 4 yards, the quarterback evaded a fierce Panther rush and got rid of a pass just as he was tackled. Tight end Kay made a leaping catch in the corner of the end zone for a 20-17 Georgia lead. All Georgia had to do was protect its three-point lead for eight minutes and 13 seconds.

Marino countered with a minidrive to midfield. On fourth-and-three at the 50, after Marino overthrew Collins down the sideline, Dooley called time-out. There was 5:37 left. The Georgia coaching staff didn't believe Pitt was going to punt and used the time-out to alert the defense. Sure enough, Flynn took a short snap and ran to his right, but Terry Hoage brought him down for no gain.

All Georgia had to do from this point was squeeze out two or three first downs. If they could keep the ball and wipe out most of the 5:29 remaining, the 'Dogs would win. Instead, after three plays Jim Broadway punted back to Pitt, which took over at the 20 with 3:46 remaining. Marino and company picked up 10 yards in two plays and then called "69-X." The Panther quarterback threw to Thomas, who broke a tackle at the 35 and ran out to the Pitt 48. "It's a simple crossing pattern by our two backs," Marino explained of 69-X. The backs become part of a five-receiver corps downfield, joining the tight end and two wide-outs. "The first time we ran it, they rushed only three men and Bryan was able to run away from a linebacker. So I got him the ball."

Pitt stalled, staring at a fourth-and-four at the Dog 46. Marino called a quarterback draw that gained 8 yards. But another potential Pitt disaster hit two plays later when Marino threw to fullback Wayne DiBartola in the right flat at the 33. Linebacker Will Forts jarred Dibartola, who fumbled. Collins recov-

ered for Pitt. After an incomplete pass, Marino was left with a fourth-and-five and 42 seconds to go at the 33.

Time-out was signalled. Sherrill felt Pitt's best shot might be an attempt at a tying field goal. "But I asked Danny what he thought, " said the coach. "He wanted to go for the win. Since he thought he could do it, I went along with him."

"It comes down to this," said Marino. "It's a 50-yard field goal and, even if we make it, which is a longshot, it's still going to be a 20-20 score. If we go for it and make the first down, then we have a shot to win the game. And if we don't make the first down, then we don't deserve to win the game."

While Marino and Sherrill were deciding on 69-X as the best shot at getting the first down, Georgia defensive coordinator Bill Lewis called for an all-out blitz. "I wanted to minimize Marino's chances for a big play," said Dooley. "That's why we blitzed. It would have worked against most quarterbacks."

Marino took the snap. His backs picked up the blitzing linebackers. The other receivers adjusted and went deep against Georgia's single coverage. Instinctively, Marino took a deeper drop than usual and singled out John Brown a former wide receiver turned tight end), who was breaking down the center of the field. "He looked like he was bending to the outside on a short route," said a red-eyed safety Steve Kelly of Brown afterward, "to pick up the first down. I got my shoulders turned around and he broke back behind me." "When I looked up," said Brown, "there was the ball."

There was also the touchdown and there was the game. "It was a terrible thing to see," said Georgia tight end Kay.

It turned out the Bulldogs couldn't control the ball against Pitt. Possession time (36:26–23:34) and virtually every other statistic was lopsidedly in the Panthers' favor. Even Georgia's awesome Walker was outrushed by Thomas (129 yards–84 yards), as Sherrill had dreamed.

To the victor, Coach Jackie Sherrill, goes the spoils.

Coach Vince Dooley can only taste defeat.

Penn State-Georgia

SATURDAY,
JANUARY 1, 1983

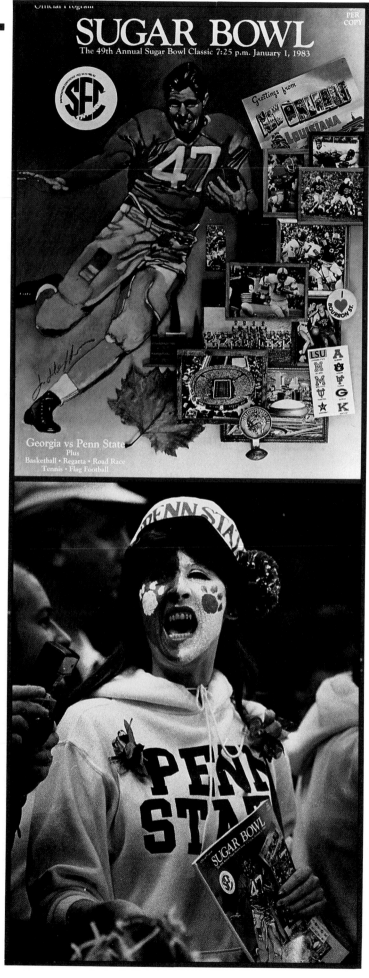

The face of the 1983 Sugar Bowl.

"If we win, I'll get a raise."

Pitt was a spectacular Sugar Bowl victor. In the Orange Bowl Clemson sealed the national championship with a victory over Nebraska. But CBS was the biggest New Year's Day winner. The Orange Bowl drowned the Sugar in the TV derby. The Sugar had 11.8 and 18 rating figures.

But even the rough spots couldn't detract from the absorbing drama of the 48th Sugar presentation.

Pittsburgh, with most of its high-octane offense and stunning defense returning, was the 1982 preseason choice for No. 1. The biggest Panther loss was its coach, Jackie Sherrill, who went to Texas A&M; his replacement was assistant Foge Fazio.

The Panthers looked to be a hurdle and an influence for the entire 1983 bowl scene. Georgia and Alabama appeared to be the best SEC teams, and a Georgia-Pitt rematch had strong appeal. As the season progressed, several possibilities arose—Georgia-LSU or Georgia-Penn State.

Pitt won consistently throughout the 1982 season against a demanding schedule. LSU became a postseason favorite by turning a 3-7-1 record (1981) into a ranking 8-2-1 (1982). Penn State started weakly, lost to Alabama by a 42-21 misleading score, and then turned into a devastating machine.

Alabama led the Nittany Lions 27-21 in the fourth quarter, though Penn State seemed ready to take command. A Lion blocker backed into a Lion punt, though, to give the Tide an easy touchdown. An interception soon after accounted for the final margin. "In the locker room after the game," center Mark Battaglia later recalled, "Coach (Joe Paterno) was very calm. He said we had six games left and we should be thinking about winning them all, one at a time. Looking back, I think that loss set the tone for the rest of the season."

Penn State didn't lose again, but even in their defeat to Alabama the Sugar Bowl scouts saw something in the Nittany Lions. "To be honest," said Penn State Athletic Director Jim Tarman, "Those of us around here thinking about bowls, started setting our sights at a different level after the Alabama game. But the Sugar Bowl people told us we were still in the picture. We have a little edge because we can deliver the TV markets in New York, Boston, Philadelphia, Washington, D.C., and Baltimore."

"We sent a representative to their game against Syracuse the week after Alabama," Mickey Holmes added. "We wanted to assure them they weren't out of it. I think it might have helped us when they saw we still were interested."

Paterno did a masterful job in throwing off the defeat to the Crimson Tide. Against one of the most difficult schedules in the country, including six bowl teams, the Lions pulled themselves together in an impressive forge down the stretch.

After Mississippi State upset LSU, making Georgia the undisputed SEC king, the Sugar was faced with the same choice it had the previous year. They would invite a combatant in the Pitt-Penn State fracus, an intense rivalry that would be played after the November 20 bowl signings.

Pitt was interested in the Cotton Bowl, but the Sugar had to decide whether to take Penn State. "There were three major factors in our decision to invite Penn State," said Holmes. "First, Penn State was finishing the season stronger. It beat Notre Dame while Pitt lost to Notre Dame. There was our gut reaction that Penn State was a better team. It was playing at home."

The Nittany Lions won, 19-10, and accepted the invitation to play the team that had risen to the top of the polls, 11-0-0. Paterno, an advocate of a national championship tournament, always seeks to have his teams play the highest-ranked opponent in a bowl. That philosophy cost him a national championship in the 1979 Sugar Bowl when his No. 1 team lost to No. 2 Alabama. Penn State got a chance to atone for that in 1982 when undefeated and 2nd-ranked Southern Methodist was tied by Arkansas. Penn State rose to No. 2.

For the sixth time in bowl history, and for the second time in five Sugar Bowls, a No. 1 and No. 2 would tee-it-up. The national championship game was scheduled for New Orleans for the fifth time in seven years.

Penn State opened a four-point favorite, the third time in five years the No. 1-ranked team was a Sugar Bowl underdog.

The main attractions would be Herschel Walker, the Heisman Trophy winner and by now the third-leading ground gainer in NCAA annals with 5,097 yards, and Curt Warner and Todd Blackledge, the leg and the arm of Penn State's success. The coaches, Paterno and Vince Dooley, were really the most compelling figures in the game.

Both were survivors in a demanding profession. Both enjoyed huge success and longevity, tributes to a pair of former journeymen quarterbacks, who were both articulate, fueled by competitive fire, long on insight, and long on discipline.

In 19 years at Georgia, Dooley had a 151-58-6 record (a winning percentage of .710), appeared in 14 bowl games, and won six conference championships. In 17 years with the Nittany Lions, Paterno's teams had made 15 bowl appearances and finished in the Top Ten 13 times while compiling a record of 161-34-1 (a winning percentage of .821).

The biggest professional difference between the men was the national title Dooley won on the Superdome carpet in the Sugar Bowl of 1981. Paterno, who coached three undefeated, untied teams, had lost his best chance at No. 1 on the same Superdome carpet in 1979. "Our fans make more of that than I do," Paterno said of his lack of No. 1 rankings. "I think we were No. 1 in 1968, 1969, and 1973. We just weren't voted No. 1."

Dooley was struck by the offensive capabilities of Penn State, comparable, in his opinion, to the Pitt team he coached against in the 1977 Sugar Bowl. That team had the best opposing offense he had seen in almost 20 years at Georgia. Paterno had to brace for Herschel Walker and John Lastinger. Georgia quarterback Lastinger completed passes at only a 42 percent clip but had a 24-0-0 record as a starter in high school and college. The Bulldog secondary had intercepted 35 passes and led the nation.

Critics said Georgia was "one-dimensional" with Walker as its only real threat, but Paterno answered,

"Anytime Vince wants balance, he'll have balance. If you have a Herschel Walker, you run a Herschel Walker."

Paterno dismissed talk of what the national championship would mean to a school (with 95 years of excellent football tradition) that had never won it, or to a coach who won 82 percent of his games but never a No. 1. "If we win, maybe I'll get a raise," he chuckled lightly for the public.

But it had to mean more. Right after the Pitt victory, Paterno's thoughts returned to the 1979 Sugar when his Lions failed to score from the 1 and let the national championship pass to Alabama.

"This time we'll score," Paterno said to Jim Tarman as they walked off the field.

Georgia fans show hopeful signs.

Lion fans cheer Warner & Co.

Penn State 27-Georgia 23

Chris McCarthy hits a wall of Nittany Lions.

"I guess dreams are meant to be that way."

"We wanted to scare them with the long pass early," said Penn State wide receiver Gregg Garrity of Joe Paterno's early strategy. Paterno's team came out passing against Georgia's secondary, catching Dooley's wounded defensive line by surprise.

Todd Blackledge, dissecting Georgia with a surgeon's precision, took the Nittany Lions on an 80-yard, seven-play scoring drive. Strokes of 27 and 33 yards to Garrity and tight end Mike McCloskey were featured in Penn State's unusual trips (three receivers to one side) formation with two tight ends.

Curt Warner swept left end for the 2-yard touchdown with 12:09 still to be played in the opening period.

"We knew what we had to do coming into the game," continued Garrity, "exactly what we were going to do."

Penn State also knew exactly what it had to do defensively, although it's a lot easier to stop Herschel Walker on paper than on the field. Defensive coordinator Jerry Sandusky installed an ever-changing defensive alignment that featured two down linemen at times, an eight-man front at other times, and var-

Curt Warner (25) circles into the end zone for Penn State's first touchdown as Todd Blackledge (14) jumps for joy.

Warner throws up arms after 9-yard touchdown run.

Punt returner Kevin Baugh (11) finally brought down by band of Bulldogs.

ied looks in between. Everything was used to disrupt the Georgia rhythm and keep Walker moving from sideline to sideline.

It didn't take immediate effect. John Lastinger took Georgia on a bruising, authoritative 80-yard drive. Georgia pushed to inside the 9 when, on second-and-eight, wide-open tight end Clarence Kay gave up on an end zone route as Lastinger's pass went incomplete. After a yard loss, Kevin Butler kicked a 27-yard field goal.

Nick Gancitano got the three points back early in the second quarter after Warner swiveled through the Bulldog trenches for 26 yards. Gancitano's 38-yard field goal made the score 10-3 with 11:47 to go until the half. And Penn State was about to uncover another weapon.

Georgia pushed to its own 41 before Jim Broadway punted to Kevin Baugh. Lion assistant John Rosenberg had put in a middle return for the Bulldogs. Baugh gathered in the punt at the Penn State 7, wiggled through a wave of Georgians, and set sail for the goal. He was finally downed at the 'Dog 27, 66 yards from the start of the return. Nothing came

of it and Gancitano missed a 47-yard field goal, but the Bulldogs had a glimpse of another Penn State menace.

The next time Broadway punted, Baugh returned it 24 yards to the Lion 35 and from there Blackledge threw to Garrity for 36 yards, a play that set up an eventual 9-yard touchdown swing by Warner. With 2:43 to go until the half, the score was 17-3. Gancitano kicked a 45-yard field goal with 44 seconds to go. Penn State held, 20-3. "They were about to run us out of there," said the startled Dooley.

Walker returned the kickoff to the Georgia 34 and the man Paterno said he most feared—Lastinger—took sudden command. The baby-faced quarterback completed a 17-yard pass to Kay, then a 13-yard pass to freshman Herman Archie to place the ball at the Penn State 36. Kevin Harris grabbed the next pass at the 20, then he lateralled to Walker who had lined up as a flanker. Walker gained 10 yards.

On the next play, Lastinger lobbed a high pass to the 6-foot-5 Archie over 5-foot-8 Dan Biondi in the corner of the end zone. Georgia sliced the score to

Warner celebrates as he hits the end zone for Penn State's second TD.

Wide open Georgia receiver Herman Archie (81) drops what could have been a touchdown pass as badly beaten Dan Biondi (39) tries to catch up.

Biondi cuts down Herschel Walker (34).

20-10 with a 39-second, 5-play drive. "That was a clear example of having to throw and doing it," said Lastinger. "Penn State will back up and give the short pass when it is ahead. We just took advantage of that."

"We felt like we were beating ourselves," Walker said of the halftime situation. "They gave us a chance and we didn't put any points on the board. We gave them a chance and they did." Other than its two scoring drives, Georgia didn't penetrate beyond its own 45 in the first half.

Georgia steamed to another touchdown on the first possession of the second half as Lastinger directed an innovative 11-play, 69-yard drive that ended when Walker went over from the one. Suddenly, it was 20-17 and Georgia had literally jumped into position for victory.

The Penn State passing lanes were shut down, partly because the Bulldog secondary closed the long routes off and partly because Blackledge, as he said, went "out of whack." Three of Georgia's five sacks came in the third quarter, contributing to the loss of poise. "I told the coach to give me a little while and I would be okay," the 6-foot-4 quarterback said. During that period Paterno said he could "feel it beginning to slip away."

Things fell back into sync for the Nittany Lions in the opening minutes of the final period. On a first-and-10 at the Bulldog 47, with Georgia in two-deep coverage and leaning for the run, Blackledge called "six-43," a routine play-action fake while four receivers streak downfield. Garrity flew past freshman cornerback Tony Flack and made a diving, skidding catch in the end zone. "Todd made a great throw, Garrity made a great catch," assessed Paterno. "It gave us some breathing room."

The only turnover Penn State would make that night, a fumbled punt return by Baugh, made things close to the end. Lastinger pushed from the Lion 43 to the 9 where he scrambled and then drew back across the field to Kay for a touchdown with 3:54 remaining.

A two-point conversion would put Georgia—with one of the nation's best kickers in Butler—in position to win with a field goal. But Walker was stopped short, leaving the score at 27-23.

Strategy from here on was simple. Georgia needed to get the ball back, Penn State had to hold it. Blackledge, on third-and-one at the 23, sneaked for 2. On the next third down, 3 yards were needed at

the 32. Instead of a plunge into the line by Warner, the call everyone expected, Blackledge said, "Let's go for it." "I just told him 'Make sure you throw it far enough,' " said Paterno.

The quarterback called a play, dropped, and threw a darter to Garrity for a 6-yard gain.

Walker said the Georgia offense was confident it could pull the game out ". . . if we could just get our hands on the ball. But when they made that last first down, I turned to the guy who was standing next to me and said, 'We won't be going out there again.' "

Penn State had finally won its national championship by demonstrating clear superiority over a worthy opponent. Defenders like end Walker Lee Ashley and safety Mark Robinson, with nine tackles and two interceptions, performed above and beyond the call of duty. Walker was 'held' to 103 yards and his longest gain was 12 yards. The figure represented the best defensive effort against Walker in his three collegiate seasons.

Warner outrushed another Heisman Trophy winner by gaining 117 yards. The previous year he outrushed USC's Marcus Allen (Heisman Trophy winner) in the Fiesta Bowl.

The midseason 42-21 defeat to Alabama would be recorded as the biggest defeat a national champion suffered, showing just how far the Nittany Lions had come. The game also was a demonstration of just how far the Sugar Bowl had come. The prime-time telecast outdrew all other postseason college games, burying its head-to-head competitor, the Orange Bowl, and a CBS movie. A 24.4 Nielson rating translated into 38 percent of the entire TV audience while the Orange Bowl (LSU-Nebraska) drew a 14 percent share.

In 1983, the Sugar Bowl also paid in excess of $1.8 million to each team, the highest of any bowl other than the Rose. It was a far cry from the early 1970s when its ratings were dismal and its pay equally poor. The Sugar Bowl, like Penn State, had recaptured its No. 1 status.

"We heard about the polls on the plane ride home," said Biondi. "We all cheered and basically went nuts." "Riding home tonight," said reciever Kenny Jackson, "all this stuff was going on and I found myself thinking, 'Wait a minute. Is this for real?'. . . I know it's the greatest feeling I've ever experienced, but, at the same time, it's unreal. I guess dreams are meant to be that way."

Gregg Garrity holds ball in triumph as Kevin Baugh (11) hugs his teammate after Garrity caught the game's winning touchdown.

Joe Paterno, king, finally, of the hill.

"They were the pathfinders."

The Sugar Bowl has traveled from the thoughts of one man in the 1920s to an enormous happening in the 1980s. It has moved from a small, barely adequate stadium to what some call "Starship Superdome." It was conceived in ridicule, but lives in acclaim. Its roots stretch from Glenn "Pop" Warner and Bernie Moore to Bear Bryant and Vince Dooley, from Monk Simons to Herschel Walker.

Not every step the Sugar Bowl has taken has been the right one. It is an association of men, and men are fallible.

An "open" bowl concept was clung to in the early and adolescent years and often New Orleans was treated to the very best in college football. Times changed. The team selections became more awkward. The Sugar Bowl considered a conference tie-up more carefully. Finally, the Southeastern Conference and the Sugar Bowl joined forces. Times may change again, but for now, it can be argued that this is truely a marriage made in football heaven.

The Sugar Bowl was struggling financially at the start of the 1970s; it could not quite shake the effects of the segregation years. By 1980, segregation was forgotten, and the Sugar Bowl paid each of its participants $1 million. The Sugar Bowl's first six games after the tie-up featured four national champions and a No. 2 team that won impressively while No. 1 was losing. That string of successes demonstrates the phenomenal artistry of selection in recent Sugar Bowls. It rivals the Sugar's early years. "We knew things would probably be easier with a tie-up," said Cliff Kern, a past president of the Sugar Bowl, "we just didn't know how much easier. It's really been incredible.

Fred Digby had a vision. Thirty-seven men forged it into reality. Considering the times in which it was born, the Sugar Bowl is a near-miracle. The founders, and their successors, have not only built a monument, they've kept a pledge. Over the course of a half-century, more often than not, the Sugar Bowl has had the best game possible.